COLI

GLASGOW
STREETFINDER
COLOUR ATLAS

Contents

HarperCollinsPublishers

Published by Collins
An imprint of HarperCollins*Publishers*
77-85 Fulham Palace Road, Hammersmith, London W6 8JB

The HarperCollins website address is:
www.**fire**and**water**.com

Copyright © HarperCollins*Publishers* Ltd 2000
Mapping © Bartholomew Ltd 1985, 1987, 1989, 1992, 1993, 1995, 1997, 2000

Collins® is a registered trademark of HarperCollins*Publishers* Limited

Bartholomew website address is: www.bartholomewmaps.com

Based upon the Ordnance Survey Mapping with the permission of The Controller of Her Majesty's
Stationery Office © Crown copyright 399302

The contents of this publication are believed correct at the time of printing. Nevertheless, the publisher
can accept no responsibility for errors or omissions, changes in the detail given, or for any expense or
loss thereby caused.

The representation of a road, track or footpath is no evidence of a right of way.

Printed in Hong Kong   ISBN 0 00 448998 5   MI 10245   ANN

e-mail: roadcheck@harpercollins.co.uk

Key to map symbols

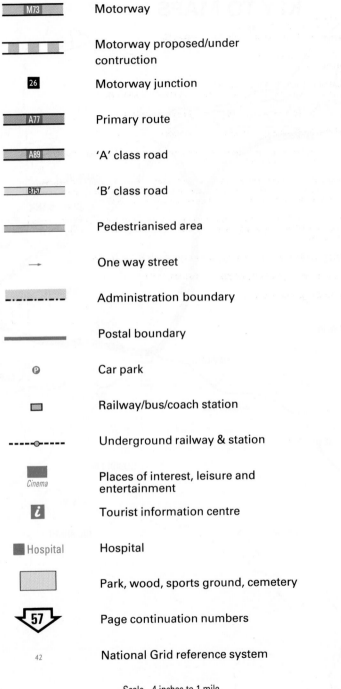

M73	Motorway
	Motorway proposed/under contruction
26	Motorway junction
A77	Primary route
A89	'A' class road
B757	'B' class road
	Pedestrianised area
→	One way street
	Administration boundary
	Postal boundary
Ⓟ	Car park
▭	Railway/bus/coach station
----○----	Underground railway & station
Cinema	Places of interest, leisure and entertainment
𝑖	Tourist information centre
Hospital	Hospital
▭	Park, wood, sports ground, cemetery
57	Page continuation numbers
42	National Grid reference system

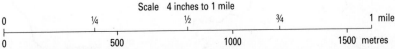

Scale 4 inches to 1 mile

0 — ¼ — ½ — ¾ — 1 mile
0 — 500 — 1000 — 1500 metres

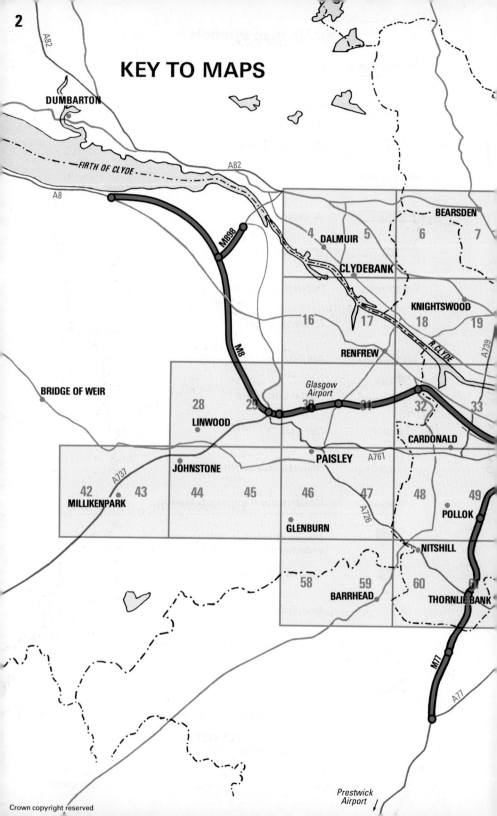

2

KEY TO MAPS

DUMBARTON

FIRTH OF CLYDE — A82

A8

A82

M898

M8

BEARSDEN

4 DALMUIR 5 6 7

CLYDEBANK

KNIGHTSWOOD

16 17 18 19

RENFREW R CLYDE A739

BRIDGE OF WEIR

Glasgow
Airport

28 29 30 31 32 33

LINWOOD CARDONALD

PAISLEY A761

JOHNSTONE

42 43 44 45 46 47 48 49

MILLIKENPARK A737 POLLOK

GLENBURN A726

NITSHILL

58 59 60 61

BARRHEAD THORNLIEBANK

M77

A77

Prestwick
Airport

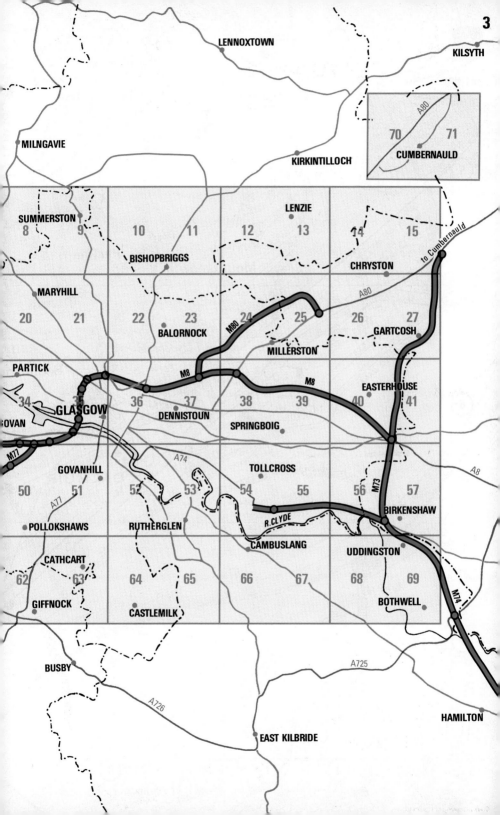

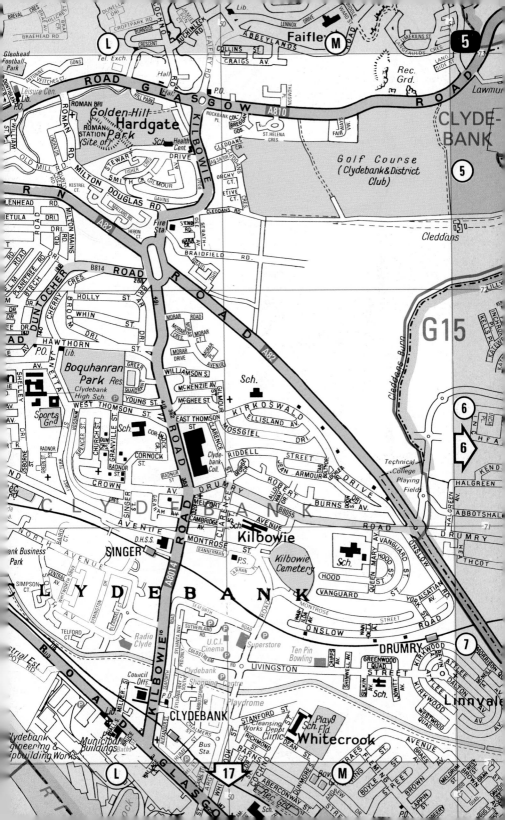

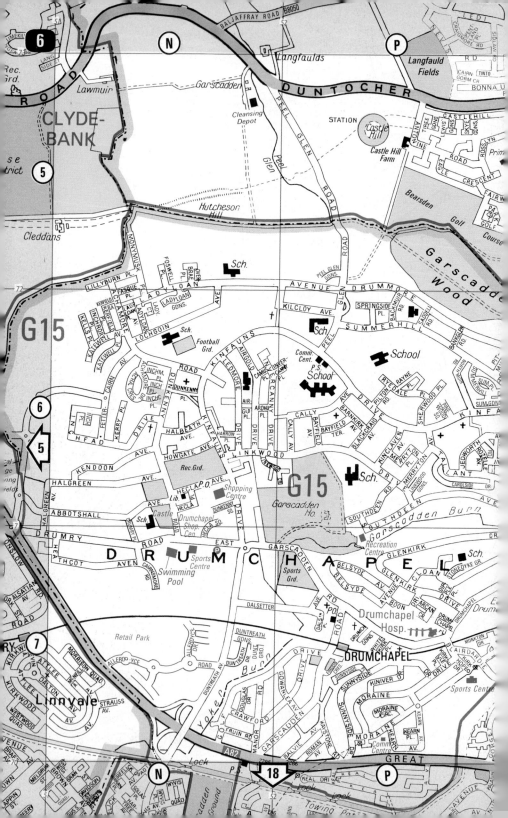

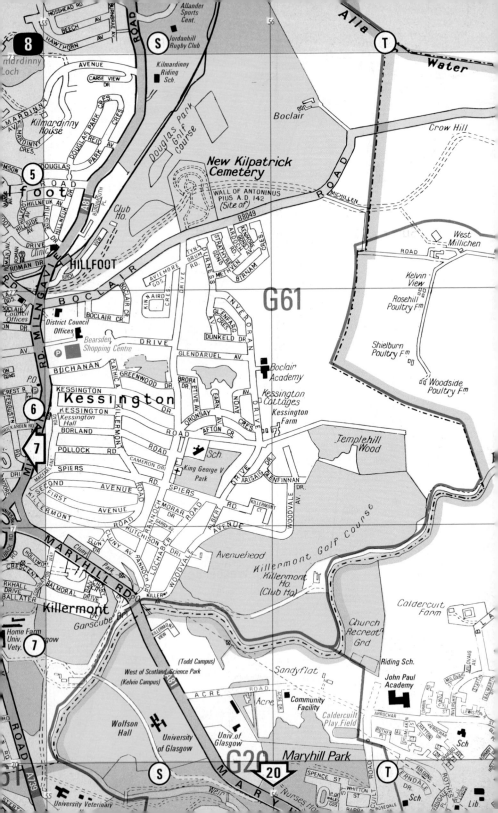

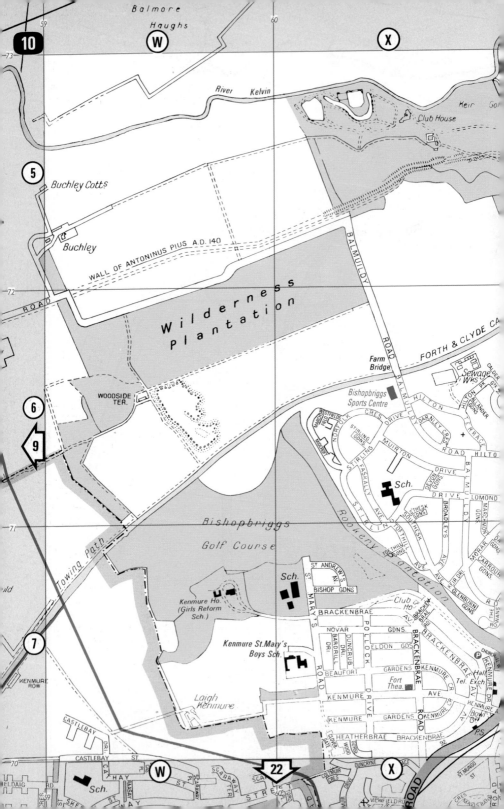

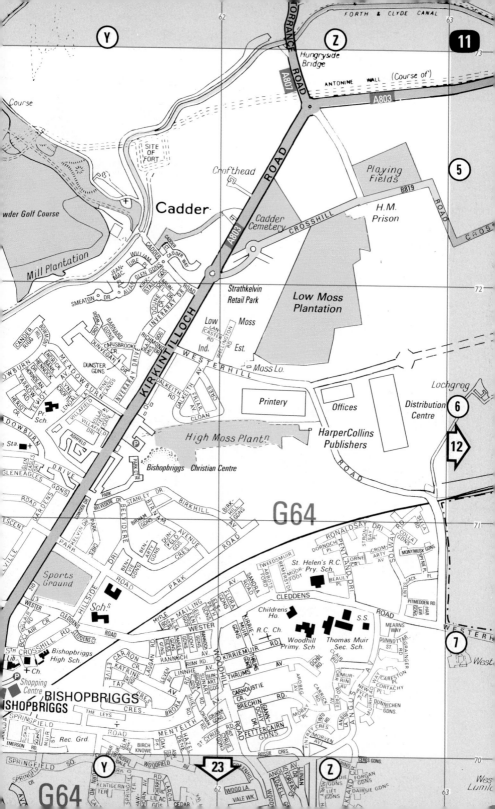

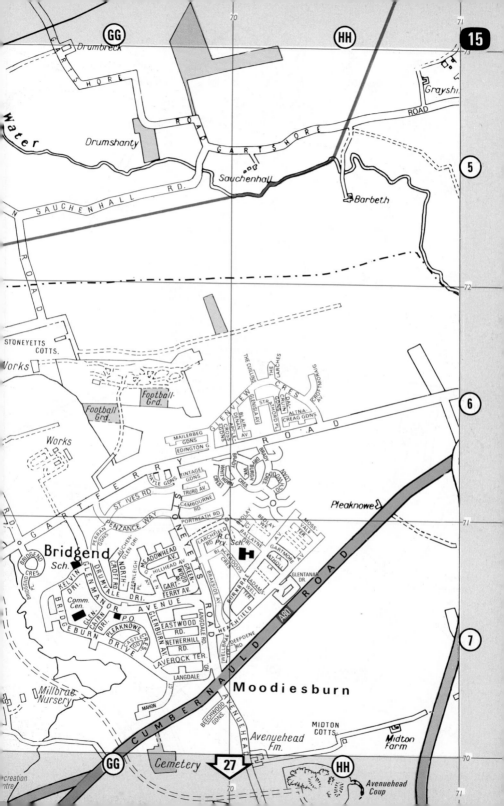

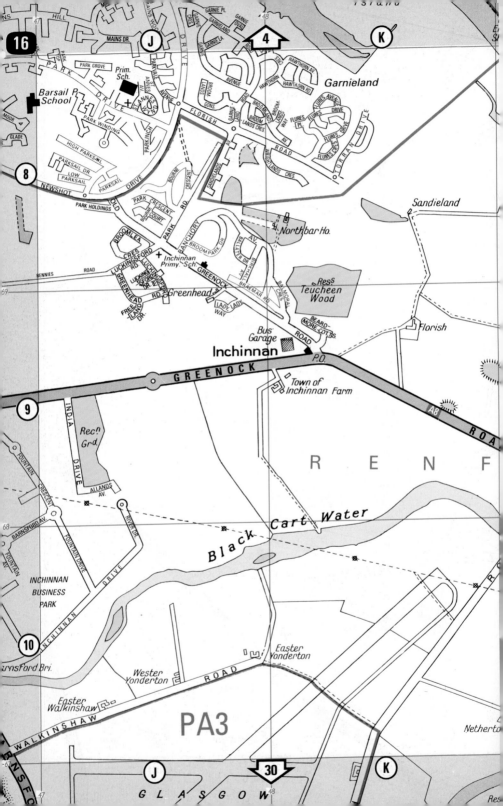

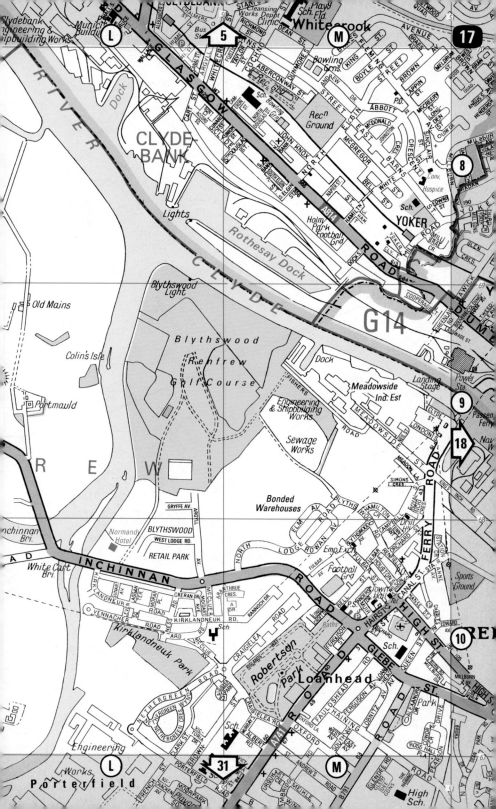

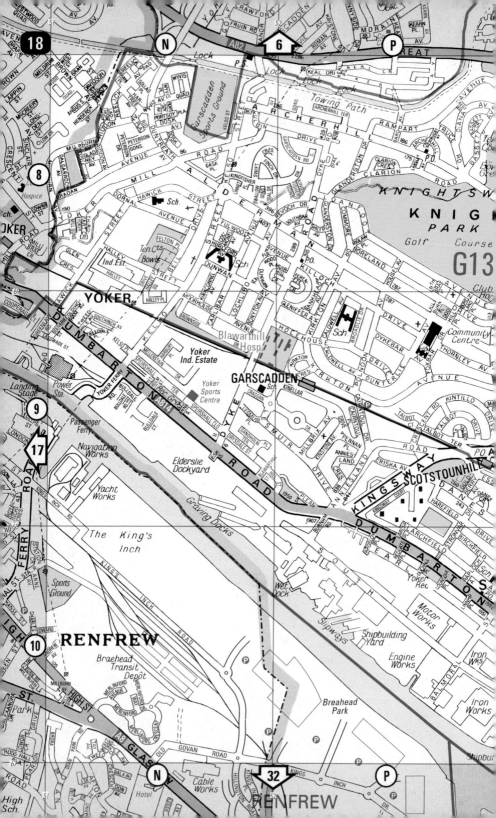

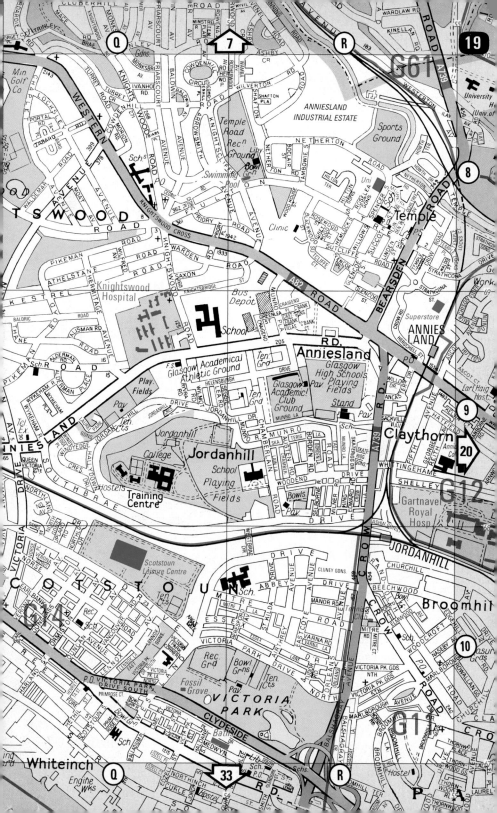

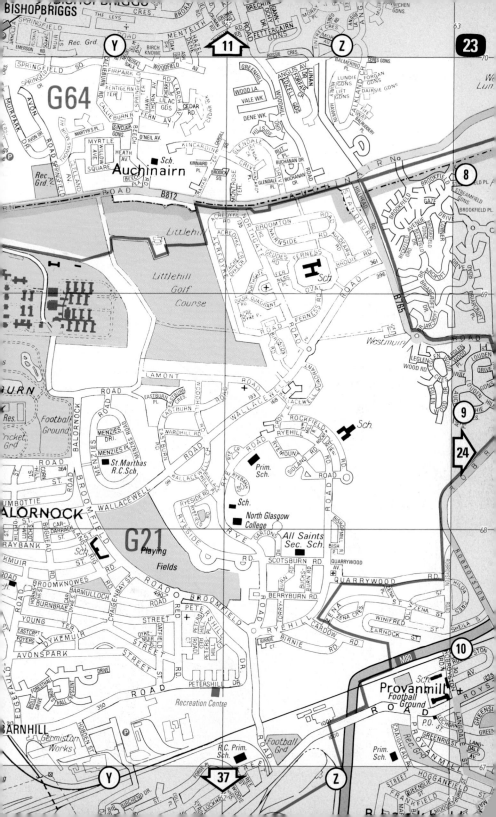

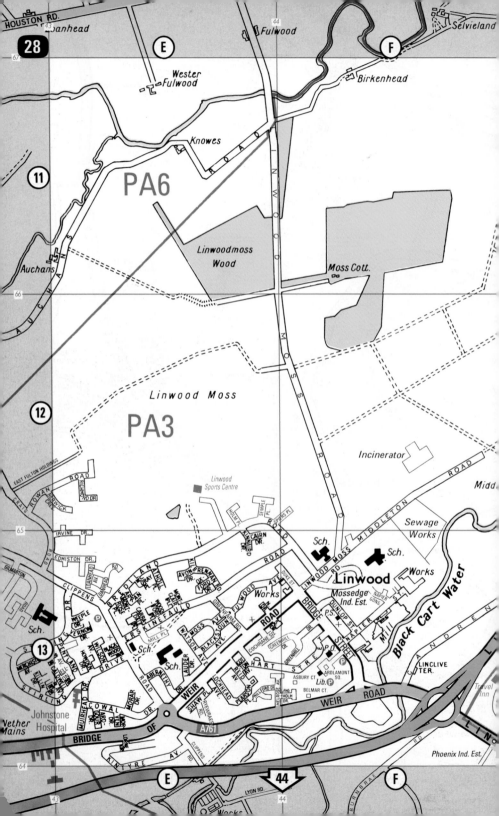

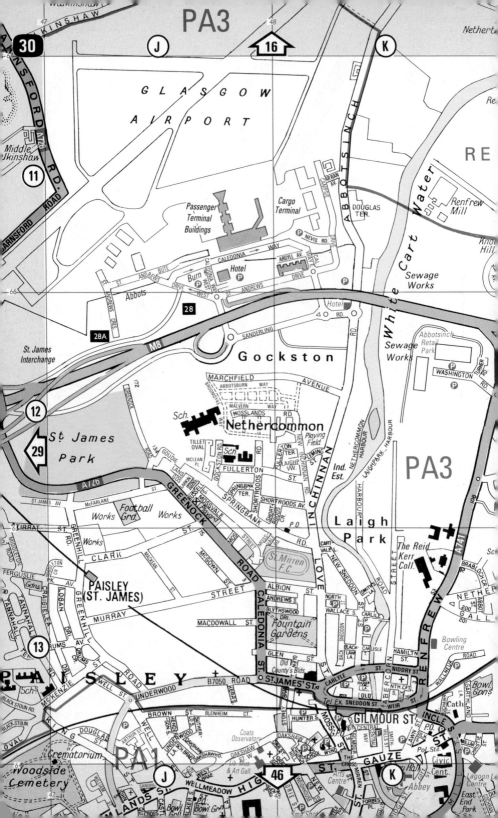

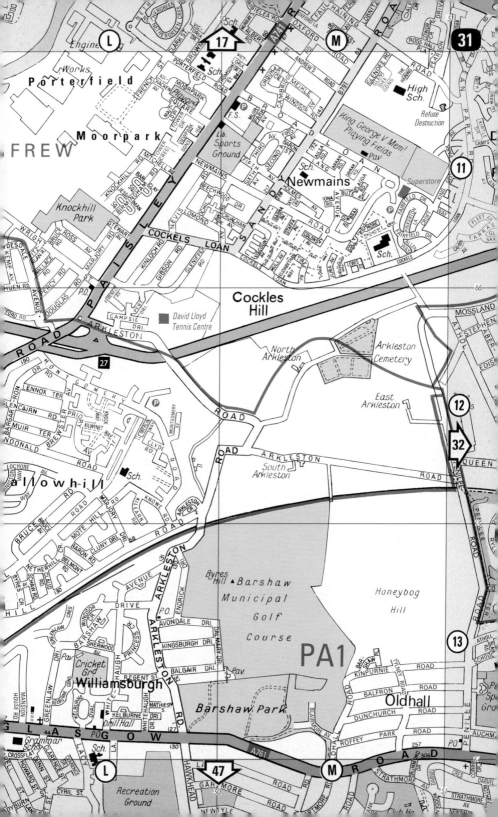

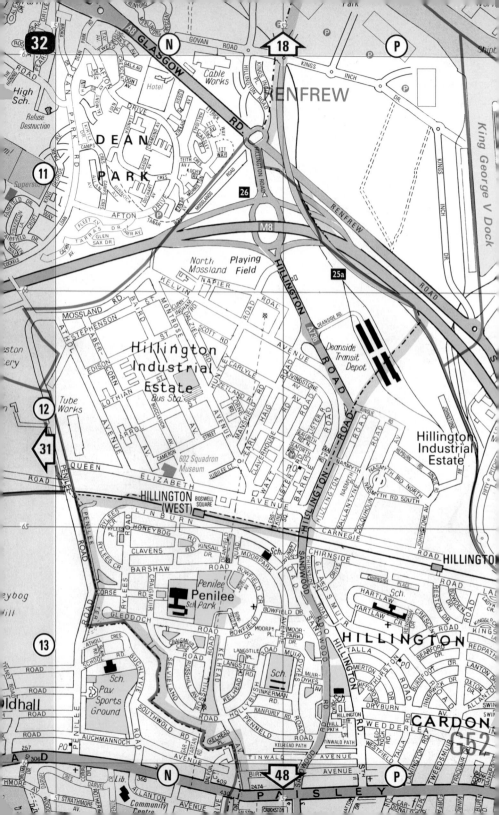

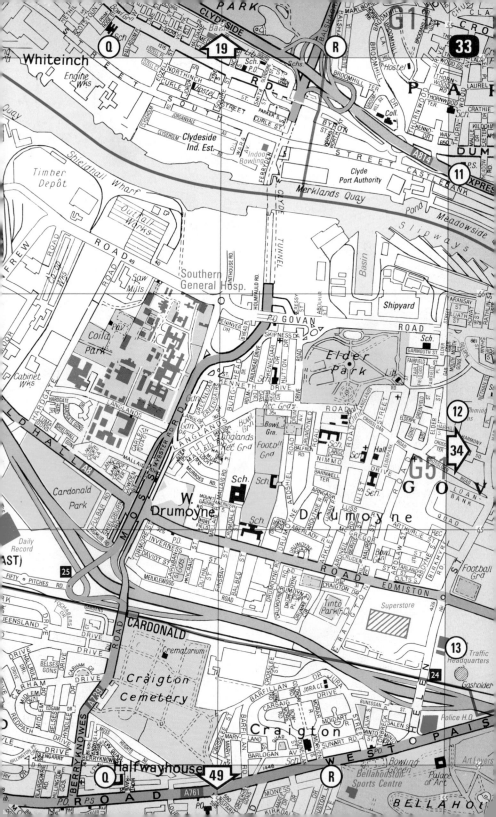

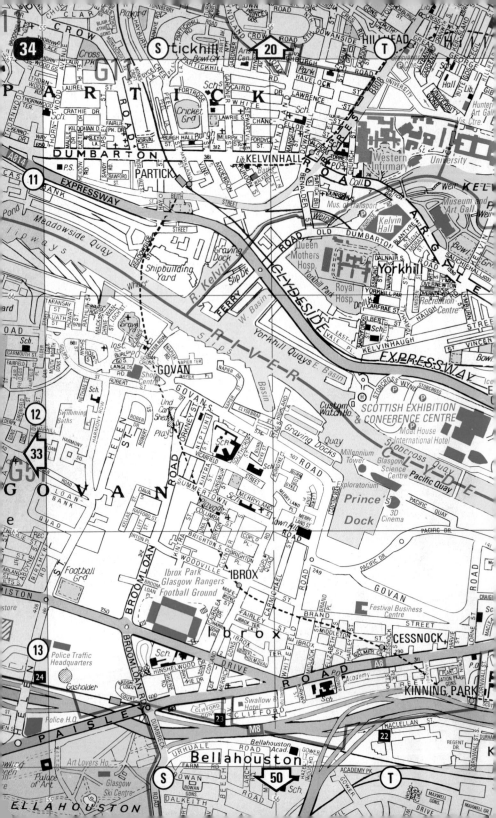

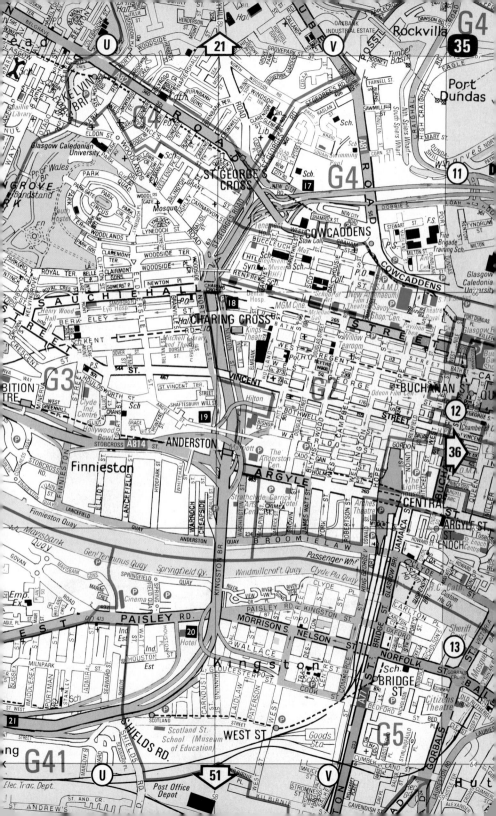

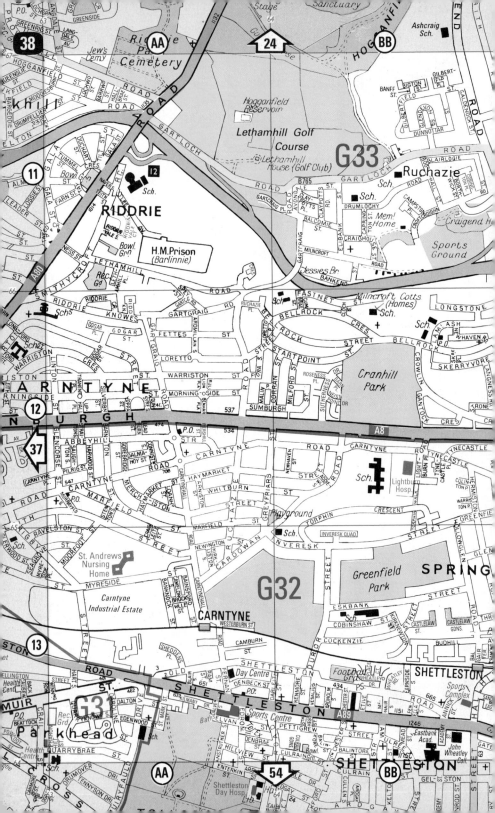

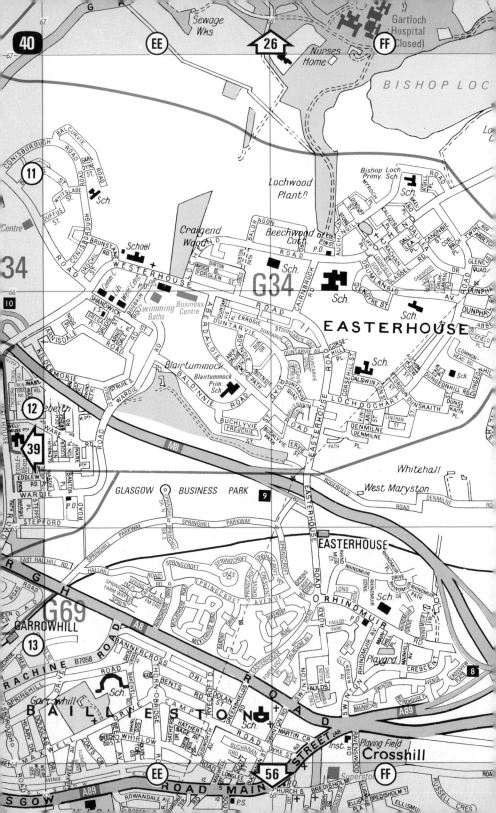

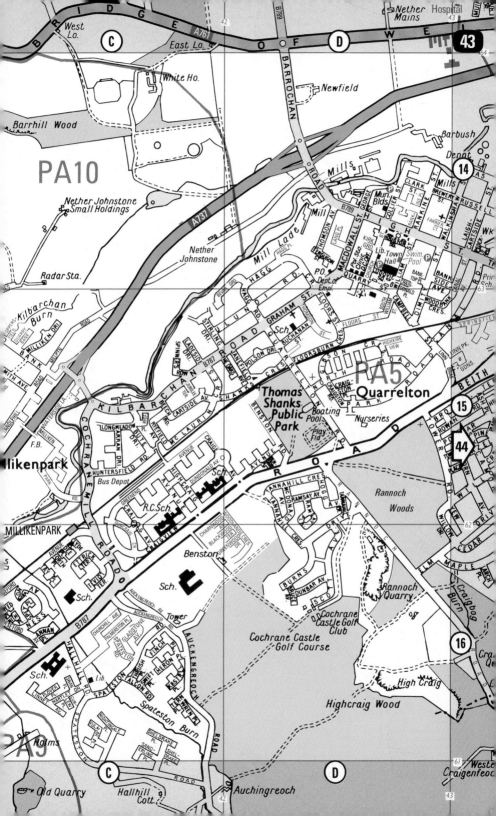

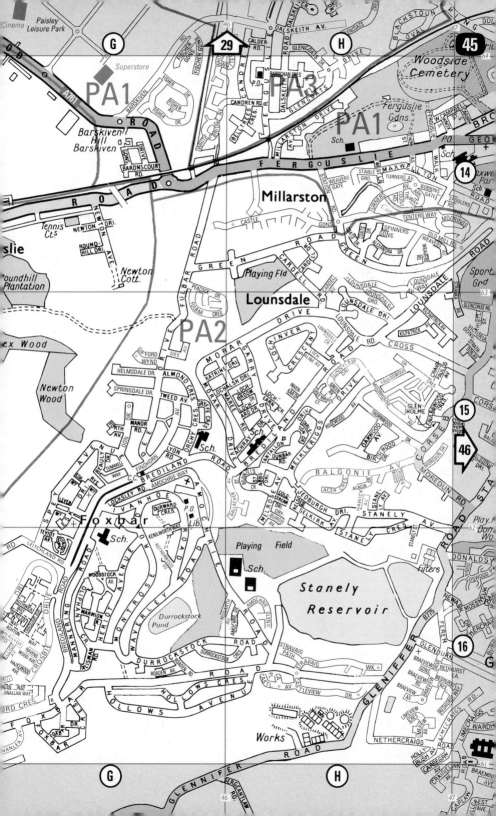

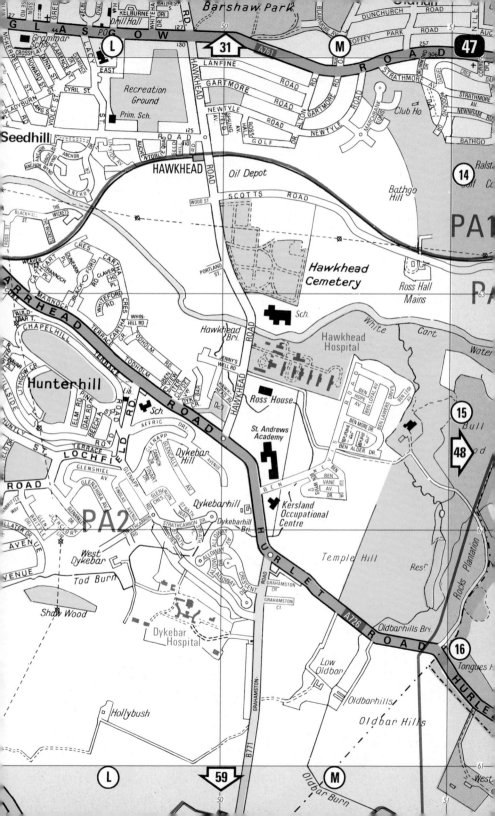

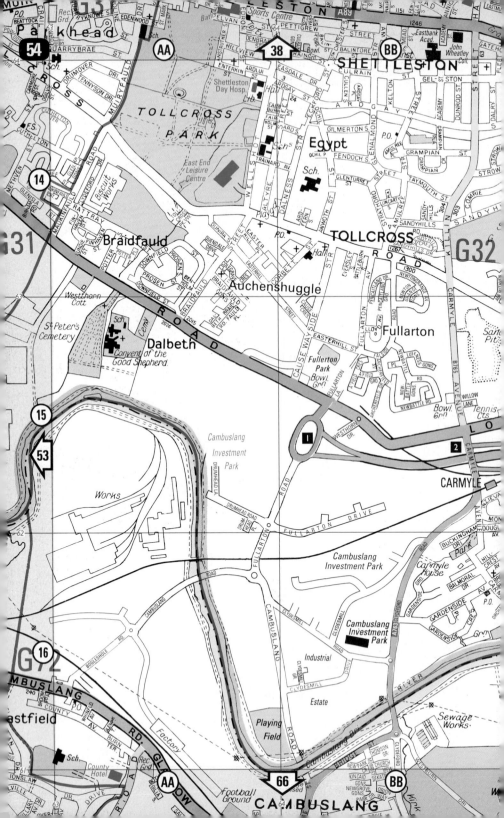

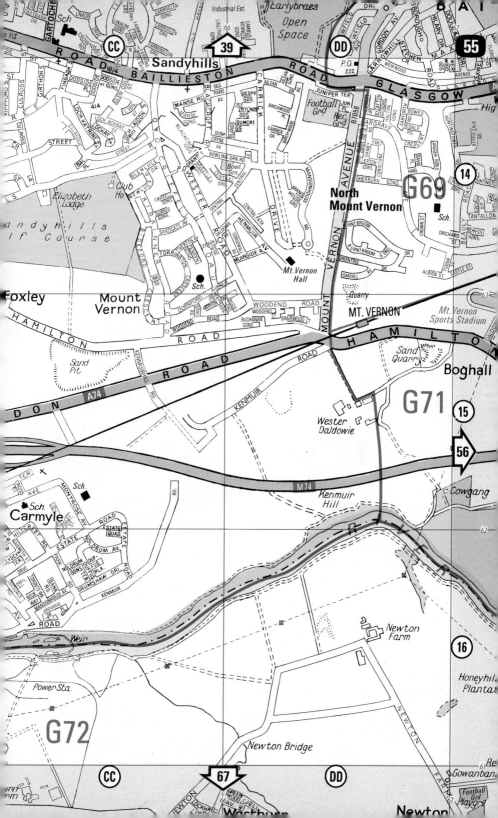

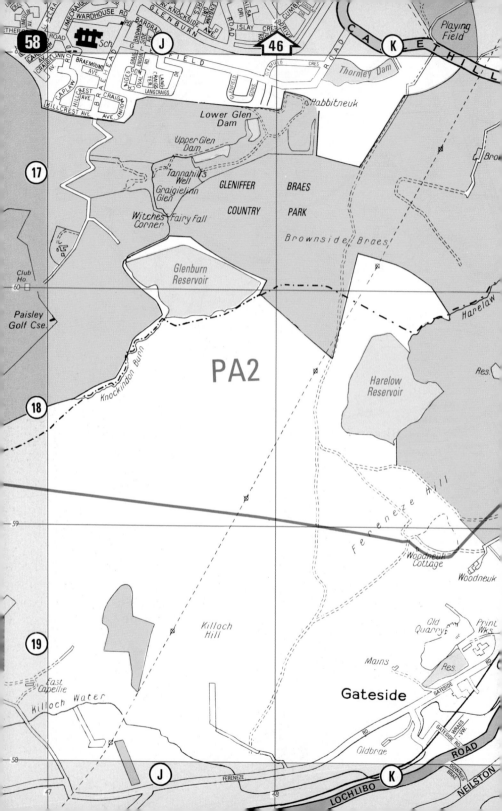

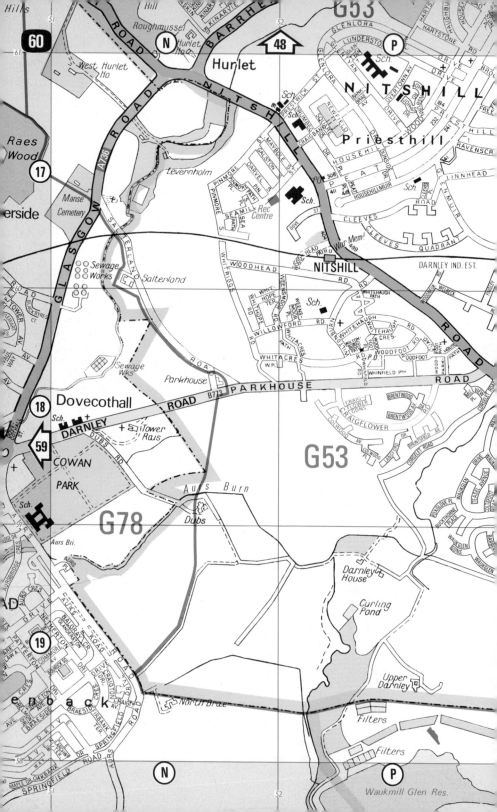

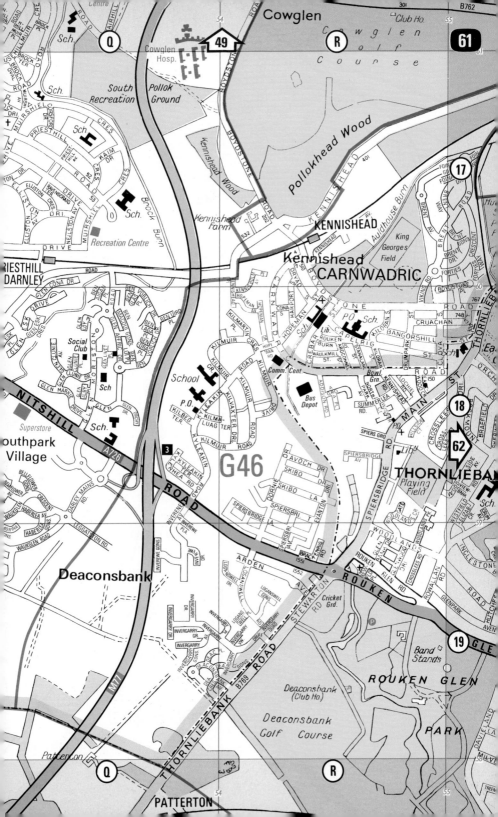

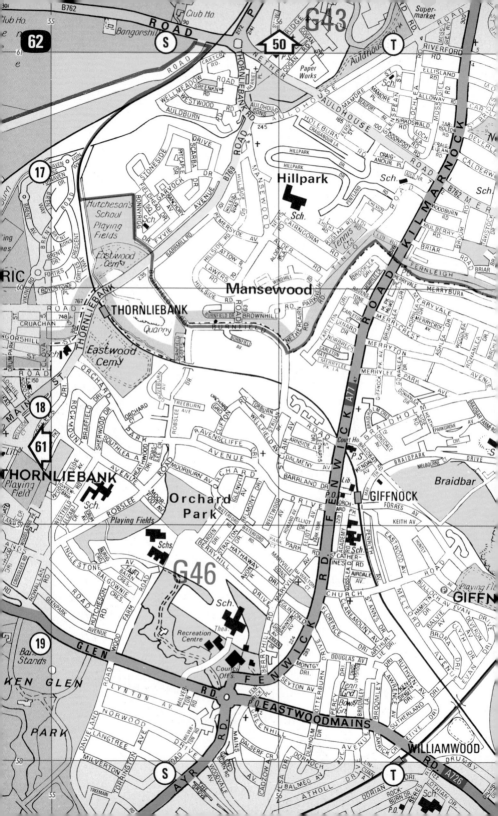

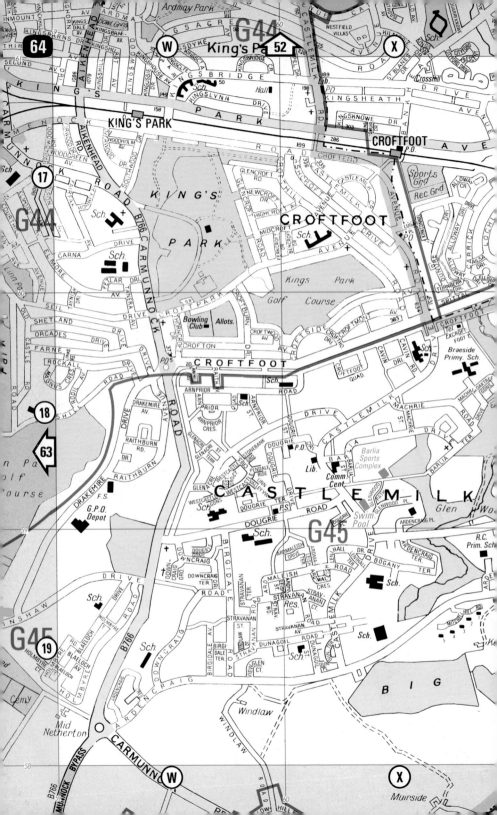

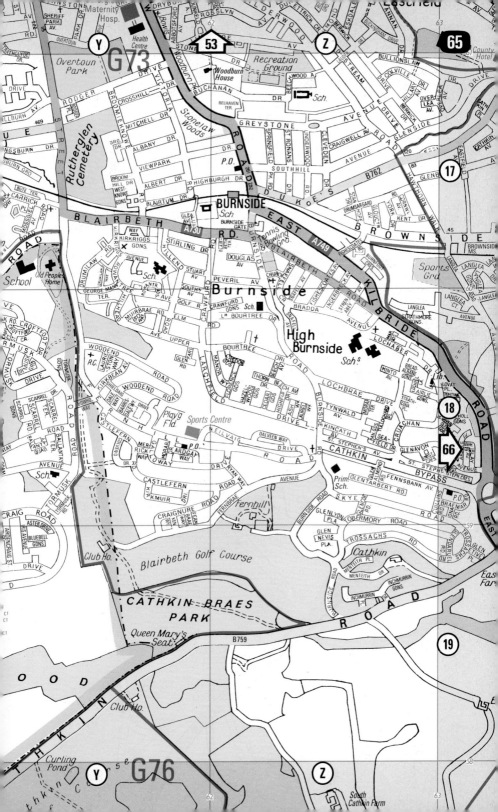

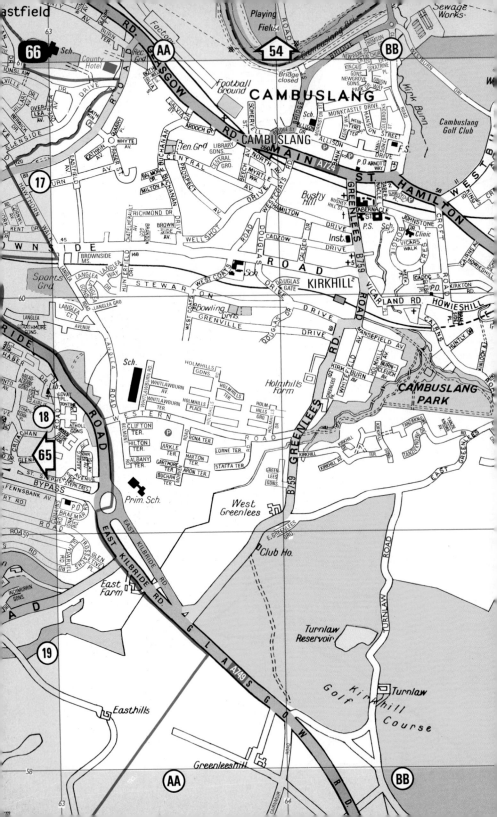

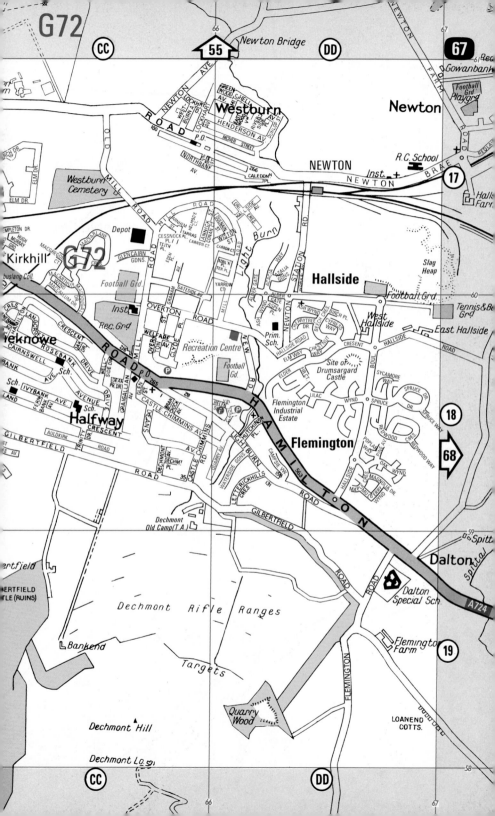

Glasgow

Information

Contents

The City of Glasgow began life as a makeshift hamlet of huts huddled round a 6thC church, built by St. Mungo on the banks of a little salmon river - the Clyde. It was called Gleschow, meaning 'beloved green place' in Celtic. The cathedral was founded in 1136; the university, the second oldest in Scotland, was established in the 15thC; and in 1454 the flourishing medieval city wedged between the cathedral and the river was made a Royal burgh. The city's commercial prosperity dates from the 17thC when the lucrative tobacco, sugar and cotton trade with the New World flourished. The River Clyde, Glasgow's gateway to the Americas, was dredged, deepened and widened in the 18thC to make it navigable to the city's heart.

By the 19thC, Glasgow was the greatest shipbuilding centre in the world. From the 1820s onwards, it grew in leaps and bounds westwards along a steep ridge of land running parallel with the river. The hillside became encased in an undulating grid of streets and squares. Gradually the individualism, expressed in one-off set pieces characteristic of the 18thC and early 19thC, gave way to a remarkable coherent series of terraced squares and crescents of epic proportions - making Glasgow one of the finest of Victorian cities. But the price paid for such rapid industrialisation, the tremendous social problems manifest in the squalor of some of the worst of 19thC slums, was high. Today the city is still the commercial and industrial capital of the West of Scotland. The most notorious of the slums have been cleared but the new buildings lack that sparkling clenchfisted Glaswegian character of the 19thC. Ironically, this character was partially destroyed when the slums were cleared for it wasn't the architecture that had failed, only the bureaucrats, who designated such areas as working class ghettos.

Districts
Little remains of medieval Glasgow, which stood on the wedge of land squeezed between the cathedral and

the River Clyde. Its business centre was The Cross, a space formed by the junction of several streets - the tall, square Tolbooth Steeple, 1626, in the middle. Opposite is Trongate, an arch astride a footpath, complete with tower and steeple salvaged from 17thC St. Mary's Church - destroyed by fire in 1793. The centre of 20thC Glasgow is George Square, a tree-lined piazza planned in 1781 and pinned down by more than a dozen statues including an 80 foot high Doric column built in 1837 to carry a statue of Sir Walter Scott. Buildings of interest: the monumental neo-Baroque City Chambers 1883-88 which takes up the east side and the Merchants' House 1874, on the west. To the south of the square, in a huddle of narrow streets, is the old Merchant City. Of interest here is the elegant Trades House, 85 Glassford Street, built by Robert Adam in 1794. An elegant Ionic portico stands on a rusticated ground storey flanked by domed towers. Hutcheson's Hospital, 158 Ingram Street, is an handsome Italianate building designed by David Hamilton in 1805. Nearby is Stirling's Library, originally an 18thC private residence, it became the Royal Exchange in 1827 when the Corinthian portico was added. To the north west is Kelvingrove, Victorian Glasgow at its best. Built around a steep saddle of land, landscaped by Paxton in 1850 and lined along its edge with handsome terraces.

Last but not least are the banks of the River Clyde. From Clyde Walkway on the north bank you can see: the Suspension Bridge of 1871 with its pylons in the form of triumphal arches; 17thC Merchants' Steeple; the Gothic Revival St. Andrew's R.C. Cathedral of 1816; the church, built 1739, in nearby St. Andrew's Square is a typical copy of London's St. Martin-in-the-Fields.

City of Glasgow Local Information Guide

Useful Information

Area of City 79 sq. miles (approx)

Population (Glasgow City)
1998 619,680

Electricity
240 volts A.C.

Emergency Services
Police, Fire and Ambulance. Dial 999
on any telephone.

Licensing Hours
Public Houses
City Centre
Daily except Sundays 11 a.m.-12 midnight
Sundays 12.30 p.m.-12 midnight

Restaurants, Hotels and Public Houses
with catering facililities; same as above
but can be extended for drinks with
meals.

Information Bureau

Tourist Information Centres:
11 George Square, Glasgow, G2 1DY
0141 204 4400

Town Hall, 9a Gilmour Street,
Paisley, PA1 1DD
0141 889 0711

Glasgow International Airport (Abbotsinch),
Paisley, PA3 2ST
0141 848 4440

7a Clyde Square, Greenock, PA15 1NB
01475 722007

Help & Advice

British Telecom Scotland (Glasgow Area)
Westergate Chambers,
11 Hope Street, Glasgow, G2 6AB.
All Enquiries 0141 220 1234
FREEFONE 0800 309 409

Chamber of Commerce
30 George Square, G2 1EQ.
0141 204 2121

Citizens Advice Bureau
48 Albion Street, Glasgow, G1 1LH
0141 552 5556

119 Main Street,
Bridgeton, Glasgow, G40 1QD
0141 554 0336

27 Dougrie Drive, Castlemilk,
Glasgow, G45 9AD
0141 634 0338/9

139 Main Street (Town Hall),
Rutherglen, G73 2JJ
0141 647 5100

216 Main Street, Barrhead, G78 1SN
0141 881 2032

1145 Maryhill Road, Glasgow, G20 9AZ
0141 946 6373

4 Shandwick Square, Easterhouse,
Glasgow, G34 9DS
0141 771 2328

Drumchapel, 49 Dunkenny Square,
G15 8NE
0141 944 2612

1361-1363 Gallowgate
Parkhead
G31 4DN
0141 554 0004

Consumer Advice Centre
Nye Bevan House,
20 India Street,
Glasgow, G2 4PF
0141 287 6681

Customs and Excise
21 India Street, G2 4PZ
0141 221 3828

Enable
(Organisation for people with learning disabilities)
6th Floor
7 Buchanan Street
Glasgow, G1 3HL
0141 226 4541

H.M. Immigration Office
Public Enquiry Office
Dumbarton Court,
Admin Block D, Argyll Avenue, Glasgow
International Airport, Paisley, PA3 2TD
0141 887 2255

Housing Aid and Advice
Shelter, 53 St. Vincent Crescent,
Glasgow, G3 8NQ
0141 221 8995

Lost Property
Trains - There is a railway switchboard
number that will put you through to Lost
Property (whichever station).
0141 335 3276

Buses - Office of bus company
Elsewhere in City - Strathclyde Police.
Lost Property Department,
173 Pitt Street, G2 4JS
0141 532 2000

Registrar of Births, Deaths and Marriages
1 Martha Street, G1 1JJ
0141 287 7652

Marriages only:
22 Park Circus, G3 6BE
0141 287 8350
Hours: Monday 9.15 a.m. - 5.00p.m.
Tuesday to Friday 9.15 a.m. - 4.00 p.m.

Births must be registered within twenty
one days, deaths within eights days and
marriages within three days. The
Registrar should be consulted at least
one month before intended date of
marriage.

Children First
c/o SCET, 74 Victoria Crescent Road,
Glasgow, G12 9JN
0141 334 2547

RNID - Royal National Institute for the Deaf
9 Clairmont Gardens, Glasgow, G3 7LW
0141 332 0343

Samaritans
210 West George Street, Glasgow,
G2 2PQ
0141 248 4488

Shopmobility
To book a free battery powered
wheelcahir or scooter, or to request a
guide at the Sauchiehall, Saint Enoch and
Buchanan Galleries Shopping Centres.
0141 332 6486

Society for the Prevention of Cruelty to Animals
Central Control Telephone Number:
0131 339 0111

Media

British Broadcasting Corporation
Queen Margaret Drive, G12 8DG
0141 339 8844

Scottish Television
Cowcaddens, G2 3PR
0141 300 3000

Morning Daily Newspapers
Daily Record
40 Anderston Quay, G3 8DA.
0141 248 7000

The Herald
195 Albion Street, G1 1QP
0141 552 6255

Scottish Daily Express
Park House, Park Circus Place,
G3 6AF
0141 332 9600

The Scotsman
Regent Court, 70 West Regent Street
G2 2QZ
0141 236 6410

Evening Daily Newspapers
Evening Times
195 Albion Street, G1 1QP
0141 552 6255

Sunday Newspapers
Scottish Sunday Express
Park House, Park Circus Place, G3 6AF
0141 332 9600

Sunday Mail
40 Anderston Quay, G3 8DA
0141 248 7000

Sunday Post
144 Port Dundas Road, G4 0HZ
0141 332 9933

Parking

Car Parking in the central area of Glasgow is controlled. Parking meters are used extensively and signs indicating restrictions are displayed at kerbsides and on entry to the central area. Traffic Wardens are on duty.

Multi-Storey Car Parks (Open 24 Hours)
Cadogan Square, G2: Cambridge Street, G2: Charing Cross, G2: Concert Square, G1: George Street, G1: Mitchell Street, G1: Oswald Street (for Central Station), G1: Sauchiehall Centre, G2:
St. Enochs Shopping Centre, G1 (not 24 Hours)

Surface Car Parks
Anderston Centre, G2: Cathedral Street, G1: Charlotte Street, G1: Dundasvale, G4: Dunlop Street, G1: Great Dovehill, G1: High Street, G1: Ingram Street, G1: King Street, G1: Little Dovehill, G1: Lilybank Gardens, G1: Moir Street, G1: Newton Street, G2: St. Andrew's Lane, G1: Spoutmouth, G1: Washington Street, G1

Post Offices

Head Post Office
47 St. Vincent Street, Glasgow G2 5QX
0141 204 3688
Open Monday to Friday 8.30a.m. - 5.45p.m. Saturdays 9 a.m. - 5.30 p.m.

Branch Offices
228 Hope Street, Glasgow G2 3PN
0141 332 4598
Open Monday - Thursday
8.30a.m. - 5.30p.m.
Friday - 9.00a.m. - 5.30p.m.
Saturday - 8.30a.m. - 5.30p.m.

87-91 Bothwell Street, Glasgow
G2 7AA
0141 221 0666
Open Monday - Friday
9.00a.m.-5.30p.m.

Taxis

Glasgow has over 1400 traditional London type taxis, all licensed by the Glasgow District Council and all fitted with meters sealed and approved by the Council. A fare card stating the current tariff is displayed in a prominent position within each taxi. At the time of publishing a three mile journey costs approximately £5. The total price of each journey is shown on the meter and is calculated by distance or time or a combination of both.Fares are normally reviewed annually by the council. Each taxi can carry a maximum of five passengers.

The major taxi companies in the city offer City tours at fixed prices, listing the places of interest to be visited, leaflets are available at all major hotel reception areas. Tours vary from 1 to 3 hours and in price between £15 and £45. A tour "Glasgow by Night" is also available.

Any passenger wishing to travel to a destination outside the Glasgow District Boundary should ascertain from the driver the fare to be charged or the method of calculating the fare PRIOR to making the journey.

Complaints
Any complaints regarding the conduct of a taxi driver should be addressed to the Taxi Enforcement Officer, City Building Department, 73 Hawthorn Street, Glasgow G22 6HY.
0141 287 3326

Local Government

East Dunbartonshire
PO Box 4, Tom Johnston House, Civic Way, Kirkintilloch, G66 4TJ
0141 578 8000

East Renfrewshire
Council Offices, Eastwood Park, Rouken Glen Road, Giffnock G46 6UG
0141 577 3000

Glasgow City
City Chambers, George Square, Glasgow G2 1DU
0141 287 2000

North Lanarkshire
Civic Centre, Motherwell, ML1 1TW
01698 302222

Renfrewshire
Cotton Street, Paisley, PA1 1BU
0141 842 5000

South Lanarkshire
Council Offices, Almada Street, Hamilton ML3 0AA
01698 454444

West Dunbartonshire
Council Offices
Garshake Road
Dumbarton
G82 3PU
01389 737000

Places of Worship

Glasgow Cathedral is a perfect example of pre-Reformation Gothic architecture. Begun in 1238, it has a magnificent choir and handsome nave with shallow projecting transepts. On a windy hill to the east is the Necropolis, a cemetery with a spiky skyline of Victoriana consisting of pillars, temples and obelisks, dominated by an 1825 Doric column carrying the statue of John Knox. Other churches of interest: Landsdowne Church built by J. Honeyman in 1863; St. George's Tron Church by William Stark 1807; Caledonian Road Church, a temple and tower atop a storey-high base, designed by Alexander Thomson in 1857; a similar design is to be found at the United Presbyterian Church, St. Vincent Street, 1858, but on a more highly articulated ground storey; Queen's Cross Church 1897 is an amalgam of Art Nouveau and Gothic Revival by the brilliant Charles Rennie Mackintosh.

Churches within the central area of Glasgow are:

Church of Scotland
Glasgow Cathedral
Castle Street, G4
Renfield St. Stephen's Church
262 Bath Street, G2
St. George's Tron Church
165 Buchanan Street, G1
St. Columba Church (Gaelic)
300 St. Vincent Street, G3

Baptist
Adelaide Place Church
209 Bath Street, G2

Episcopal Church in Scotland
Cathedral Church of St. Mary
300 Great Western Road

First Church of Christ Scientist
Berkeley Street, G3

Free Church of Scotland
265 St. Vincent Street, G2

German Speaking Congregation
Services held at 7 Hughenden Terrace, G12

Greek Orthodox Cathedral
St. Luke's, 27 Dundonald Road, G12

Islamic Centre
Glasgow Central Mosque, Mosque Avenue, G5

Jewish Orthodox Synagogue
Garnethill, 29 Garnet Street, G3

Methodist
Woodlands Church
229 Woodlands Road, G3

Roman Catholic
St. Andrew's Cathedral
190 Clyde Street, G1
St. Aloysius' Church
25 Rose Street, G3

Unitarian Church
72 Berkeley Street, G3

United Free
Candlish Wynd
62 Daisy Street, G42

Buildings & Shops

Interesting Buildings

Victorian Glasgow was extremely eclectic architecturally. Good examples of the Greek Revival style are Royal College of Physicians 1845, by W.H. Playfair and the Custom House 1840, by G.L. Taylor. The Queen's Room 1857, by Charles Wilson, is a handsome temple used now as a Christian Science church. The Gothic style is seen at its most exotic in the Stock Exchange 1877, by J. Burnet. The new Victorian materials and techniques with glass, wrought and cast iron were also ably demonstrated in the buildings of the time. Typical are: Gardener's Stores 1856, by J. Baird; the Buck's Head, Argyle Street, an amalgam of glass and cast iron; and the Egyptian Halls of 1873, in Union Street, which has a masonry framework. Both are by Alexander Thomson. The Templeton Carpet Factory 1889, Glasgow Green, by William Leiper, is a Venetian Gothic building complete with battlemented parapet.

Glasgow University

The great genius of Scottish architecture is Charles Rennie Mackintosh whose major buildings are in Glasgow. In the Scotland Street School 1904-6, he punctuated a 3-storey central block with flanking staircase towers in projecting glazed bays. His most famous building - Glasgow School of Art 1897-9 - is a magnificent Art Nouveau building of taut stone and glass; the handsome library, with its gabled facade, was added later in 1907-9.

Stirling's Library

Galleries & museums

Scotland's largest tourist attraction, The Burrell Collection, is situated in Pollok Country Park, Haggs Road and has more than 8,000 objects, housed in an award winning gallery. The Museum and Art Gallery, Kelvingrove Park, Argyle Street, a palatial sandstone building with glazed central court, has one of the best municipal collections in Britain; superb Flemish, Dutch and French paintings, drawings, prints, also ceramics, silver, costumes and armour, as well as a natural history section. The McLellan Galleries in Sauchiehall Street provide an important venue for touring and temporary art exhibitions. Provand's Lordship c1471, in Castle Street, is Glasgow's oldest house and now a museum of 17th-18thC furniture and household articles (Please note; Provand's Lordship will be closed for major structural repairs, throughout 1999/2000). Pollok House, Pollok Country Park, a handsome house designed by William Adam in 1752, has paintings by William Blake and a notable collection of Spanish paintings, including works by El Greco. The Museum of Transport, housed in Kelvin Hall, Bunhouse Road, has a magnificent collection of trams, cars, ships models, bicycles, horse-drawn carriages and 7 steam locos. The People's Palace, Glasgow Green built 1898 with a huge glazed Winter Garden, has a lively illustrated history of the city. But the oldest museum in Glasgow is the Hunterian Museum, University of Glasgow, University Avenue, opened in 1807, it has a fascinating collection of manuscripts, early painted books, as well as some fine archaeological and geological exhibits.

Streets & shopping

The Oxford Street of Glasgow is Sauchiehall (meaning 'willow meadow') Street. This together with Buchanan Street, The Buchanan Galleries Shopping Centre, Argyle Street, Princes Square and St. Enoch Centre form the main shopping area. Here you will find the department stores, boutiques and

Old Sheriff Court

general shops. All three streets are largely pedestrianised, but the most exhilarating is undoubtedly Buchanan Street. Of particular interest is the spatially elegant Argyll Arcade 1828, the Venetian Gothic-style Stock Exchange 1877, the picturesque Dutch gabled Buchanan Street Bank building 1896 and the Glasgow Royal Concert Hall (opened 1990). In Glasgow Green is The Barras, the city's famous street market, formed by the junction of London Road and Kent Street. The Market is open weekends.

Museum & Art Gallery Kelvingrove

Entertainment

As Scotland's commercial and industrial capital, Glasgow offers a good choice of leisure activities. The city now has many theatres where productions ranging from serious drama to pantomime, pop and musicals are performed. The Theatre Royal, Hope Street is Scotland's only opera house and has been completely restored to its full Victorian splendour. The Royal Scottish National Orchestra gives classical music concerts at the Glasgow Royal Concert Hall between October and April and is the venue for the proms in June. Cinemas are still thriving in Glasgow, as are the many public houses, some of which provide meals and live entertainment. In the city centre and Byres Road, West End, there is a fair number of restaurants where traditional home cooking, as well as international cuisines, can be sampled. More night life can be found at the city's discos and dance halls.

Outdoors, apart from the many parks and nature trails, there is Calderpark Zoological Gardens, situated 6 miles from the centre between Mount Vernon and Uddingston. Here you may see white rhinos, black panthers and iguanas among many species. Departing from Anderston Quay, you can also cruise down the Clyde in 'P.S. Waverley' - the last sea-going paddle- steamer in the world.

Cinemas

ABC Cinema, 380 Clarkston Road
0141 633 2123
Glasgow Film Theatre
12 Rose Street
0141 332 6535
Grosvenor Cinema
Ashton Lane
0141 339 4298
Kelburne Cinema
(Manager), Glasgow Road, Paisley
PA1 3BD.
Odeon Film Centre
56 Renfield Street 0141 332 8701
UCG
The Forge Shopping Centre
1221 Gallowgate,
G31 4EB
0141 556 4282

Halls

City Halls, Candleriggs, G1
Couper Institute
86 Clarkston Road, G44
Langside Hall, 5 Langside Avenue, G41
Partick Burgh Hall, 9 Burgh Hall Street, G11
Woodside Hall, Glenfarg Street, G20

More information about the above G.C.C. halls contact,
Cultural and Leisure Services, 1st Floor,
32 Albion Srteet, Glasgow,
G1 5LH
0141 287 5008

Glasgow Royal Concert Hall
2 Sauchiehall Street, G2 3NY
0141 333 9123
Henry Wood Hall, 73 Claremont Street,
Glasgow, G3 7JB
0141 225 3555

Theatres

Arches Theatre
30 Midland Street G1 4PR
0141 221 9736
Citizens' Theatre
119 Gorbals Street G5 9DS
0141 429 0022
King's Theatre
297 Bath Street, G2 4JN
0141 287 5022
Mitchell Theatre and Moir Hall
Granville Street G3 7DR
0141 287 4855
New Athenaeum Theatre
100 Renfrew Street G2 3DB
0141 332 5057
Pavilion Theatre
121 Renfield Street G2 3AX
0141 332 1846
Theatre Royal
282 Hope Street G2 3QA
0141 332 9000
Tramway
25 Albert Drive G41 2PE
0141 422 2023
Tron Theatre
63 Trongate, Glasgow G1 5HB
0141 552 4267

The Ticket Centre
Candleriggs, G1 1NQ
Glasgow's Central Box Office for Centre for Contemporary Arts, Citizens' Theatre, City Hall at Candleriggs, Cottier Theatre, King's Theatre, Mitchell Theatre, Tron Theatre, Scottish Exhibition Centre and Glasgow Royal Concert Hall.
Counter Service and telephone lines open:
Mon.- Sat. 9.00a.m. - 9.00 p.m. Sun. 10.00a.m. - 5.00 p.m.
0141 287 5511

Weather

The City of Glasgow is on the same latitude as the City of Moscow, but because of its close proximity to the warm Atlantic Shores, and the prevailing westerly winds, it enjoys a more moderate climate. Summers are generally cool and winters mostly mild, this gives Glasgow fairly consistent summer and winter temperatures. Despite considerable cloud the City is sheltered by hills to the south-west and north and the average rainfall for Glasgow is usually less than 40 inches per year. The following table shows the approximate average figures for sunshine, rainfall and temperatures to be expected in Glasgow throughout the year.

Weather Forecasts
For the Glasgow Area including Loch Lomond and the Clyde Coast:
Weatherline 0891 232 791 (Recording)
The Glasgow Weather Centre (Meteorological Office), St. Vincent Street, G2 5QD
0141 248 3451

Month	Hours of Sunshine	Inches of Rainfall	Temperature °C		
			Ave. Max.	Ave. Min.	High/Low
January	36	3.8	5.5	0.8	-18
February	62	2.8	6.3	0.8	-15
March	94	2.4	8.8	2.2	21
April	147	2.4	11.9	3.9	22
May	185	2.7	15.1	6.2	26
June	181	2.4	17.9	9.3	30
July	159	2.9	18.6	10.8	29
August	143	3.5	18.5	10.6	31
September	106	4.1	16.3	9.1	-4
October	76	4.1	13.0	6.8	-8
November	47	3.7	8.7	3.3	-11
December	30	4.2	6.5	1.9	-12

Sport & Recreation

For both spectator and participant, football is Glasgow's favourite sport. Both Celtic and Rangers, Scotland's most famous rival teams, have their grounds within the City. Glasgow houses Scotland's national football stadium at Hampden Park.

Badminton

Scottish Badminton Union's Cockburn Centre, 40 Bogmoor Place, G51 4TQ.
0141 445 1218

Bowling Greens

There are greens in all the main Parks. Information about clubs from the Scottish Bowling Association: 50 Wellington Street, G2 6EF.
0141 221 8999

Cricket Grounds

Huntershill Crowhill Road, Bishopbriggs, G64
Pollok Dawholm, 2060 Pollokshaws Road, G43.
West of Scotland Peel Street, G11.

Football Grounds

Broadwood (Clyde F.C.) Cumbernauld, G68
Celtic Park (Celtic F.C.) 95 Kerrydale Street, G40 3RE
Firhill Park (Partick Thistle F.C.) Firhill Road, G20 7AL
Hampden Park (Queen's Park F.C.) Somerville Drive, G42 9BA
Ibrox Stadium (Rangers F.C.) Edmiston Drive, G51 2XD
St. Mirren Park (St. Mirren F.C.) Love Street, Paisley, PA3 2EJ

Golf Courses

9 holes
Alexandra Park, Sannox Gardens, G31
Cambuslang, Westburn Drive, Cambuslang G72
King's Park, Carmunnock Road, Croftfoot, G44
Knightswood, Lincoln Avenue,G13
Ruchill, Brassey Street, G20

18 holes
Barshaw, Glasgow Road, Paisley, PA1
Douglaston, Strathblane Road,Milngavie, G62 (Five miles from Glasgow).
Elderslie, Main Road, Elderslie, PA5
Lethamhill, Cumbernauld Road, G33
Littlehill, Auchinairn Road, G74
Linn Park, Simshill Road, G44
Pollok, Barrhead Road, Pollokshaws, G43

Putting Greens
There are putting greens in some of the main parks.

Pitch & Putt
Courses at Bellahouston Park, Queen's Park and several others.

Rugby Grounds

Auldhouse (Hutchesons'/Aloysians) Thornliebank
Cartha Queens Park Haggs Road, G41
Garscube Estate Switchback Road, Maryhill, Glasgow, G61
Hughenden (Hillhead High School) Hughenden Road, G12.
New Anniesland (Glasgow Acad.) Helensburgh Drive, G13.
Old Anniesland (Glasgow High School F.P. & Kelvinside Academicals) Crow Road, G11.

Sports Centres

Barrhead, Main Street, Barrhead G78 1SW
0141 881 1900

Bellahouston 31 Bellahouston Drive, G52 1HH.
0141 427 5454
Burnhill 60 Toryglen Road, Rutherglen, G73 2JH.
0141 643 0327
Crownpoint Crownpoint Road, Bridgeton, G40 1HH.
0141 554 8274
Linwood, Brediland Road, Linwood PA3 3RA.
01505 329 461
Springburn Key Street, Springburn, G21 1LY.
0141 557 5878
Tryst, Tryst Walk, Cumbernauld G67 1EW.
01236 728138

Swimming Pools

Drumchapel, 199 Drumry Road East, G15 8NS.
0141 944 5812
Easterhouse, Bogbain Road, G34 9OU. 0141 771 7978
Elderslie, 3 Stoddard Square, Elderslie. PA5 9AS
01505 328133
Lagoon Leisure Centre, Mill St., Paisley PA1 1LZ.
0141 889 4000
North Woodside, Braid Square, G4 9YB. 0141 332 8102
Pollok Leisure Pool, Cowglen Road, G53. 0141 881 3313
Renfrew Victory Baths, Inchinnan Road, Renfrew PA4 8ND.
0141 886 2088
Scotstoun Leisure Centre 72 Danes Drive, Scotstoun, G14 9HO. 0141 959 4000
Tollcross Park Leisure Centre Wellshot Road, Tollcross G32 7QR 0141 763 1222

Tennis

There are courts in some of the main parks. Information about clubs from the Secretary of the West of Scotland Lawn Tennis Association: Mr J Stevenson 01505 814337.

Anniesland College
Hatfield Drive, Glasgow, G12 OYE
0141 357 3969

Ayr College
Dam Park, Ayr, KA8 OEU
01292 265184

Bell College of Technology
Almada Street, Hamilton, Lanarkshire,
ML3 OJB
01698 283100

**Cardonald College of Further
Education**
690 Mosspark Drive, Glasgow, G52 3AY
0141 272 3333

Central College of Commerce
300 Cathedral Street, Glasgow, G1 2TA
0141 552 3941

Clydebank College
Kilbowie Road, Clydebank,
Dunbartonshire, G81 2AA
0141 952 7771

Coatbridge College
Kildonan Street, Coatbridge,
Lanarkshire, ML5 3LS
01236 422316

Cumbernauld College
Town Centre, Cumbernauld, Glasgow,
G67 1HU
01236 731811

Glasgow Caledonian University
70 Cowcaddens Road, Glasgow, G4 0BA
0141 331 3000

**Glasgow College of Building and
Printing**
60 North Hanover Street, Glasgow,
G1 2BP
0141 332 9969

**Glasgow College of Food
Technology**
230 Cathedral Street, Glasgow, G1 2TG
0141 552 3751

Glasgow College of Nautical Studies
21 Thistle Street, Glasgow, G5 9XB
0141 565 2500

James Watt College
Finnart Street, Greenock, Renfrewshire,
PA16 8HF
01475 724433

John Wheatley College
1346 Shettleston Road, Glasgow,
G32 9AT
0141 778 2426

Kilmarnock College
Holehouse Road, Kilmarnock, Ayrshire,
KA3 7AT
01563 523501

Langside College
50 Prospecthill Road, Glasgow, G42 9LB
0141 649 4991

Motherwell College
Dalzell Drive, Motherwell, Lanarkshire,
ML1 2DD
01698 232323

North Glasgow College
110 Flemington Street, Glasgow,
G21 4BX
0141 558 9001

Reid Kerr Gollege, The
Renfrew Road, Paisley, Renfrewshire,
PA3 4DR
0141 581 2222

South Lanarkshire College
Hamilton Road, Cambuslang, Glasgow,
G72 7BS
0141 641 6600

Stow College
43 Shamrock Street, Glasgow, G4 9LD
0141 332 1786

University of Glasgow
University Avenue, Glasgow, G12 8QQ
0141 339 8855

University of Paisley
High St, Paisley, PA1 2BE
0141 848 3000

University of Strathclyde
16 Richmond Street, Glasgow, G1 1XQ
0141 552 4400

Parks & Gardens

There are over 70 public parks within the city. The most famous is Glasgow Green. Abutting the north bank of the River Clyde, it was acquired in 1662. Of interest are the Winter Gardens attached to the People's Palace. Kelvingrove Park is an 85-acre park laid out by Sir Joseph Paxton in 1852. On the south side of the city is the 148-acre Queen's Park, Victoria Road, established 1857-94. Also of interest: Rouken Glen, Thornliebank, with a spectacular waterfall, walled garden, nature trail and boating facilities; Victoria Park, Victoria Park Drive, with its famous Fossil Grove, flower gardens and yachting pond. In Great Western Road are the Botanic Gardens. Founded in 1817, the gardens' 42 acres are crammed with natural attractions, including the celebrated Kibble Palace glasshouse with its fabulous tree ferns, exotic plants and white marble Victorian statues.

Alexandra
671 Alexandra Parade, G31.

Barshaw
Glasgow Road, Paisley.

Bellahouston
Dumbreck Road, G51.

Botanic Gardens
730 Great Western Road, G12.

Hogganfield
Cumbernauld Road, G33.

Glasgow Green
Greendyke Street, G40.

Kelvingrove
Sauchiehall Street, G3.

King's
325 Carmunnock Road, G44.

Linn
Clarkston Road at Netherlee Road, G44.

Pollok Country Park
Pollokshaws Road, G43

Queen's
Victoria Road, G42.

Rouken Glen
Rouken Glen Road, G46.

Springburn
Broomfield Road, G21.

Tollcross
461 Tollcross Road, G32.

Victoria
Victoria Park Drive North, G14.

Kibble Palace

Public Transport

The City of Glasgow has one of the most advanced, fully integrated public transport systems in the whole of Europe. The Strathclyde Transport network consists of: the local railway network, the local bus services and the fully modernised Glasgow Underground, with links to Glasgow International Airport and the Steamer and Car Ferry Services.
For information contact:
Strathclyde Transport Travel Centre
Buchanan Bus Station, Killermont Street, G2 0141 332 7133
Open everyday 6.30 a.m. - 9.30 p.m.
Telephone enquiries everyday 7.00 a.m. - 9.30 p.m.

For City services, ferry services, local train services. Free timetables are available.

Bus Services and Tours
Long Distance Coach Service
Citylink 0990 505050
National Express 0990 808080
Scottish Citylink Coaches Ltd and National Express provide express services to London and most parts of Scotland including Campbeltown, Tarbert, Ardrishaig, Inverary, Oban, Fort William, Skye, Stirling, Perth, Dundee, Arbroath, Montrose, Aberdeen, Aviemore, Inverness and Edinburgh.

Local Bus Services
A comprehensive network of local bus services is provided by a variety of operators within the City of Glasgow and also direct to the following destinations:
Airdrie, Ardrossan, Ayr, Balfron, Barrhead, Bearsden, Beith, Bellshill, Bishopbriggs, Bishopton, Blantyre, Bo'ness, Caldercruix, Cambuslang, Campsie Glen, Carluke, Clydebank, Coatbridge, Cumbernauld, Denny, Drymen, Dunfermline, Duntocher, Eaglesham, East Kilbride, Erskine, Falkirk, Glenrothes, Grangemouth, Hamilton, Irvine, Johnstone, Kilbarchan, Kilbirnie, Killearn, Kilmarnock, Kilsyth, Kirkintilloch, Kirkcaldy, Lanark, Largs, Larkhall, Lennoxtown, Lochwinnoch, Motherwell, Milngavie, Newton Mearns, Old Kilpatrick, Paisley, Prestwick, Renfrew, Saltcoats, Shotts, Stirling, Strathblane, Strathaven, Uddingston, Wishaw.

These services depart from City Centre bus stops or from Buchanan Bus Station. 0141 332 7133

Coach Hire and Day, Half Day and Extended Tours
Scottish Citylink Coaches Ltd
Private hire and seasonal tours
0990 505050

Haldane's of Cathcart
12, Delvin Road, Cathcart, G44 3AA
Private hire and tours
0141 637 2234

First Glasgow
4 Glencryan Road, South Carbrain, Cumbernauld, G67 2UL.
Private hire and seasonal tour
01236 782491

Railway Services
National Rail Passenger enquiries:
0345 484 950
ScotRail enquiries: 0345 550 033

ScotRail trains serve over 170 stations in Glasgow and Strathclyde (see map). ScotRail services operate to most destinations in Scotland.
East Coast Ltd., West Coast Ltd. and Cross Country Trains Ltd. operate services to England.

Glasgow Queen Street Station
for services to Cumbernauld, Edinburgh, Falkirk, Stirling, Perth, Dundee, Arbroath, Montrose, Aberdeen, Pitlochry, Aviemore, Inverness, Durnbarton, Balloch, Helensburgh, Oban, Fort William, Mallaig, Coatbridge, Airdrie.

Glasgow Central Station
for services to Gourock (ferry connection to Dunoon), Greenock, Wemyss Bay (ferry connection to Rothesay), Paisley, Johnstone, Largs, Ardrossan (ferry connection to Brodick), Irvine, Ayr, Girvan, Stranraer, East Kilbride, Kilmarnock, Dumfries, Motherwell, Hamilton, Lanark, Carlisle, Shotts, Edinburgh, Berwick, Newcastle.
London and destinations on West and East Coast Main Lines.

Strathclyde Transport

JOIN US ON A JOURNEY

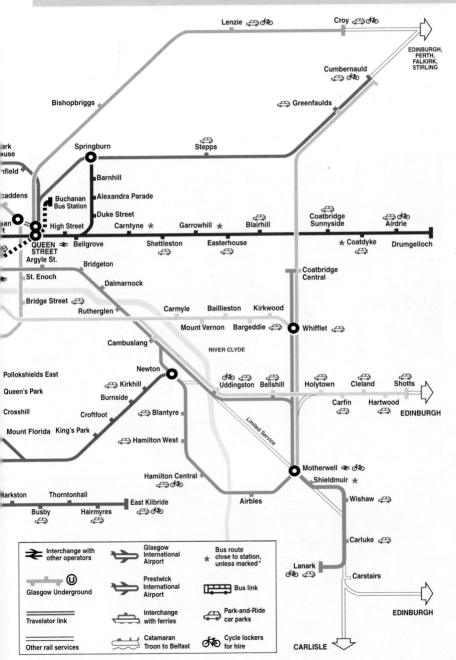

Lenzie

Croy

EDINBURGH,
PERTH,
FALKIRK,
STIRLING

Cumbernauld

Greenfaulds

Bishopbriggs

Springburn

Stepps

Park
ouse

field

caddens

Barnhill

Alexandra Parade

Buchanan
Bus Station

Duke Street

Coatbridge
Sunnyside

Airdrie

an
t

High Street

Carntyne ★

Garrowhill ★

Blairhill

QUEEN
STREET

Bellgrove

Shettleston

Easterhouse

★ Coatdyke

Drumgelloch

Argyle St.

Coatbridge
Central

Bridgeton

St. Enoch

Dalmarnock

Bridge Street

Rutherglen

Carmyle

Baillieston

Kirkwood

Mount Vernon

Bargeddie

Whifflet

Cambuslang

RIVER CLYDE

Pollokshields East

Newton

Queen's Park

Kirkhill

Uddingston

Bellshill

Holytown

Cleland

Shotts

Burnside

Carfin

Hartwood

Crosshill

Croftfoot

Blantyre

EDINBURGH

Mount Florida

King's Park

Limited Service

Hamilton West

arkston

Thorntonhall

Hamilton Central

Motherwell

Shieldmuir ★

Busby

Hairmyres

East Kilbride

Airbles

Wishaw

Carluke

Lanark

Carstairs

EDINBURGH

CARLISLE

Legend

≷	Interchange with other operators	✈	Glasgow International Airport	★	Bus route close to station, unless marked*
Ⓤ Glasgow Underground		✈	Prestwick International Airport	🚌	Bus link
Travelator link		⛴	Interchange with ferries	🚗	Park-and-Ride car parks
Other rail services		⛴	Catamaran Troon to Belfast	🚲	Cycle lockers for hire

Current at November 1999

87

Glasgow International Airport

Glasgow International Airport is located eight miles (13km) west of Glasgow alongside the M8 motorway at Junction 28. It is linked by a bus service to Buchanan Bus Station, which runs every 10 minutes from 8.00 a.m.-5.00p.m. Monday to Saturday and less frequently at off peak times. There is a frequent coach service linking the Airport with all major bus and rail terminals in the City. Gilmour Street railway station in Paisley is 2 miles away and is linked by a frequent local bus service or by taxi.

Car parking is available with a graduated scale of charges. The Airport telephone number is 0141 887 1111

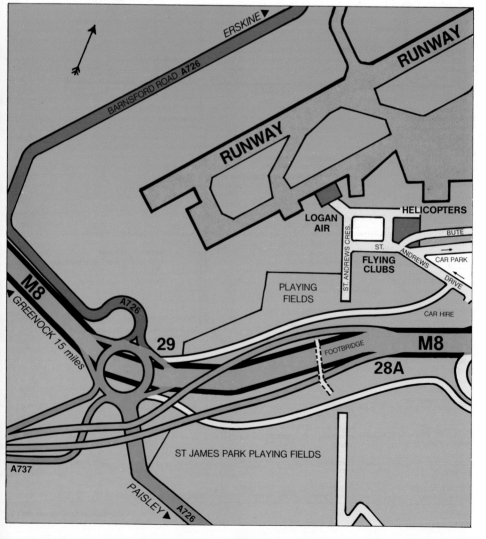

Airlines

Aer Lingus Flights to: Dublin
Reservations 0645 737 747
Air Canada Flights to: Toronto
Reservations 0990 247 226
KLM U.K. Flights to: Amsterdam and
London Stansted.
Reservations 0870 507 4074
British Airways Flights to:
London Gatwick, London Heathrow,
Manchester, Birmingham, Bristol,
Cardiff, Belfast, Londonderry and Inter
Scottish Routes.
Reservations 0345 222111

British Midland Flights to: London
Heathrow, East Midlands, Manchester,
Leeds Bradford, Jersey and
Copenhagen
Reservations 0870 607 0555
Easy Jet Flights to: London Luton.
Reservatons 01582 445566
Icelandair Flights to: Reykjavik.
Reservations 020 7874 1000
Manx Airlines Flights to: Isle of Man
Reservations 0845 725 6256
Sabena Flights to: Brussels
Reservations 0845 601 0933

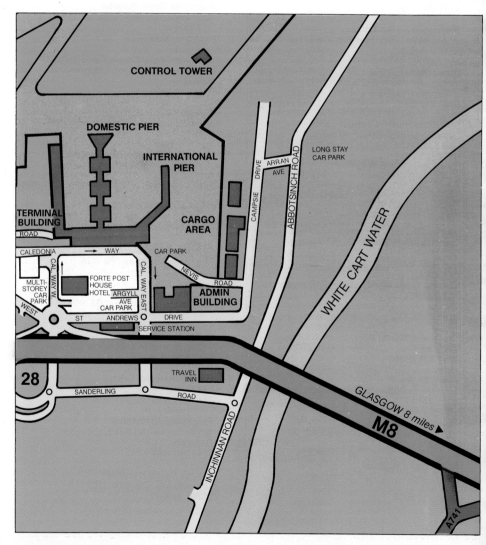

Hospitals and Health Centres

Greater Glasgow Health Board
(Administration)
Dalian House, P.O. Box 15329, 350 St.
Vincent Street, Glasgow, G3 8YZ
0141 201 4444

Acorn Street Psychiatric Day Hospital
23 Acorn Street, Bridgeton, Glasgow, G40
4AA
0141 556 4789

Baillieston Health Centre
20 Muirside Road, Glasgow, G69 7AD
0141 531 8000

Blawarthill Hospital
129 Holehouse Drive, Blawarthill,
Glasgow, G13 3TG
0141 954 9000

Bridgeton Health Centre
201 Abercromby Street, Glasgow,
G40 2AD
0141 531 6500

Canniesburn Hospital
Switchback Road, Bearsden, Glasgow,
G61 1QL
0141 211 5600

Castlemilk Health Centre
Dougrie Drive, Castlemilk, Glasgow,
G45 9AW
0141 531 8500

Charing Cross Clinic
8 Woodside Crescent, Glasgow,
G3 7UL
0141 211 8100

Clydebank Health Centre
Kilbowie Road, Clydebank, G81 2TQ
0141 531 6400

Cowglen Hospital
10 Boydstone Road, Glasgow, G53 6XJ
0141 211 9200

Douglas Inch Centre
2 Woodside Terrace, Glasgow, G3 7UY
0141 211 8000

Drumchapel Hospital
129 Drumchapel Road, Glasgow,
G15 6PX
0141 211 6000

Easterhouse Health Centre
9 Auchinlea Road, Glasgow, G34 9QU
0141 531 8100

Gartnavel General Hospital
1053 Great Western Road, Glasgow,
G12 0YN
0141 211 3000

Gartnavel Royal Hospital
1055 Great Western Road, Glasgow,
G12 0XH
0141 211 3600

Glasgow Dental Hospital and School
378 Sauchiehall Street, Glasgow,
G2 3JZ
0141 211 9600

Glasgow Eye Infirmary
3 Sandyford Place, Glasgow, 63 7NB
0141 211 3000

Glasgow Homeopathic Hospital
1053 Great Western Road, Glasgow,
G12 0XQ
0141 211 1600

Glasgow Royal Infirmary
84 Castle Street, Glasgow, G4 0SF
0141 211 4000

Glasgow Royal Maternity Hospital
Rottenrow, Glasgow, G4 0NA
0141 211 5400

Gorbals Health Centre
45 Pine Place, Glasgow, G5 0BQ
0141 531 8200

Govan Health Centre
5 Drumoyne Road, Glasgow G51 4BJ
0141 531 8400

Govanhill Health Centre
233 Calder Street, Glasgow, G42 7DR
0141 531 8300

Knightswood Hospital
125 Knightswood Road, Glasgow,
G13 2XB
0141 211 6900

Lennox Castle Hospital
Lennoxtown, Glasgow, G65 7LB
01360 313000

Lenzie Hospital
Auchinloch Road, Kirkintilloch, Glasgow,
G66 5UF
0141 211 8200

Leverndale Hospital
510 Crookston Road, Glasgow,
G53 7TU
0141 211 6400

Lightburn Hospital
966 Carntyne Road, Glasgow, G32 6ND
0141 221 1500

Maryhill Health Centre
41 Shawpark Street, Glasgow, G20 9DR
0141 531 8700

Mansionhouse Geriatric Unit
100 Mansionhouse Road, Glasgow,
G44 3DX
0141 201 6111

Parkhead Health Centre
101 Salamanca Street, Glasgow,
G31 5NA
0141 531 9000

Parkhead Hospital
81 Salamanca Street, Glasgow,
G31 5ES
0141 211 8300

Pollock Health Centre
21 Cowglen Road, Glasgow, G53 6EQ
0141 531 6800

Possilpark Health Centre
85 Denmark Street, Glasgow, G22 5EG
0141 531 6120

Queen Mother's Hospital
Yorkhill, Glasgow, G3 8SJ
0141 201 0550

Royal Hospital for Sick Children
Yorkhill, Glasgow, G3 8SJ
0141 201 0000

Rutherglen Health Centre
130 Stonelaw Road, Rutherglen,
Glasgow, G73 2PQ
0141 531 6000

Rutherglen Maternity Hospital
120 Stonelaw Road, Rutherglen,
Glasgow, G73 2PG   0141 201 6060

Shettleston Health Centre
420 Old Shettleston Road, Glasgow,
G32 7JZ
0141 531 6200

Southern General Hospital
1345 Govan Road, Glasgow, G51 4TF
0141 201 1100

Springburn Health Centre
200 Springburn Way, Glasgow, G21 1RT
0141 531 6700

Stobhill Hospital
133 Balornock Road, Glasgow, G21 3UW
0141 201 3000

Thornliebank Health Centre
20 Kennishead Road, Glasgow, G46 8NY
0141 531 6900

Townhead Health Centre
16 Alexandra Parade, Glasgow, G31 2ES
0141 531 8900

Victoria Infirmary
Langside Road, Glasgow, G42 9TY
0141 201 6000

Western Infirmary
Dumbarton Road, Partick, Glasgow,
G11 6NT
0141 211 2000

Woodilee Hospital
Lenzie, Glasgow, G66 3UG
0141 531 3100

Woodside Health Centre
Barr Street, Glasgow, G20 7LR
0141 531 9200

Renfrew District

A selection of leisure, recreational and cultural attractions in Renfrew District:

Barrhead Sports' Centre
The Centre contains swimming pools, sports halls, activity rooms and saunasuite. Bar and restaurant facilities add to the wide range of sporting and leisure activities available. 0141 580 1175

Barshaw Park, Glasgow Road, Paisley
The park is extensive with formal and informal areas. It adjoins the public golf course and incorporates a boating pond, playgrounds, model "ride-on" railway and a nature corner. 0141 840 2908

Braehead Shopping & Leisure Centre, King's Inch Road
Retail and leisure centre opened in 1999 including over 100 shops, 4000 seat ice arena, skating and curling rinks. 0141 885 4600

Castle Semple Visitor Centre, Lochwinnoch
Castle Semple Loch is a popular feature for sailing and fishing. Canoes, rowing boats and sailing boards for hire. Fishing permits available. 01505 842882

Coats Observatory
The Observatory has traditionally recorded astronomical and meteorological information since 1882. Now installed with a satellite picture receiver, it is one of the best equipped Observatories in the country. Open Tuesday - Saturday 10 a.m. - 5 p.m. Sunday 2p.m. - 5p.m. 0141 889 2013

Erskine Bridge (Toll)
The bridge is an impressive high level structure opened by HRH Princess Anne in 1971 and provides a direct link from Renfrew District to Loch Lomond and the Trossachs. The bridge replaced the Erskine Ferry and affords extensive views up and down river to pedestrian users.

Finlaystone Country Estate
Off the A8 at Langbank. Gardens and woodland walks. The house has connections with John Knox and Robert Burns and is open by appointment only. Estate open all year round 10.30a.m. -5p.m. 0147 540505

Gleniffer Braes Country Park, Glenfield Road, Paisley
1,000 breathtaking acres including Glen Park nature trail, picnic and children's play areas. Open dawn till dusk, the park affords extensive walks and spectacular views from this elevated moorland area, and contains an area reserved for model aero flying. 0141 884 3794

Houston Village
Houston was developed in the 18th century as an estate village. The traditional smiddy building, village pubs and terraced houses combine to create a quiet, sleepy atmosphere which has successfully survived the development of extensive modern housing on its periphery.

Inchinnan Bridges
Early 19th century stone bridges over the White Cart and Black Cart rivers close to St. Conval's stone, and the site of the Inchinnan Church which houses the graves of the Knights Templar, whose order was introduced to Scotland in 1153 by King David I.

Johnstone Castle
The remnants of a 1700 building formerly a much larger structure but demolished in the 1950's. The castle has significant historical links with the Cochrane and Houston families, major landowners who were instrumental in the development of the Burgh of Johnstone.

Kilbarchan Village
A good example of an 18th Century weaving village with many original buildings still fronting the narrow streets. A focal point is the steeple building in the square, originally a school and meal market and now used as public meeting rooms. A cycle route/footpath system links it to Glasgow and the Clyde Coast.

Lagoon Leisure Centre, Paisley
Ultra-modern complex housing superb ice rink and extensive "fun" pool featuring artificial wave machine and water slides. Also has cafe/bar facilities. Unique within the area, the complex is easily reached by public transport and has ample parking. Monday - Friday 10 a.m. - 10 p.m., Saturday and Sunday 9.30 a.m. - 5.00 p.m. 0141 889 4000

Linwood Sports Centre

A wide range of indoor and outdoor sporting activities include football and rugby pitches, running track, games hall, squash courts, BMX track, fitness trail, tennis courts and conditioning suite.
01505 329 461

Lochwinnoch Village

An attractive rural village close to the Castle Semple Water Park, Muirshiel Country Park and the R.S.P.B. nature reserve, Lochwinnoch contains a small local museum with displays reflecting agricultural, social and industrial aspects of village life. Museum open Monday, 10 a.m. - 1 p.m., 2 - 5 p.m. and 6 - 8 p.m. Saturday 10 a.m. - 1 p.m. and 2- 5 p.m.
01505 842615

Muirshiel Country Park

Four miles north of Lochwinnoch, the park features trails of varying length radiating from the Information Centre. Open daily 9a.m.-4.30 p.m. (Winter), 9a.m. - 7.30 p.m. (Summer). 01505 842803

Paisley Abbey

Birthplace of the Stewart Dynasty, the Abbey dates, in part, to the 12th century and features regimental flags, relics, the Barochan Cross and beautiful stained glass windows.
Monday - Saturday 10 a.m. - 3.30 p.m., Sunday1.30- 3.30 p.m.
0141 889 3630

Paisley Arts Centre

Converted 18th century church the Laigh Kirk. Performing arts, works by local artists and participatory events, includes bar and bistro. Open Monday - Saturday 10a.m. - 8p.m.   Further information
0141 887 1010

Paisley Museum and Art Gallery, High Street, Paisley

In addition to the world famous collection of Paisley shawls, the Museum traces the history of the Paisley pattern, the development of weaving techniques and houses collections of local and natural history, ceramics and paintings.
Tuesday- Saturday 10 a.m - 5 p.m.
Sunday 2p.m. - 5p.m.
0141 889 3151

Paisley Town Hall

A Renaissance style building by the River Cart in the heart of Paisley, it features a slim clock tower and houses a Tourist Information Centre. It accommodates many exhibitions during the year and it is also available for conferences and functions.
Monday - Friday 9 a.m. - 5 p.m.
0141 887 1007

Paisley Town Trail

An easy to follow route taking in the town's historic and architecturally significant buildings. Visitors can spend an hour or two walking round the trail and referring to a printed guide and wall plaques on the main buildings.

Renfrew Town Hall

The Town Hall has a "fairy-tale" style to its 105 feet high spire and was the administrative centre of the Royal Burgh of Renfrew. Originally the principal town in the area, Renfrew was strategically placed on the River Clyde, and a passenger ferry continues to operate daily.

Robert Tannahill, Weaver Poet

The works of Tannahill rank with those of Burns. Born in 1774 he took his own life in 1810 and is buried in a nearby graveyard. Visitors can visit his early home, site of his death, and his grave, and read his works in Paisley Library.

Royal Society for Protection of Birds, Lochwinnoch

An interesting visitor centre with observation tower, hides, displays and gift shop.
Open every day 10a.m. - 5 p.m.
01505 842663

Sma' Shot Cottages, Paisley

Fully restored and furnished artisan's house of the Victorian era; exhibition room displaying photographs plus artefacts of local interest. 18th Century weaver's loomshop with combined living quarters.
Open Wednesday & Saturday
April- September 1-5 p.m. Group visits arranged by appointment.
0141 889 1708

The Clyde Estuary

Visitors travelling along the rural route to the Old Greenock Road above Langbank village at the western end of the District are able to take advantage of extensive views of the upper and lower Clyde Estuary, the Gareloch and the mountains beyond.

Thomas Coats Memorial Church

Another gift from the Coats family to Paisley, the church was built in 1894 and constructed of red sandstone, is one of the finest Baptist Churches in the country.
Open May - September
Monday, Wednesday and Friday 2-4p.m.
Sunday 11a.m.-12 midday
0141 889 9980

Wallace Monument, Elderslie

The monument was erected in 1912 and marks the birthplace of the Scottish Patriot, Sir William Wallace. It stands adjacent to the reconstructed foundation plan of the Wallace Buildings which dated from the 17th Century.

Weaver's Cottage, Kilbarchan

This cottage, built in 1723, houses the last of the village's 800 looms and demonstrations are still given. It contains displays of weaving and domestic utensils, with Cottage garden and refreshments.
Open daily May - September and weekends in October 1.30p.m. - 5.30p.m.
01505 705588

INDEX TO STREETS

General Abbreviations

Arc.	Arcade	Dr.	Drive	Lo.	Lodge	St.	Street,Saint
Av.	Avenue	E.	East	Mans.	Mansions	Sta.	Station
Bk.	Bank	Est.	Estate	Ms.	Mews	Ter.	Terrace
Bldgs.	Buildings	Ex.	Exchange	N.	North	Trd.	Trading
Boul.	Boulevard	Fm.	Farm	Par.	Parade	Twr.	Tower
Bri.	Bridge	Gdns.	Gardens	Pas.	Passage	Vill.	Villa
Cen.	Centre,Central	Gra.	Grange	Pk.	Park	Vills.	Villas
Cft.	Croft	Grn.	Green	Pl.	Place	Vw.	View
Circ.	Circus	Gro.	Grove	Quad.	Quadrant	W.	West
Clo.	Close	Ho.	House	Rd.	Road	Wd.	Wood
Cor.	Corner	Hts.	Heights	Ri.	Rise	Wds.	Woods
Cotts.	Cottages	Ind.	Industrial	S.	South	Wf.	Wharf
Cres.	Crescent	La.	Lane	Sch.	School	Wk.	Walk
Ct.	Court	Ln.	Loan	Sq.	Square		

Postal Town Abbreviations

Clyde.	Clydebank	Ersk.	Erskine	Pais.	Paisley
Coat.	Coatbridge	John.	Johnstone	Renf.	Renfrew

Locality Abbreviations

Abbots.	Abbotsinch	Clark.	Clarkston	Kirk.	Kirkintilloch
Bail.	Baillieston	Cumb.	Cumbernauld	Linw.	Linwood
Barr.	Barrhead	Cumb.V.	Cumbernauld Village	Mill.Pk.	Milliken Park
Bears.	Bearsden	Dunt.	Duntocher	Mood.	Moodiesburn
Bishop.	Bishopbriggs	Elder.	Elderslie	Muir.	Muirhead
Blan.	Blantyre	Gart.	Gartcosh	Old Kil.	Old Kilpatrick
Both.	Bothwell	Giff.	Giffnock	Ruther.	Rutherglen
Camb.	Cambuslang	Inch.	Inchinnan	Thorn.	Thornliebank
Chry.	Chryston	Kilb.	Kilbarchan	Udd.	Uddingston

NOTES

Postal district information is included for all streets and so Abbey Dr. is to be found in postal district G14. In some cases the additional locality information is included in brackets following the street name. Where this has been abbreviated please consult the locality abbreviations listed above. For streets outwith the Glasgow post town area, the appropriate post town abbreviation is also used with the postal district. Thus Abbey Close is located within the Paisley post town, district PA1 and it will be found on page 46 in square K14.

This index contains some street names in standard text which are followed by another street named in italics. In these cases the street in standard text does not actually appear on the map due to insufficient space but can be located close to the street named in italics. Thus Abbot St. G41 is to be found off Frankfort St. page 51 grid square U15.

Abbey Clo., Pais. PA1	46	K14	Abernethy St. G31	37	Z12	Advie Pl. G42	51	V16
Abbey Dr. G14	19	R10	Aberuthven Dr. G32	54	BB14	*Prospecthill Rd.*		
Abbey Rd. (Elder.), John. PA5	44	F15	Abiegail Pl. (Blan.) G72	68	FF19	Affric Dr., Pais. PA2	47	L15
Abbeycraig Rd. G34	40	FF11	Aboukir St. G51	33	R12	Afton Cres. (Bears.) G61	8	S6
Abbeydale Way (Ruther.) G73	65	Z18	Aboyne Dr., Pais. PA2	46	K15	Afton Dr., Renf. PA4	18	N10
Neilvaig Dr.			Aboyne St. G51	33	R13	Afton Rd. (Cumb.) G67	71	PP2
Abbeyhill St. G32	38	AA12	Acacia Dr. (Barr.) G78	59	L17	Afton St. G41	51	U16
Abbot St. G41	51	U15	Acacia Dr., Pais. PA2	45	H15	Agamemnon St., Clyde. G81	4	K7
Frankfort St.			Acacia Pl., John. PA5	44	E16	Agnew La. G42	51	V15
Abbot St., Pais. PA3	30	K13	Acacia Way (Camb.) G72	67	DD17	*Albert Rd.*		
Abbotsburn Way, Pais. PA3	30	J12	Academy Pk. G41	50	T14	Aigas Cotts. G13	19	R9
Abbotsford (Bishop.) G64	11	Z7	Academy Rd. (Giff.) G46	62	T19	*Crow Rd.*		
Abbotsford Av. (Ruther.) G73	53	Y16	Academy St. G32	54	BB14	Aikenhead Rd. G42	51	V14
Abbotsford Ct. (Cumb.) G67	70	NN4	Acer Cres., Pais. PA2	45	H15	Aikenhead Rd. G44	64	W17
Abbotsford Cres., Pais. PA2	44	F16	Achamore Cres. G15	6	N6	Ailean Dr. G32	55	DD14
Abbotsford La. G5	51	V14	Achamore Dr. G15	6	N6	Ailean Gdns. G32	55	DD14
Cumberland St.			Achamore Pl. G15	6	N6	Ailort Av. G44	63	V17
Abbotsford Pl. G5	35	V13	*Achamore Rd.*			*Lochinver Dr.*		
Abbotsford Pl. (Cumb.) G67	70	NN4	Achamore Rd. G15	6	N6	Ailsa Dr. G42	51	U16
Abbotsford Rd. (Bears.) G61	7	Q5	Achray Dr., Pais. PA2	45	H15	Ailsa Dr. (Both.) G71	69	HH18
Abbotsford Rd. (Cumb.) G67	70	NN4	Acorn Ct. G40	52	X14	Ailsa Dr. (Ruther.) G73	64	X17
Abbotsford Rd., Clyde. G81	5	L7	*Acorn St.*			Ailsa Dr., Clyde. G81	5	M5
Abbothall Av. G15	6	N6	Acorn St. G40	52	X14	Ailsa Dr., Pais. PA2	46	J16
Abbotsinch Rd., Pais. PA3	30	K11	Acre Dr. G20	8	T7	Ailsa Rd. (Bishop.) G64	11	Y7
Abbotsinch Rd., Renf. PA4	30	K11	Acre Rd. G20	8	S7	Ailsa Rd., Renf. PA4	31	M11
Abbott Cres., Clyde. G81	17	M8	Acredyke Cres. G21	23	Z8	Ainslie Rd. G52	32	P12
Aberconway St., Clyde. G81	17	M8	Acredyke Pl. G21	23	Z9	Ainslie Rd. (Cumb.) G67	71	QQ2
Abercorn Av. G52	32	N12	Acredyke Rd. G21	23	Y8	Airdale Av. (Giff.) G46	62	T19
Abercorn Pl. G23	9	U7	Acredyke Rd. (Ruther.) G73	52	X16	Aird's La. G1	36	W13
Abercorn St., Pais. PA3	30	K13	Adams Ct. La. G1	35	V12	*Bridgegate*		
Abercrombie Cres. (Bail.) G69	41	GG13	*Howard St.*			Airgold Dr. G15	6	N6
Abercromby Dr. G40	36	X13	Adamswell St. G21	22	X10	Airgold Pl. G15	6	N6
Abercromby Sq. G40	36	X13	Adamswell Ter. (Chry.)	15	HH7	Airlie Gdns. (Ruther.) G73	65	Z18
Abercromby St. G40	36	X13	G69			Airlie La. G12	20	S10
Aberdalgie Path G34	40	EE12	Addiewell St. G32	38	BB12	*Clarence Dr.*		
Aberdalgie Rd. G34	40	EE12	Addison Gro. (Thorn.) G46	61	R18	Airlie Rd. (Bail.) G69	56	EE14
Aberdour St. G31	37	Z12	Addison Pl. (Thorn.) G46	61	R18	Airlie St. G12	20	S10
Aberfeldy St. G31	37	Z12	Addison Rd. G12	20	T10	Airlour Rd. G43	63	U17
Aberfoyle St. G31	37	Z12	Addison Rd. (Thorn.) G46	61	R18	Airth Dr. G52	49	R14
Aberlady Rd. G51	33	R12	Adelaide Ct. (Old Kil.) G60	4	J5	Airth La. G52	49	R14
Abernethy Dr. (Linw.), Pais.	28	E13	Adelphi St. G5	36	W13	Airth Pl. G52	49	R14
PA3			Admiral St. G41	35	U13	Airthrey Av. G14	19	R10

Street	Page	Grid
Airthrey La. G14	19	Q10
Airthrey Av.		
Aitken St. G31	37	Z12
Aitkenhead Av., Coat. ML5	57	HH14
Aitkenhead Rd. (Udd.) G71	57	HH16
Alasdair Ct. (Barr.) G78	59	M19
Albany Av. G32	39	CC13
Albany Cotts. G13	19	R9
Crow Rd.		
Albany Dr. (Ruther.) G73	65	Y17
Albany Pl. (Both.) G71	69	HH19
Marguerite Gdns.		
Albany Quad. G32	39	CC13
Mansionhouse Dr.		
Albany St. G40	53	Y14
Albany Ter. (Camb.) G72	66	AA18
Albany Way, Pais. PA3	30	K12
Abbotsburn Way		
Albert Av. G42	51	U15
Albert Bri. G1	36	W13
Albert Bri. G5	36	W13
Albert Ct. G41	51	U14
Albert Dr.		
Albert Cross G41	51	U14
Albert Dr. G41	50	T15
Albert Dr. (Bears.) G61	8	S7
Albert Dr. (Ruther.) G73	65	Y17
Albert Rd. G42	51	V15
Albert Rd. (Lenzie) G66	13	CC6
Albert Rd., Clyde. G81	5	L6
Albert Rd., Renf. PA4	17	M10
Alberta Ter. G12	20	T10
Saltoun St.		
Albion Gate, Pais. PA3	30	J13
Mossvale St.		
Albion St. G1	36	W12
Albion St. (Bail.) G69	55	DD14
Albion St., Pais. PA3	30	J13
Alcaig Rd. G52	49	R16
Alder Av. (Kirk.) G66	12	BB5
Alder Ct. (Barr.) G78	59	M19
Alder Gate (Camb.) G72	67	DD17
Alder Pl. G43	62	T17
Alder Pl., John. PA5	44	E15
Alder Rd. G43	62	T17
Alder Rd. (Cumb.) G67	71	QQ3
Alder Rd., Clyde. G81	4	K5
Alderman Pl. G13	19	Q9
Alderman Rd. G13	18	N8
Alderside Dr. (Udd.) G71	57	GG16
Aldersyde Pl. (Blan.) G72	68	FF19
Alexander Cres. G5	52	W14
Alexander St., Clyde. G81	5	L7
Alexandra Av. (Stepps) G33	25	CC9
Alexandra Av. (Lenzie) G66	13	CC6
Alexandra Ct. G31	37	Y12
Roebank St.		
Alexandra Cross G31	37	Y12
Duke St.		
Alexandra Dr., Pais. PA2	45	H14
Alexandra Dr., Renf. PA4	17	M10
Alexandra Gdns. (Kirk.) G66	13	CC6
Alexandra Par. G31	37	Y12
Alexandra Pk. (Kirk.) G66	13	CC6
Alexandra Pk. St. G31	37	Y12
Alexandra Rd. (Lenzie) G66	13	CC6
Alford St. G21	22	W10
Alfred La. G12	20	T10
Cecil St.		
Algie St. G41	51	U16
Alice St., Pais. PA2	46	K15
Aline Ct. (Barr.) G78	59	L18
Allan Av., Renf. PA4	32	N11
Allan Glen Gdns. (Bishop.) G64	11	Y6
Allan Pl. G40	53	Y14
Allan St. G40	53	Y15
Allander Gdns. (Bishop.) G64	10	X6
Allander Rd. (Bears.) G61	7	Q6
Allander St. G22	22	W10
Allands Av. (Inch.), Renf. PA4	16	J9
Allanfauld Rd. (Cumb.) G67	70	NN2
Allanton Av., Pais. PA1	48	N14
Allanton Dr. G52	32	P13
Allen Way, Renf. PA4	31	M11
Allerdyce Dr. G15	6	N7
Allerdyce Rd. G15	6	N7
Allerton Gdns. (Bail.) G69	55	DD14
Alleysbank Rd. (Ruther.) G73	53	Y15
Allison Dr. (Camb.) G72	66	BB17
Allison Pl. G42	51	V15
Prince Edward St.		
Allison Pl. (Gart.) G69	27	GG10
Allison St. G42	51	V15
Allnach Pl. G34	41	GG12
Alloway Av., Pais. PA2	47	L16
Alloway Cres. (Ruther.) G73	64	X17
Alloway Cres., Pais. PA2	47	L16
Alloway Dr. (Ruther.) G73	64	X17
Alloway Dr., Clyde. G81	5	M6
Alloway Dr., Pais. PA2	47	L16
Alloway Rd. G43	62	T17
Alma St. G40	37	Y13
Almond Av., Renf. PA4	32	N11
Almond Bk. (Bears.) G61	7	Q7
Almond Rd.		
Almond Cres., Pais. PA2	45	G15
Almond Dr. (Kirk.) G66	12	BB5
Almond Rd. G33	25	CC9
Almond Rd. (Bears.) G61	7	Q7
Almond St. G33	37	Z11
Almond Vale (Udd.) G71	57	HH16
Hamilton Vw.		
Alness Cres. G52	49	R14
Alpine Gro. (Udd.) G71	57	GG16
Alsatian Av., Clyde. G81	5	M7
Alston La. G40	36	X13
Claythorn St.		
Altnacreag Gdns. (Chry.) G69	15	HH6
Alton Gdns. G12	20	T10
Great George St.		
Alton Rd., Pais. PA1	47	M14
Altpatrick Gdns. (Elder.), John. PA5	44	E14
Altyre St. G32	54	AA14
Alva Gdns. G52	49	R15
Alva Gate G52	49	R15
Alva Pl. (Lenzie) G66	13	DD6
Alyth Gdns. G52	49	R14
Ambassador Way, Renf. PA4	31	M11
Cockels Ln.		
Amisfield St. G20	21	U9
Amochrie Dr., Pais. PA2	45	H16
Amochrie Glen, Pais. PA2	45	H16
Amochrie Rd., Pais. PA2	45	G15
Amochrie Way, Pais. PA2	45	G15
Amulree Pl. G32	54	BB14
Amulree St. G32	38	BB13
Ancaster Dr. G13	19	R9
Ancaster La. G13	19	Q8
Great Western Rd.		
Anchor Av., Pais. PA1	47	L14
Anchor Cres., Pais. PA1	47	L14
Anchor Dr., Pais. PA1	47	L14
Anchor La. G1	36	W12
St. Vincent Pl.		
Anchor Wynd, Pais. PA1	47	L14
Ancroft St. G20	21	V10
Anderson Dr., Renf. PA4	17	M10
Anderson Gdns. (Blan.) G72	69	GG19
Station Rd.		
Anderson St. G11	34	S11
Anderston Cross Cen. G2	35	V12
Anderston Quay G3	35	U13
Andrew Av. (Lenzie) G66	13	CC6
Andrew Av., Renf. PA4	18	N10
Andrew Dr., Clyde. G81	17	M8
Andrew Sillars Av. (Camb.) G72	67	CC17
Andrews St., Pais. PA3	30	J13
Angela Way (Udd.) G71	69	GG17
Angle Gate G14	19	Q10
Angus Av. G52	48	P14
Angus Av. (Bishop.) G64	23	Z8
Angus Gdns. (Udd.) G71	57	GG16
Angus La. (Bishop.) G64	11	Z7
Angus Oval G52	48	P14
Angus Pl. G52	48	P14
Angus St. G21	22	X10
Angus St., Clyde. G81	18	N8
Angus Wk. (Udd.) G71	57	HH16
Annan Dr. (Bears.) G61	7	Q6
Annan Dr. (Ruther.) G73	53	Z16
Annan Pl., John. PA5	43	C16
Annan St. G42	51	V16
Annandale St. G42	51	V14
Annbank Pl. G31	36	X13
Annbank St.		
Annbank St. G31	36	X13
Anne Av., Renf. PA4	17	M10
Anne Cres. (Lenzie) G66	13	CC6
Annette St. G42	51	V15
Annfield Gdns. (Blan.) G72	68	FF19
Annfield Pl. G31	36	X12
Annick Dr. (Bears.) G61	7	Q7
Annick St. G32	38	BB13
Annick St. (Camb.) G72	67	CC17
Anniesdale Av. (Stepps) G33	25	CC9
Anniesland Cres. G14	18	P9
Anniesland Mans. G13	19	R9
Ancaster Dr.		
Anniesland Rd. G13	19	Q9
Anniesland Rd. G14	18	P9
Anson St. G40	52	X14
Anson Way, Renf. PA4	31	M11
Britannia Way		
Anstruther St. G32	38	AA13
Anthony St. G2	35	V12
Cadogan St.		
Antonine Gdns., Clyde. G81	5	L5
Antonine Rd. (Bears.) G61	6	P5
Anwoth St. G32	54	BB14
Apartments, The (Giff.) G46	62	S19
Milverton Rd.		
Appin Cres. G31	37	Y12
Appin Rd. G31	37	Y12
Appin Ter. (Ruther.) G73	65	Z18
Lochaber Dr.		
Appin Way (Both.) G71	69	HH18
Bracken Ter.		
Appleby St. G22	21	V10
Eltham St.		
Applecross Gdns. (Chry.) G69	15	GG6
Applecross St. G22	21	V10
Appledore Cres. (Both.) G71	69	HH18
Apsley La. G11	34	S11
Apsley St. G11	34	S11
Aranthrue Cres., Renf. PA4	17	M10
Aranthrue Dr., Renf. PA4	17	M10
Aray St. G20	20	T9
Arbroath Av. G52	48	P14
Arcadia St. G40	36	X13
Arcan Cres. G15	6	P7
Archerfield Av. G32	54	BB15
Archerfield Cres. G32	54	BB15
Archerfield Dr. G32	54	BB15
Archerfield Gro. G32	54	BB15
Archerhill Av. G13	18	N8
Archerhill Cotts. G13	18	P8
Archerhill Rd.		
Archerhill Cres. G13	18	P8
Archerhill Gdns. G13	18	P8
Archerhill Rd.		
Archerhill Rd. G13	18	P8
Archerhill Sq. G13	18	N8
Kelso St.		
Archerhill St. G13	18	P8
Archerhill Rd.		
Archerhill Ter. G13	18	P8
Archerhill Rd.		
Ard Rd., Renf. PA4	17	L10
Ard St. G32	54	BB14
Ardargie Dr. G32	55	CC16
Ardargie Pl. G32	55	CC16
Ardbeg Av. (Bishop.) G64	11	Z7
Ardbeg Av. (Ruther.) G73	66	AA18
Ardbeg La. G42	51	V15
Coplaw St.		
Ardbeg St. G42	51	V15
Ardconnel St. (Thorn.) G46	61	R18
Arden Av. (Thorn.) G46	61	R19
Arden Dr. (Giff.) G46	62	S19
Arden Pl. (Thorn.) G46	61	R19
Stewarton Rd.		
Ardencraig Cres. G45	64	W19
Ardencraig Dr. G45	64	X19
Ardencraig La. G45	64	W19
Ardencraig Rd.		
Ardencraig Pl. G45	64	X18
Ardencraig Quad. G45	64	X19
Ardencraig Rd. G45	64	W19
Ardencraig St. G45	65	Y19
Ardencraig Ter. G45	64	X19
Ardenlea (Udd.) G71	57	GG16
Ardenlea St. G40	53	Y14
Ardery St. G11	34	S11
Apsley St.		
Ardessie Pl. G20	20	T9
Ardessie St. G23	8	T7
Torrin Rd.		
Ardfern St. G32	54	BB14
Ardgay Pl. G32	54	BB14
Ardgay St. G32	54	BB14
Ardgay Way (Ruther.) G73	65	Y18

Street	Page	Grid
Ardgour Dr. (Linw.), Pais. PA3	28	E13
Ardgowan Av., Pais. PA2	46	K14
Ardgowan Dr. (Udd.) G71	57	GG16
Ardgowan St., Pais. PA2	46	K15
Ardgowan Ter. La. G3	34	T11
Gray St.		
Ardholm St. G32	38	BB13
Ardhu Pl. G15	6	N6
Ardlamont Sq. (Linw.), Pais. PA3	28	F13
Ardlaw St. G51	33	R13
Ardle Rd. G43	63	U17
Ardlui St. G32	54	AA14
Ardmaleish Cres. G45	64	X19
Ardmaleish Rd. G45	64	W19
Ardmaleish St. G45	64	X19
Ardmaleish Ter. G45	64	X19
Ardmay Cres. G44	52	W16
Ardmillan St. G33	38	AA12
Ardmory Av. G42	52	W16
Ardmory La. G42	52	X16
Ardmory Pl. G42	52	X16
Ardnahoe Av. G42	52	W16
Ardnahoe Pl. G42	52	W16
Ardneil Rd. G51	33	R13
Ardnish St. G51	33	R12
Ardo Gdns. G51	34	S13
Ardoch Gro. (Camb.) G72	66	AA17
Ardoch Rd. (Bears.) G61	8	S5
Ardoch St. G22	22	W10
Ardoch Way (Chry.) G69	15	GG7
Braeside Av.		
Ardshiel Rd. G51	33	R12
Ardsloy La. G14	18	P10
Ardsloy Pl.		
Ardsloy Pl. G14	18	P10
Ardtoe Cres. G33	25	DD9
Ardtoe Pl. G33	25	DD9
Arduthie Rd. G51	33	R12
Ardwell Rd. G52	49	R14
Argosy Way, Renf. PA4	31	M11
Britannia Way		
Argyle St. G2	35	V12
Argyle St. G3	34	T11
Argyle St., Pais. PA1	46	J14
Argyll Arc. G2	35	V12
Argyll Av. (Abbots.), Pais. PA3	30	K11
Argyll Av., Renf. PA4	17	L10
Argyll Rd., Clyde. G81	5	M7
Arisaig Dr. G52	49	R14
Arisaig Dr. (Bears.) G61	8	S6
Arisaig Pl. G52	49	R14
Ark La. G31	36	X12
Arkle Ter. (Camb.) G72	66	AA18
Arkleston Cres., Pais. PA3	31	L12
Arkleston Rd., Pais. PA1	31	L13
Arkleston Rd., Pais. PA3	31	M12
Arkleston Rd., Renf. PA4	31	L12
Arklet Rd. G51	33	R13
Arkwrights Way, Pais. PA1	45	H14
Turners Av.		
Arlington St. G3	35	U11
Armadale Ct. G31	37	Y12
Townmill Rd.		
Armadale Path G31	37	Y12
Armadale Pl. G31	37	Y12
Armadale St. G31	37	Y12
Armaleish Dr. G45	64	X19
Armour Pl., John. PA5	44	E14
Armour Sq., John. PA5	44	E14
Armour St. G31	36	X13
Armour St., John. PA5	44	E14
Armstrong Cres. (Udd.) G71	57	HH16
Arngask Rd. G51	33	R12
Arnhall Pl. G52	49	R14
Arnhem St. (Camb.) G72	67	CC17
Arnholm Pl. G52	49	R14
Arnisdale Pl. G34	40	EE12
Arnisdale Rd. G34	40	EE12
Arnisdale Way (Ruther.) G73	65	Y18
Shieldaig Dr.		
Arniston St. G32	38	AA12
Arniston Way, Pais. PA3	31	L12
Arnol Pl. G33	39	DD12
Arnold Av. (Bishop.) G64	11	Y7
Arnold St. G20	21	V9
Arnott Way (Camb.) G72	66	BB17
Arnprior Cres. G45	64	W18
Arnprior Gdns. (Chry.) G69	15	GG7
Braeside Av.		
Arnprior Quad. G45	64	W18
Arnprior Rd. G45	64	W18
Arnprior St. G45	64	W18
Arnside Av. (Giff.) G46	62	T18
Arnwood Dr. G12	20	S9
Aron Ter. (Camb.) G72	66	AA18
Aros Dr. G52	49	R15
Aros La. G52	49	Q15
Aros Dr.		
Arran Av. (Abbots.), Pais. PA3	30	K11
Arran Dr. (Giff.) G46	62	S19
Arran Dr. G52	49	R14
Arran Dr. (Cumb.) G67	70	MM4
Arran Dr., John. PA5	43	C15
Arran Dr., Pais. PA2	46	K16
Arran La. (Chry.) G69	15	HH7
Burnbrae Av.		
Arran Pl., Clyde. G81	5	M7
Arran Pl. (Linw.), Pais. PA3	28	E13
Arran Rd., Renf. PA4	31	M11
Arran Ter. (Ruther.) G73	64	X17
Arran Way (Both.) G71	69	GG19
Arriochmill Rd. G20	20	T10
Kelvin Dr.		
Arrochar Ct. G23	21	U8
Sunningdale Rd.		
Arrochar Dr. G23	8	T7
Arrochar St. G23	20	T8
Arrol Pl. G40	53	Y14
Arrol Rd. G40	53	Y14
Arrol St. G52	32	N12
Arrowsmith Av. G13	19	Q8
Arthur Av. (Barr.) G78	59	L19
Arthur Rd., Pais. PA2	46	K16
Arthur St. G3	34	T11
Arthur St., Pais. PA1	30	J13
Arthurlie Av. (Barr.) G78	59	M19
Arthurlie Dr. (Giff.) G46	62	T19
Arthurlie St. G51	33	R12
Arthurlie St. (Barr.) G78	59	M19
Arundel Dr. G42	51	V16
Arundel Dr. (Bishop.) G64	11	Y6
Asbury Ct. (Linw.), Pais. PA3	28	F13
Ascaig Cres. G52	49	R15
Ascog Rd. (Bears.) G61	7	R7
Ascog St. G42	51	V15
Ascot Av. G12	19	R9
Ascot Ct. G12	20	S9
Ash Gro. (Bishop.) G64	11	Y7
Ash Gro. (Kirk.) G66	12	BB5
Ash Gro. (Bail.) G69	41	GG13
Ash Gro. (Udd.) G71	57	HH16
Ash Pl., John. PA5	44	E15
Ash Rd. (Cumb.) G67	71	QQ1
Ash Rd. (Bail.) G69	56	EE14
Ash Rd., Clyde. G81	4	K5
Ash Wk. (Ruther.) G73	65	Z18
Ash Wynd (Camb.) G72	67	DD18
Ashburton La. G12	20	S9
Ashburton Rd.		
Ashburton Rd. G12	20	S9
Ashby Cres. G13	7	R7
Ashcroft Dr. G44	64	X17
Ashdale Dr. G52	49	R14
Ashdene Rd. G22	21	V8
Ashfield (Bishop.) G64	11	Y6
Ashfield St. G22	22	W10
Ashgill Pl. G22	22	W9
Ashgill Rd. G22	21	V9
Ashgrove (Mood.) G69	41	GG13
Ashgrove St. G40	53	Y15
Ashkirk Dr. G52	49	R14
Ashlea Dr. (Giff.) G46	62	T18
Ashley Dr. (Both.) G71	69	HH19
Ashley La. G3	35	U11
Woodlands Rd.		
Ashley St. G3	35	U11
Ashmore Rd. G43	63	U17
Ashmore Rd. G44	63	U17
Ashton Gdns. G12	34	T11
Ashton Gdns. (Gart.) G69	27	GG9
Ashton La. G12	34	T11
University Av.		
Ashton La. N. G12	34	T11
University Av.		
Ashton Pl. G12	20	T10
Byres Rd.		
Ashton Rd. G12	34	T11
University Av.		
Ashton Rd. (Ruther.) G73	53	Y15
Ashton Ter. G12	34	T11
University Av.		
Ashton Way, Pais. PA2	45	G16
Ashtree Rd. G43	50	T16
Ashvale Cres. G21	22	X10
Ashwood Gdns. G13	19	R9
Aspen Dr. G21	23	Y10
Aspen Pl. (Camb.) G72	67	DD18
Aspen Pl., John. PA5	44	E15
Aster Dr. G45	65	Y18
Aster Gdns. G53	61	Q18
Waukglen Cres.		
Athelstane Dr. (Cumb.) G67	70	MM4
Athelstane Rd. G13	19	Q8
Athena Way (Udd.) G71	57	HH16
Athol Av. G52	32	N12
Athole Gdns. G12	20	T10
Athole La. G12	20	T10
Saltoun St.		
Atholl Cres., Pais. PA1	32	N13
Atholl Gdns. (Bishop.) G64	11	Y6
Atholl Gdns. (Ruther.) G73	66	AA18
Atholl La. (Chry.) G69	15	HH7
Atholl Pl. (Linw.), Pais. PA3	28	E13
Atholl Ter. (Udd.) G71	57	GG15
Atlas Pl. G21	22	X10
Atlas Rd. G21	22	X10
Atlas Sq. G21	22	X10
Ayr St.		
Atlas St., Clyde. G81	17	L8
Cart St.		
Attlee Av., Clyde. G81	5	M7
Attlee Pl., Clyde. G81	5	M7
Attlee Av.		
Attow Rd. G43	62	S17
Auburn Dr. (Barr.) G78	59	M19
Auchans Rd. (Houston), John. PA6	28	E12
Auchenbothie Cres. G21	24	AA9
Auchenbothie Pl. G21	24	AA9
Auchencrow St. G34	40	FF12
Auchengeich Rd. (Mood.) G69	14	FF6
Auchenglen Dr. (Chry.) G69	15	GG7
Auchengreoch Av., John. PA5	43	C16
Auchengreoch Rd., John. PA5	43	C16
Auchenlodment Rd., John. PA5	44	E15
Auchentorlie Quad., Pais. PA1	47	L14
Auchentorlie St. G11	33	R11
Dumbarton Rd.		
Auchentoshan Av., Clyde. G81	4	K5
Auchentoshan Ter. G21	36	X11
Auchentoshen Cotts. (Old Kil.) G60	4	J5
Auchinairn Rd. (Bishop.) G64	22	X8
Auchinbee Way (Cumb.) G68	70	LL2
Auchingill Path G34	40	FF11
Auchingill Rd.		
Auchingill Pl. G34	40	FF11
Auchingill Rd. G34	40	FF11
Auchinlea Rd. G34	39	DD11
Auchinleck Av. G33	24	AA9
Auchinleck Cres. G33	24	AA9
Auchinleck Dr. G33	24	AA9
Auchinleck Gdns. G33	24	AA9
Auchinleck Rd. G33	24	AA9
Auchinloch Rd. (Lenzie) G66	13	CC6
Auchinloch St. G21	22	X10
Auchmannoch Av., Pais. PA1	32	N10
Auckland Pl., Clyde. G81	4	J6
Auckland St. G22	21	V10
Auld Rd., The (Cumb.) G67	71	PP2
Auld St., Clyde. G81	4	K6
Auldbar Rd. G52	49	R14
Auldbar Ter., Pais. PA2	47	L15
Auldburn Pl. G43	62	S17
Auldburn Rd.		
Auldburn Rd. G43	62	S17
Auldearn Rd. G21	23	Z8
Auldgirth Rd. G52	49	R14
Auldhouse Av. G43	62	S17
Thornliebank Rd.		
Auldhouse Gdns. G43	62	S17
Auldhouse Rd. G43	62	S17
Auldhouse Ter. G43	62	S17
Auldhouse Rd.		
Auldkirk Rd. (Camb.) G72	67	CC18
Aultbea St. G22	21	V8
Aultmore Rd. G33	39	DD12
Aurs Cres. (Barr.) G78	59	M19
Aurs Dr. (Barr.) G78	59	M19

Aurs Glen (Barr.) G78 59 M19
Aurs Pl. (Barr.) G78 59 M19
Aurs Rd. (Barr.) G78 59 M18
Aursbridge Cres. (Barr.) G78 59 M19
Aursbridge Dr. (Barr.) G78 59 M19
Austen La. G13 19 R9
Skaterig La.
Austen Rd. G13 19 R9
Avenel Rd. G13 7 R7
Avenue, The (Kilb.), John. 42 B15
PA10
Low Barholm
Avenue End Rd. G33 24 BB10
Avenue St. G40 37 Y13
Avenue St. (Ruther.) G73 53 Y15
Avenuehead Rd. (Chry.) G69 15 GG7
Avenuepark St. G20 21 U10
Aviemore Gdns. (Bears.) G61 8 S5
Aviemore Rd. G52 49 R15
Avoch Dr. (Thorn.) G46 61 R18
Avoch St. G34 40 EE11
Avon Av. (Bears.) G61 8 S6
Avon Dr. (Bishop.) G64 23 Y8
Avon Dr. (Linw.), Pais. PA3 28 E13
Avon Rd. (Giff.) G46 62 S19
Avon Rd. (Bishop.) G64 23 Y8
Avon St. G5 35 U13
Avonbank Rd. (Ruther.) G73 52 X16
Avondale Dr., Pais. PA1 31 L13
Avondale St. G33 38 BB11
Avonhead Av. (Cumb.) G67 70 MM4
Avonhead Gdns. (Cumb.) 70 MM4
G67
Avonhead Pl. (Cumb.) G67 70 MM4
Avonhead Rd. (Cumb.) G67 70 MM4
Avonspark St. G21 23 Y10
Aylmer Rd. G43 63 U17
Ayr Rd. (Giff.) G46 62 S19
Ayr St. G21 22 X10
Aytoun Rd. G41 50 T14
Azalia Gdns. (Camb.) G72 67 DD17

B

Back Causeway G31 37 Z13
Back Sneddon St., Pais. PA3 30 K13
Backmuir Rd. G15 6 P6
Bagnell St. G21 22 X9
Baillie Dr. (Both.) G71 69 HH18
Baillie Wynd (Udd.) G71 57 HH16
Baillieston Rd. G32 55 CC14
Baillieston Rd. (Udd.) G71 56 EE14
Bain Sq. G40 36 X13
Bain St.
Bain St. G40 36 X13
Bainsford St. G32 38 AA13
Baird Av. G52 32 N12
Baird Ct., Clyde. G81 5 L7
North Av.
Baird Dr. (Bears.) G61 7 Q5
Baird St. G4 36 W11
Bairdsbrae G4 21 V10
Possil Rd.
Baker Pl. G41 51 U15
Baker St.
Baker St. G41 51 U15
Bakewell Rd. (Bail.) G69 40 EE13
Balaclava St. G2 35 V13
McAlpine St.
Balado Rd. G33 39 DD12
Balbeg St. G51 33 R13
Balbeggie Pl. G32 55 CC14
Balbeggie St. G32 55 CC14
Balblair Rd. G52 49 R15
Balcarres Av. G12 20 T9
Balcomie St. G33 38 BB11
Balcurvie Rd. G34 40 EE11
Baldinnie Rd. G34 40 EE12
Baldorran Cres. (Cumb.) G68 70 LL2
Baldovan Cres. G33 39 DD12
Baldovie Rd. G52 49 Q14
Baldragon Rd. G34 40 EE11
Baldric Rd. G13 19 Q9
Baldwin Av. G13 7 Q7
Balerno Dr. G52 49 R14
Balfluig St. G34 39 DD11
Balfour St. G20 20 T9
Balfron Rd. G51 33 R12
Balfron Rd., Pais. PA1 31 M13
Balgair Dr., Pais. PA1 31 L13
Balgair St. G22 21 V9
Balgair Ter. G32 38 BB13

Balglass St. G22 21 V10
Balgonie Av., Pais. PA2 45 H15
Balgonie Dr., Pais. PA2 46 J15
Balgonie Rd. G52 49 R14
Balgonie Wds., Pais. PA2 46 J15
Balgownie Cres. (Thorn.) G46 62 S19
Balgray Cres. (Barr.) G78 60 N19
Balgraybank St. G21 23 Y10
Balgrayhill Rd. G21 22 X9
Balintore St. G32 38 BB13
Baliol La. G3 35 U11
Woodlands Rd.
Baliol St. G3 35 U11
Ballaig Av. (Bears.) G61 7 Q5
Ballaig Cres. (Stepps) G33 25 CC9
Ballantay Quad. G45 65 Y18
Ballantay Rd. G45 65 Y18
Ballantay Ter. G45 65 Y18
Ballantyne Rd. G52 32 P12
Ballater Dr. (Bears.) G61 7 R7
Ballater Dr., Pais. PA2 47 L15
Ballater Dr. (Inch.), Renf. PA4 16 J8
Ballater Pl. G5 52 W14
Ballater St. G5 36 W13
Ballayne Dr. (Chry.) G69 15 HH7
Ballindalloch Dr. G31 37 Y12
Ballindarroch La. G31 37 Y12
Meadowpark St.
Balloch Gdns. G52 49 R14
Balloch Loop Rd. (Cumb.) 70 MM2
G68
Balloch Vw. (Cumb.) G67 70 NN3
Ballochmill Rd. (Ruther.) G73 53 Z16
Ballochmyle Cres. G53 48 P16
Ballochmyle Dr. G53 48 P15
Ballochmyle Gdns. G53 48 P15
Ballogie Rd. G44 51 V16
Balmartin Rd. G23 8 T7
Balmerino Pl. (Bishop.) G64 23 Z8
Balmoral Cres. G42 51 V15
Queens Dr.
Balmoral Cres. (Inch.), Renf. 16 K9
PA4
Balmoral Dr. G32 54 BB16
Balmoral Dr. (Bears.) G61 8 S7
Balmoral Dr. (Camb.) G72 66 AA17
Balmoral Gdns. (Udd.) G71 57 GG15
Balmoral Gdns. (Blan.) G72 68 FF19
Balmoral Rd. (Elder.), John. 44 E15
PA5
Balmoral St. G14 18 P10
Balmoral Pl. G22 21 V9
Balmore Rd.
Balmore Rd. G22 21 V8
Balmore Rd. G23 9 U7
Balmore Rd. (Milngavie) G62 9 U5
Balmore Sq. G22 21 V9
Balmuildy Rd. G23 9 V6
Balmuildy Rd. (Bishop.) G64 9 V6
Balornock Rd. G21 23 Y9
Balruddery Pl. (Bishop.) G64 23 Z8
Balshagray Av. G11 19 R10
Balshagray Cres. G14 33 R11
Dumbarton Rd.
Balshagray Dr. G11 19 R10
Balshagray La. G11 19 R10
Balshagray Pl. G11 19 R10
Balshagray Dr.
Baltic Ct. G40 53 Y14
Baltic St.
Baltic La. G40 53 Y14
Baltic Pl. G40 52 X14
Baltic St. G40 53 Y14
Balure St. G31 37 Z12
Balvaird Cres. (Ruther.) G73 53 Y16
Balvaird Dr. (Ruther.) G73 53 Y16
Balveny St. G33 39 CC11
Balvicar Dr. G42 51 U15
Balvicar St. G42 51 U15
Balvie Av. G15 6 P7
Balvie Av. (Giff.) G46 62 T19
Banavie Rd. G11 20 S10
Banchory Av. G43 62 S17
Banchory Av. (Inch.), Renf. 16 J8
PA4
Banchory Cres. (Bears.) G61 8 S7
Banff St. G33 38 BB11
Bangorshill St. (Thorn.) G46 61 R18
Bank Rd. G32 55 CC16
Bank St. G12 35 U11
Bank St. (Camb.) G72 66 BB17
Bank St. (Barr.) G78 59 M19

Bank St., Pais. PA1 46 K14
Bankbrae Av. G53 60 P17
Bankend St. G33 38 BB11
Bankfoot Dr. G52 48 P14
Bankfoot Rd. G52 48 P14
Bankfoot Rd., Pais. PA3 29 H13
Bankglen Rd. G15 6 P6
Bankhall St. G42 51 V15
Bankhead Av. G13 18 P9
Bankhead Dr. (Ruther.) G73 53 Y16
Bankhead Rd. (Ruther.) G73 64 X17
Bankier St. G40 36 X13
Banknock St. G32 38 AA13
Bankside Av., John. PA5 43 D14
Banktop Pl., John. PA5 43 D14
Banling Grn. Rd. G44 63 V17
Clarkston Rd.
Bannatyne Av. G31 37 Y12
Banner Dr. G13 7 Q7
Banner Rd. G13 7 Q7
Bannercross Av. (Bail.) G69 40 EE13
Bannercross Dr. (Bail.) G69 40 EE13
Bannercross Gdns. (Bail.) G69 40 EE13
Bannercross Dr.
Bannerman Pl., Clyde. G81 5 M7
Bannerman St., Clyde. G81 5 M7
Bantaskin St. G20 20 T8
Banton Pl. G33 40 EE12
Barassie Ct. (Both.) G71 69 GG19
Barassie Cres. (Cumb.) G68 70 NN1
Barbae Pl. (Both.) G71 69 HH18
Hume Dr.
Barberry Av. G53 60 P19
Barberry Gdns. G53 60 P19
Barberry Av.
Barberry Pl. G53 60 P19
Barberry Av.
Barbreck Rd. G42 51 U15
Pollokshaws Rd.
Barcaldine Av. (Chry.) G69 14 EE7
Barclay Av. (Elder.), John. 44 E15
PA5
Barclay Sq., Renf. PA4 31 L11
Barclay St. G21 22 X9
Lenzie St.
Barcraigs Dr., Pais. PA2 46 K16
Bard Av. G13 18 P8
Bardowie St. G22 21 V10
Bardrain Av. (Elder.), John. 44 F15
PA5
Bardrain Rd., Pais. PA2 46 J16
Bardrill Dr. (Bishop.) G64 10 X7
Bardykes Rd. (Blan.) G72 68 FF19
Barfillan Dr. G52 33 R13
Barfillan Rd. G52 33 R13
Bargany Rd. G53 48 P15
Bargaran Rd. G53 48 P14
Bargarron Dr., Pais. PA3 31 L12
Bargeddie St. G33 37 Z11
Barholm Sq. G33 39 CC11
Barke Rd. (Cumb.) G67 71 PP2
Barlanark Av. G32 39 CC12
Barlanark Cres. G33 39 CC12
Barlanark Dr. G33 39 CC12
Barlanark Pl. G32 39 CC13
Hallhill Rd.
Barlanark Pl. G33 39 DD12
Barlanark Rd. G33 39 CC12
Barlia Dr. G45 64 X18
Barlia St. G45 64 X18
Barlia Ter. G45 64 X18
Barloch St. G22 22 W10
Barlogan Av. G52 33 R13
Barlogan Quad. G52 33 R13
Barmulloch Rd. G21 23 Y10
Barn Grn. (Kilb.), John. 42 B14
PA10
Barnard Gdns. (Bishop.) G64 11 Y6
Barnard Ter. G40 53 Y14
Barnbeth Rd. G53 48 P15
Barnes Rd. G20 21 V9
Barnes St. (Barr.) G78 59 L19
Barness Pl. G33 38 BB12
Barnflat St. (Ruther.) G73 53 Y15
Barnhill Dr. G21 23 Y10
Foresthall Dr.
Barnkirk Av. G15 6 P6
Barns St., Clyde. G81 5 M7
Barnsford Av. (Inch.), Renf. 16 J9
PA4
Barnsford Rd. (Abbots.), 29 H12
Pais. PA3

97

Bentinck St. G3 35 U11
Bents Rd. (Bail.) G69 40 EE13
Benvie Gdns. (Bishop.) G64 11 Y7
Benview St. G20 21 U10
Benview Ter., Pais. PA2 47 L15
Berelands Cres. (Ruther.) G73 52 X16
Berelands Pl. (Ruther.) G73 52 X16
Beresford Av. G14 19 R10
Berkeley St. G3 35 U12
Berkeley Ter. La. G3 35 U11
Elderslie St.
Berkley Dr. (Blan.) G72 68 FF19
Bernard Path G40 53 Y14
Bernard St. G40 53 Y14
Bernard Ter. G40 53 Y14
Berneray St. G22 22 W8
Berridale Av. G44 63 V17
Berriedale Av. (Bail.) G69 56 EE14
Berryburn Rd. G21 23 Z10
Berryhill Dr. (Giff.) G46 62 S19
Berryhill Rd. (Giff.) G46 62 S19
Berryhill Rd. (Cumb.) G67 70 NN3
Berryknowes Av. G52 33 Q13
Berryknowes Av. (Chry.) G69 26 FF8
Berryknowes La. G52 33 Q13
Berryknowes Rd. G52 49 Q14
Bertram St. G41 51 U15
Bertrohill Ter. G33 39 CC12
Stepps Rd.
Bervie St. G51 33 R13
Berwick Cres. (Linw.), Pais. 28 E12
PA3
Berwick Dr. G52 48 P14
Berwick Dr. (Ruther.) G73 53 Z16
Betula Dr., Clyde. G81 5 L5
Bevan Gro., John. PA5 43 C15
Beverley Rd. G43 62 T17
Bevin Av., Clyde. G81 5 M7
Bideford Cres. G32 55 CC14
Biggar St. G31 37 Y13
Bigton St. G33 38 BB11
Bilsland Ct. G20 21 V9
Bilsland Dr.
Bilsland Dr. G20 21 U9
Binend Rd. G53 49 Q16
Binnie Pl. G40 36 X13
Binniehill Rd. (Cumb.) G68 70 MM2
Binns Rd. G33 39 CC11
Birch Cres., John. PA5 44 E15
Birch Dr. (Lenzie) G66 13 CC5
Birch Dr. (Camb.) G72 67 CC17
Birch Gro. (Udd.) G71 57 HH16
Burnhead St.
Birch Knowe (Bishop.) G64 11 Y7
Birch Pl. (Camb.) G72 67 DD18
Birch Rd., Clyde. G81 5 L5
Birch St. G5 52 W14
Silverfir St.
Birch Vw. (Bears.) G61 8 S5
Birchend Dr. G21 37 Y11
Birchend Pl. G21 37 Y11
Birchfield Dr. G14 18 P10
Birchlea Dr. (Giff.) G46 62 T18
Birchwood Av. G32 55 DD14
Birchwood Dr., Pais. PA2 45 H15
Birchwood Pl. G32 55 DD14
Birdston Rd. G21 23 Z9
Birgidale Av. G45 64 W19
Birgidale Rd. G45 64 W19
Birgidale Ter. G45 64 W19
Birkdale Ct. (Both.) G71 69 GG19
Birken Rd. (Lenzie) G66 13 DD6
Birkenshaw St. G31 37 Y12
Birkenshaw Way, Pais. PA3 30 K12
Abbotsburn Way
Birkhall Av. G52 48 N14
Birkhall Av. (Inch.), Renf. PA4 16 J8
Birkhall Dr. (Bears.) G61 7 R7
Birkhill Av. (Bishop.) G64 11 Y6
Birkhill Gdns. (Bishop.) G64 11 Z6
Birkmyre Rd. G51 33 R13
Birks Rd., Renf. PA4 31 L11
Tower Dr.
Birkwood St. G40 53 Y15
Birmingham Rd., Renf. PA4 31 L11
Birnam Av. (Bishop.) G64 11 Y6
Birnam Cres. (Bears.) G61 8 S5
Birnam Gdns. (Bishop.) G64 11 Y7
Birnam Rd. G31 53 Z14
Birness Dr. G43 50 T16
Birness St. G43 50 T16
Birnie Ct. G21 23 Z10

Birnie Rd. G21 23 Z10
Birnock Av., Renf. PA4 32 N11
Birsay Rd. G22 21 V8
Bishop Gdns. (Bishop.) G64 10 X7
Bishop St. G3 35 V12
Bishopmill Pl. G21 23 Z10
Bishopmill Rd. G21 23 Z10
Bishopsgate Dr. G21 22 X8
Bishopsgate Gdns. G21 22 X8
Bishopsgate Pl. G21 22 X8
Bishopsgate Rd. G21 22 X8
Bissett Cres., Clyde. G81 4 K5
Black St. G4 36 W11
Blackburn Sq. (Barr.) G78 59 M19
Blackburn St. G51 34 T13
Blackbyres Ct. (Barr.) G78 59 M18
Blackbyres Rd. (Barr.) G78 59 M17
Blackcraig Av. G15 6 P6
Blackcroft Gdns. G32 55 CC14
Blackcroft Rd. G32 55 CC14
Blackfaulds Rd. (Ruther.) G73 52 X16
Blackford Rd., Pais. PA2 47 L15
Blackfriars St. G1 36 W12
Blackhall La., Pais. PA1 46 K14
Blackhall St., Pais. PA1 46 K14
Blackhill Cotts. G23 9 V7
Blackhill Pl. G33 37 Z11
Blackhill Rd. G23 8 T7
Blackie St. G3 34 T11
Blackland Gro., Pais. PA2 46 J16
Blacklands Pl. (Lenzie) G66 13 DD6
Blacklaw La., Pais. PA3 30 K13
Blackstone Av. G53 49 Q16
Blackstone Cres. G53 49 Q15
Blackstone Rd., Pais. PA3 29 H12
Blackstoun Av. (Linw.), Pais. 28 E13
PA3
Blackstoun Oval, Pais. PA3 29 H13
Blackstoun Rd., Pais. PA3 29 H13
Blackthorn Av. (Kirk.) G66 12 BB5
Blackthorn Gro. (Kirk.) G66 12 BB5
Blackthorn Rd. (Cumb.) G67 71 QQ2
Blackthorn St. G22 22 X9
Blackwood Av. (Linw.), Pais. 28 E13
PA3
Blackwood St. G13 19 R8
Blackwood St. (Barr.) G78 59 L19
Blackwood Ter., John. PA5 43 C16
Blackwoods Cres. (Mood.) 15 GG7
G69
Blacurvie Rd. G34 40 EE11
Bladda La., Pais. PA1 46 K14
Blades Ct. (Gart.) G69 27 HH9
Moraine Av.
Bladnoch Dr. G15 7 Q7
Blaeloch Av. G45 64 W19
Blaeloch Dr. G45 64 W19
Blaeloch Ter. G45 64 W19
Blair Cres. (Bail.) G69 56 EE14
Blair Rd., Pais. PA1 32 N13
Blair St. G32 38 AA13
Blairatholl Av. G11 20 S10
Blairatholl Gdns. G11 20 S10
Blairbeth Dr. G44 51 V16
Blairbeth Rd. (Ruther.) G73 65 Y17
Blairbeth Ter. (Ruther.) G73 65 Y18
Blairdardie Rd. G13 7 Q7
Blairdardie Rd. G15 6 P7
Blairdenan Av. (Chry.) G69 15 HH6
Blairdenon Dr. (Cumb.) G68 70 MM2
Blairgowrie Rd. G52 49 Q14
Blairhall Av. G41 51 U16
Blairhill Av. (Kirk.) G66 14 EE5
Blairlogie St. G33 38 BB11
Blairmore Av., Pais. PA1 31 M13
Blairston Av. (Both.) G71 69 HH19
Blairston Gdns. (Both.) G71 69 HH19
Blairston Av.
Blairtum Dr. (Ruther.) G73 65 Y17
Blairtummock Rd. G33 39 CC12
Blake St. (Both.) G71 69 PP3
Blane St. G4 36 W11
Blantyre Mill Rd. (Both.) G71 69 GG19
Blantyre Rd. (Both.) G71 69 HH19
Blantyre St. G3 34 T11
Blaven Ct. (Bail.) G69 56 FF14
Bracadale Rd.
Blawarthill St. G14 18 N9
Blenheim Av. (Stepps) G33 25 CC9
Blenheim Ct. (Stepps) G33 25 DD9
Blenheim Av.
Blenheim Ct., Pais. PA1 30 J13

Blenheim La. (Stepps) G33 25 DD9
Blesdale Ct., Clyde. G81 5 L7
Blochairn Rd. G21 37 Y11
Bluebell Gdns. G45 65 Y19
Bluevale St. G31 37 Y13
Blyth Pl. G33 39 CC13
Blyth Rd. G33 39 DD13
Blythswood Av., Renf. PA4 17 M10
Blythswood Dr. G2 35 V12
Cadogan St.
Blythswood Dr., Pais. PA3 30 J13
Blythswood Rd., Renf. PA4 17 M9
Blythswood Sq. G2 35 V12
Blythswood St. G2 35 V12
Bobbins Gate, Pais. PA1 45 H14
Boclair Av. (Bears.) G61 7 R6
Boclair Cres. (Bears.) G61 8 S6
Boclair Cres. (Bishop.) G64 11 Y7
Boclair Rd. (Bears.) G61 8 S6
Boclair Rd. (Bishop.) G64 11 Y7
Boclair St. G13 19 R8
Boden St. G40 53 Y14
Bodmin Gdns. (Chry.) G69 15 GG6
Gartferry Rd.
Bogany Ter. G45 64 X19
Bogbain Rd. G34 40 EE12
Boggknowe (Udd.) G71 56 FF16
Old Edinburgh Rd.
Boghall Rd. (Udd.) G71 56 EE15
Boghall St. G33 38 BB11
Boghead Rd. G21 23 Y10
Boghead Rd. (Kirk.) G66 12 BB6
Bogleshole Rd. (Camb.) G72 54 AA16
Bogmoor Rd. G51 33 Q12
Bogside Pl. (Bail.) G69 40 FF12
Whamflet Av.
Bogside Rd. G33 24 BB9
Bogside St. G40 53 Y14
Bogton Av. G14 63 U18
Bogton Av. La. G44 63 U18
Bogton Av.
Boleyn Rd. G41 51 U15
Bolivar Ter. G42 52 W16
Bolton Dr. G42 51 V16
Bon Accord Sq., Clyde. G81 17 L8
Bonawe St. G20 21 U10
Boness St. G40 53 Y14
Bonhill St. G22 21 V10
Bonnar St. G40 53 Y14
Bonnaughton Rd. (Bears.) G61 6 P5
Bonnyrigg Dr. G43 48 P14
Bonnyrigg Dr. G43 62 S17
Bonyton Av. G13 18 N9
Boon Dr. G15 6 P7
Boquhanran Pl., Clyde. G81 5 L6
Albert Rd.
Boquhanran Rd., Clyde. G81 4 K7
Borden La. G13 19 R9
Borden Rd. G13 19 R9
Boreland Dr. G13 18 P8
Boreland Pl. G13 18 P9
Borgie Cres. (Camb.) G72 66 BB17
Borland Rd. (Bears.) G61 8 S6
Borron St. G4 22 W10
Borthwick St. G33 38 BB11
Boswell Ct. G42 51 U16
Boswell Sq. G52 32 N12
Botanic Cres. G20 20 T10
Bothlin Dr. (Stepps) G33 25 CC9
Bothlyn Cres. (Gart.) G69 27 GG8
Bothlyn Rd. (Chry.) G69 26 FF8
Bothwell La. G2 35 V12
West Campbell St.
Bothwell Pk. Rd. (Both.) G71 69 HH19
Bothwell Rd. (Udd.) G71 69 GG17
Bothwell St. G2 35 V12
Bothwell St. (Camb.) G72 66 AA17
Bothwell Ter. G12 35 U11
Bank St.
Bothwellpark Ind. Est. (Udd.) 69 HH18
G71
Bothwick Way, Pais. PA2 45 G16
Boundary Rd. (Ruther.) G73 52 X15
Rutherglen Rd.
Bourne Cres. (Inch.), Renf. PA4 16 J8
Bourne Cres. (Inch.), Renf. 16 J8
PA4
Bourock Sq. (Barr.) G78 60 N19
Bourtree Dr. (Ruther.) G73 65 Z18
Bouverie St. G14 18 N9
Bouverie St. (Ruther.) G73 52 X16
Bowden Dr. G52 32 P13

Name		
Bower St. G12	21	U10
Bowes Cres. (Bail.) G69	55	DD14
Bowfield Av. G52	32	N13
Bowfield Cres. G52	32	N13
Bowfield Dr. G52	32	N13
Bowfield Pl. G52	32	N13
Bowfield Ter. G52	32	N13
Bowfield Cres.		
Bowhouse Way (Ruther.) G73	65	Y18
Bowling Grn. La. G14	19	Q10
Westland Dr.		
Bowling Grn. Rd. G14	19	Q10
Bowling Grn. Rd. G32	55	CC14
Bowling Grn. Rd. G44	63	V17
Bowling Grn. Rd. (Chry.) G69	26	FF8
Bowman St. G42	51	V15
Bowmont Gdns. G12	20	T10
Bowmont Hill (Bishop.) G64	11	Y6
Bowmont Ter. G12	20	T10
Bowmore Gdns. (Udd.) G71	57	GG16
Bowmore Gdns. (Ruther.) G73		
Bowmore Rd. G52	33	R13
Boyd St. G42	51	V15
Boydstone Pl. (Thorn.) G46	61	R17
Boydstone Rd. G43	61	R17
Boydstone Rd. (Thorn.) G46	61	R17
Boydstone Rd. G53	61	R17
Boyle St., Clyde. G81	17	M8
Boylestone Rd. (Barr.) G78	59	L18
Boyndie Path G34	40	EE12
Boyndie St. G34	40	EE12
Brabloch Cres., Pais. PA3	30	K13
Bracadale Dr. (Bail.) G69	56	FF14
Bracadale Gdns. (Bail.) G69	56	FF14
Bracadale Gro. (Bail.) G69	56	FF14
Bracadale Rd. (Bail.) G69	56	FF14
Bracken St. G22	21	V9
Bracken Ter. (Both.) G71	69	HH18
Brackenbrae Av. (Bishop.) G64	10	X7
Brackenbrae Av. (Bishop.) G64	10	X7
Brackenrig Rd. (Thorn.) G46	61	R19
Brackla Av. G13	18	N8
Brackla Av., Clyde. G81	18	N8
Bracora Pl. G20	20	T9
Glenfinnan Dr.		
Bradan Av. G13	18	N8
Bradan Av., Clyde. G81	18	N8
Bradda Av. (Ruther.) G73	65	Z18
Bradfield Av. G12	20	T9
Brady Cres. (Mood.) G69	15	HH6
Braeface Rd. (Cumb.) G67	70	NN3
Braefield Dr. (Thorn.) G46	62	S18
Braefoot Cres., Pais. PA2	46	K16
Braehead Rd. (Cumb.) G67	71	PP2
Braehead Rd., Pais. PA2	58	J17
Braehead St. G5	52	W14
Braemar Av., Clyde. G81	4	K6
Braemar Ct. G44	63	U18
Braemar Cres. (Bears.) G61	7	R7
Braemar Cres., Pais. PA2	46	K16
Braemar Dr. (Elder.), John. PA5	44	E15
Braemar Rd. (Ruther.) G73	66	AA18
Braemar Rd. (Inch.), Renf. PA4	16	J8
Braemar St. G42	51	U16
Braemar Vw., Clyde. G81	4	K5
Braemount Av., Pais. PA2	58	J17
Braes Av., Clyde. G81	17	M8
Braeside Av. (Chry.) G69	15	GG7
Braeside Av. (Ruther.) G73	53	Z16
Braeside Cres. (Bail.) G69	41	GG13
Braeside Cres. (Barr.) G78	60	N19
Braeside Dr. (Barr.) G78	59	M19
Braeside Pl. (Camb.) G72	66	BB18
Braeside St. G20	21	U10
Braeview Av., Pais. PA2	45	H16
Braeview Dr., Pais. PA2	45	H16
Braeview Gdns., Pais. PA2	45	H16
Braeview Rd., Pais. PA2	45	H16
Braid Sq. G4	35	V11
Braid St. G4	35	V11
Braidbar Fm. Rd. (Giff.) G46	62	T18
Braidbar Rd. (Giff.) G46	62	T18
Braidcraft Pl. G53	49	Q16
Braidcraft Rd. G53	49	Q15
Braidfauld Gdns. G32	54	AA14
Braidfauld Pl. G32	54	AA15
Braidfauld St. G32	54	AA15
Braidfield Gro., Clyde. G81	5	L5
Braidfield Rd., Clyde. G81	5	L5
Braidholm Cres. (Giff.) G46	62	T18
Braidholm Rd. (Giff.) G46	62	T18
Braidpark Cres. (Giff.) G46	62	T18
Braidpark Dr. (Giff.) G46	62	T18
Braids Dr. G53	48	N15
Braids Gait, Pais. PA2	46	J15
Braids Rd., Pais. PA2	46	K15
Bramley Pl. (Lenzie) G66	13	DD6
Branchock Av. (Camb.) G72	67	CC18
Brand Pl. G51	34	T13
Brand St. G51	34	T13
Brandon Gdns. (Camb.) G72	66	AA17
Brandon St. G31	36	X13
Branscroft (Kilb.), John. PA10	42	B14
Brassey St. G20	21	U9
Breadalbane Gdns. (Ruther.) G73	65	Z18
Breadalbane St. G3	35	U12
St. Vincent St.		
Brechin (Bishop.) G64	11	Z7
Brechin St. G3	35	U12
Breck Av., Pais. PA2	44	F16
Brediland Rd., Pais. PA2	45	G15
Brediland Rd. (Linw.), Pais. PA3	28	E13
Bredisholm Dr. (Bail.) G69	56	FF14
Bredisholm Rd. (Bail.) G69	56	FF14
Bredisholm Ter. (Bail.) G69	56	FF14
Brenfield Av. G44	63	U18
Brenfield Dr. G44	63	U18
Brenfield Rd. G44	63	U18
Brent Av. (Thorn.) G46	61	R17
Brent Dr. (Thorn.) G46	61	R17
Brent Gdns. (Thorn.) G46	62	S17
Brent Rd. (Thorn.) G46	61	R17
Brent Way (Thorn.) G46	61	R17
Brentwood Av. G53	60	P18
Brentwood Dr. G53	60	P18
Brentwood Sq. G53	60	P18
Brentwood Dr.		
Brereton St. G42	52	W15
Bressey Rd. G33	39	DD13
Brewery St., John. PA5	43	D14
Brewster Av., Pais. PA3	31	L12
Briar Dr., Clyde. G81	5	L6
Briar Gdns. G43	62	T17
Briar Gro. G43	62	T17
Briar Neuk (Bishop.) G64	23	Y8
Briar Rd. G43	62	T17
Briarcroft Dr. G33	23	Z8
Briarcroft Pl. G33	24	AA9
Briarcroft Rd. G33	23	Z9
Briarlea Dr. (Giff.) G46	62	T18
Briarwood Ct. G32	55	DD15
Briarwood Gdns. G32	55	DD15
Woodend Rd.		
Brick La., Pais. PA3	30	K13
Bridge of Weir Rd. (Linw.), Pais. PA3	28	E13
Bridge St. G5	35	V13
Bridge St. (Camb.) G72	66	BB17
Bridge St., Clyde. G81	4	K6
Bridge St., Pais. PA1	46	K14
Bridge St. (Linw.), Pais. PA3	28	E13
Bridgeburn Dr. (Chry.) G69	15	GG7
Bridgegate G1	36	W13
Bridgend Cres. (Mood.) G69	15	GG7
Bridgend Pl. (Mood.) G69	15	GG7
Bridgeton Cross G40	36	X13
Brigham Pl. G23	21	U8
Broughton Rd.		
Bright St. G21	36	X11
Brighton Pl. G51	34	S13
Brighton St. G51	34	S13
Brightside Av. (Udd.) G71	69	HH17
Brisbane Ct. (Giff.) G46	62	T18
Braidpark Dr.		
Brisbane St. G42	51	V16
Brisbane St., Clyde. G81	4	J6
Britannia Way, Renf. PA4	31	M11
Briton St. G51	34	S13
Broad Pl. G40	36	X13
Broad St.		
Broad St. G40	36	X13
Broadford St. G4	36	W11
Harvey St.		
Broadholm St. G22	21	V9
Broadleys Av. (Bishop.) G64	10	X6
Broadlie Dr. G13	18	P9
Broadloan, Renf. PA4	31	M11
Broadwood Dr. G44	63	V17
Brock Oval G53	61	Q17
Brock Pl. G53	49	Q16
Brock Rd. G53	49	Q16
Brock Ter. G53	61	Q17
Brock Way (Cumb.) G67	71	PP3
North Carbrain Rd.		
Brockburn Rd. G53	48	P15
Brockburn Ter. G53	49	Q16
Brockville St. G32	38	AA13
Brodick Sq. (Bishop.) G64	23	Y8
Brodick St. G21	37	Y11
Brodie Av., Pais. PA2	46	K15
Brodie Pk. Cres., Pais. PA2	46	J15
Brodie Pk. Gdns., Pais. PA2	46	K15
Brodie Pl., Renf. PA4	31	L11
Brodie Rd. G21	23	Z8
Brogknowe (Udd.) G71	56	FF16
Glasgow Rd.		
Bron Way (Cumb.) G67	71	PP3
Brook St. G40	36	X13
Brookfield Av. G33	23	Z8
Brookfield Cor. G33	23	Z8
Brookfield Dr. G33	23	Z8
Brookfield Gdns. G33	23	Z8
Brookfield Gate G33	23	Z8
Brookfield Pl. G33	23	Z8
Brooklands Av. (Udd.) G71	57	GG16
Brooklea Dr. (Giff.) G46	62	T17
Brookside St. G40	37	Y13
Broom Cres. (Barr.) G78	59	L17
Broom Dr., Clyde. G81	5	L6
Broom Gdns. (Kirk.) G66	12	BB5
Broom Path (Bail.) G69	55	DD14
Tudor St.		
Broom Rd. G43	62	T17
Broom Rd. (Cumb.) G67	71	QQ1
Broom Ter., John. PA5	43	D15
Broomdyke Way, Pais. PA3	30	J12
Broomfield Av. G21	23	Y10
Broomfield Rd.		
Broomfield Av. (Camb.) G72	53	Z16
Broomfield La. G21	22	X9
Broomfield Rd.		
Broomfield Pl. G21	22	X9
Broomfield Rd.		
Broomfield Rd. G21	22	X9
Broomfield Ter. (Udd.) G71	57	GG15
Broomhill Av. G11	33	R11
Broomhill Av. G32	54	BB16
Broomhill Dr. G11	19	R10
Broomhill Dr. (Ruther.) G73	65	Y17
Broomhill Gdns. G11	19	R10
Broomhill La. G11	19	R10
Broomhill Path G11	33	R11
Broomhill Ter.		
Broomhill Pl. G11	19	R10
Broomhill Ter. G11	33	R11
Broomieknowe Dr. (Ruther.) G73	65	Y17
Broomieknowe Rd. (Ruther.) G73	65	Y17
Broomielaw G1	35	V13
Broomknowe (Cumb.) G68	70	MM2
Broomknowe Pl. (Lenzie) G66	13	DD6
Broomknowes Rd. G21	23	Y10
Broomlands Av., Ersk. PA8	16	J8
Broomlands Cres., Ersk. PA8	16	J8
Broomlands Gdns., Ersk. PA8	16	J8
Broomlands Rd. (Cumb.) G67	71	PP4
Broomlands St., Pais. PA1	46	J14
Broomlands Way, Ersk. PA8	16	K8
Broomlea Cres. (Inch.), Renf. PA4	16	J8
Broomley Dr. (Giff.) G46	62	T19
Broomley La. (Giff.) G46	62	T19
Broomloan Ct. G51	34	S13
Broomloan Pl. G51	34	S13
Broomloan Rd. G51	34	S13
Broompark Circ. G31	36	X12
Broompark Dr. G31	36	X12
Broompark Dr. (Inch.), Renf. PA4	16	J8
Broompark La. G31	36	X12
Craigpark		
Broompark St. G31	36	X12
Broomton Rd. G21	23	Z8
Broomward Dr., John. PA5	44	E14
Brora Dr. (Giff.) G46	62	T19
Brora Dr. (Bears.) G61	8	S6
Brora Dr., Renf. PA4	18	N10

Entry		
Brora Gdns. (Bishop.) G64	11	Y7
Brora La. G33	37	Z11
Brora St.		
Brora Rd. (Bishop.) G64	11	Y7
Brora St. G33	37	Z11
Broughton Dr. G23	21	U8
Broughton Gdns. G23	9	U7
Broughton Rd. G23	21	U8
Brown Av., Clyde. G81	17	M8
Brown Pl. (Camb.) G72	66	BB17
Allison Dr.		
Brown Rd. (Cumb.) G67	70	NN3
Brown St. G2	35	V12
Brown St., Pais. PA1	30	J13
Brown St., Renf. PA4	31	L11
Brownhill Rd. G43	62	S18
Brownlie St. G42	51	V16
Browns La., Pais. PA1	46	K14
Brownsdale Rd. (Ruther.) G73	52	X16
Brownside Av. (Camb.) G72	66	AA17
Brownside Av. (Barr.) G78	59	L17
Brownside Av., Pais. PA2	46	J16
Brownside Cres. (Barr.) G78	59	L17
Brownside Dr. G13	18	N9
Brownside Dr. (Barr.) G78	59	L17
Brownside Gro. (Barr.) G78	59	L17
Brownside Ms. (Camb.) G72	66	AA17
Brownside Rd. (Camb.) G72	65	Z17
Brownside Rd. (Ruther.) G73	65	Z17
Bruce Av., John. PA5	43	D16
Bruce Av., Pais. PA3	31	L12
Bruce Rd. G41	51	U14
Bruce Rd., Pais. PA3	31	L13
Bruce Rd., Renf. PA4	31	L11
Bruce St., Clyde. G81	5	L7
Bruce Ter. (Blan.) G72	69	GG19
Brucefield Pl. G34	40	FF12
Brunstane Rd. G34	40	EE11
Brunswick Ho., Clyde. G81	4	J5
Perth Cres.		
Brunswick La. G1	36	W12
Brunswick St.		
Brunswick St. G1	36	W12
Brunton St. G44	63	V17
Brunton Ter. G44	63	U18
Bruntsfield Av. G53	60	P18
Bruntsfield Gdns. G53	60	P18
Bruntsfield Av.		
Brydson Pl. (Linw.), Pais. PA3	28	E13
Fulwood Av.		
Buccleuch Av. G52	32	N12
Buccleuch La. G3	35	V11
Scott St.		
Buccleuch St. G3	35	V11
Buchan St. G5	35	V13
Norfolk St.		
Buchan Ter. (Camb.) G72	66	AA18
Buchanan Cres. (Bishop.) G64	23	Z8
Buchanan Dr. (Bears.) G61	8	S6
Buchanan Dr. (Bishop.) G64	23	Z8
Buchanan Dr. (Lenzie) G66	13	CC6
Buchanan Dr. (Camb.) G72	66	AA17
Buchanan Dr. (Ruther.) G73	65	Y17
Buchanan Gdns. G32	55	DD15
Buchanan Gro. (Bail.) G69	40	EE13
Buchanan St. G1	35	V12
Buchanan St. (Bail.) G69	56	EE14
Buchanan St., John. PA5	43	D15
Buchley (Bishop.) G64	10	W5
Buchlyvie Gdns. (Bishop.) G64	22	X8
Buchlyvie Path G34	40	EE12
Buchlyvie Rd., Pais. PA1	32	N13
Buchlyvie St. G34	40	EE12
Buckingham Bldgs. G12	20	T10
Great Western Rd.		
Buckingham Dr. G32	54	BB16
Buckingham Dr. (Ruther.) G73	53	Z16
Buckingham St. G12	20	T10
Buckingham Ter. G12	20	T10
Bucklaw Gdns. G52	49	Q14
Bucklaw Pl. G52	49	Q14
Bucklaw Ter. G52	49	Q14
Buckley St. G22	22	W9
Bucksburn Rd. G21	23	Z10
Buckthorne Pl. G53	60	P18
Buddon St. G40	53	Z14
Budhill Av. G32	38	BB13
Bulldale Ct. G14	18	N9
Bulldale Rd. G14	18	N9
Bulldale St. G14	18	N9
Bullionslaw Dr. (Ruther.) G73	65	Z17
Bulloch Av. (Giff.) G46	62	T19
Bullwood Av. G53	48	N15
Bullwood Ct. G53	48	N15
Bullwood Dr. G53	48	N15
Bullwood Gdns. G53	48	N15
Bullwood Pl. G53	48	N15
Bunessan St. G52	33	R13
Bunhouse Rd. G3	34	T11
Burgh Hall La. G11	34	S11
Fortrose St.		
Burgh Hall St. G11	34	S11
Burgh La. G12	20	T10
Vinicombe St.		
Burghead Dr. G51	33	R12
Burghead Pl. G51	33	R12
Burgher St. G31	37	Z13
Burleigh Rd. (Both.) G71	69	HH18
Burleigh St. G51	34	S12
Burlington Av. G12	20	S9
Burmola St. G22	21	V10
Burn Pl. (Camb.) G72	54	AA16
Burn Ter.		
Burn Ter. (Camb.) G72	54	AA16
Burn Vw. (Cumb.) G67	71	QQ2
Burnacre Gdns. (Udd.) G71	57	GG16
Burnawn Gdns. G33	23	Z8
Brookfield Dr.		
Burnawn Pl. G33	23	Z8
Brookfield Av.		
Burnbank Dr. (Barr.) G78	59	M19
Burnbank Gdns. G20	35	U11
Burnbank Pl. G4	36	X12
Drygate		
Burnbank Ter. G20	35	U11
Burnbrae, Clyde. G81	5	L5
Burnbrae Av. (Mood.) G69	15	HH7
Burnbrae Av. (Linw.), Pais. PA3	28	F13
Bridge St.		
Burnbrae Ct. (Lenzie) G66	13	CC6
Auchinloch Rd.		
Burnbrae Dr. (Ruther.) G73	65	Z17
East Kilbride Rd.		
Burnbrae Rd. (Kirk.) G66	13	DD7
Burnbrae Rd. (Chry.) G69	14	EE7
Burnbrae Rd. (Linw.), Pais. PA3	44	F14
Burnbrae St. G21	23	Y10
Burncleuch Av. (Camb.) G72	66	BB18
Burncrooks Ct., Clyde. G81	4	K5
Burndyke Ct. G51	34	T12
Burndyke Sq. G51	34	T12
Burndyke St. G51	34	S12
Burnett Rd. G33	39	DD12
Burnfield Av. (Thorn.) G46	62	S18
Burnfield Cotts. (Thorn.) G46	62	S18
Burnfield Dr. G43	62	S18
Burnfield Gdns. (Giff.) G46	62	T18
Burnfield Rd.		
Burnfield Rd. G43	62	S17
Burnfield Rd. (Thorn.) G46	62	S18
Burnfoot Cres. (Ruther.) G73	65	Z17
Burnfoot Cres., Pais. PA2	46	J16
Burnfoot Dr. G52	32	P13
Burngreen Ter. (Cumb.) G67	71	PP1
Burnham Rd. G14	18	P10
Burnham Ter. G14	18	P10
Burnham Rd.		
Burnhead Rd. G43	63	U17
Burnhead Rd. (Cumb.) G68	70	MM4
Burnhead St. (Udd.) G71	57	HH16
Burnhill Quad. (Ruther.) G73	52	X16
Burnhill St. (Ruther.) G73	52	X16
Burnhouse St. G20	20	T9
Kelvindale Rd.		
Burnmouth Ct. G33	39	DD13
Pendeen Rd.		
Burnmouth Pl. (Bears.) G61	8	S5
Burnmouth Rd. G33	39	DD13
Burnpark Av. (Udd.) G71	56	FF16
Burns Dr., John. PA5	43	D16
Burns Gdns. (Blan.) G72	68	FF19
Burns Gro. (Thorn.) G46	62	S19
Burns Rd. (Cumb.) G67	71	PP3
Burns St. G4	35	V11
Burns St., Clyde. G81	4	K6
Burnside Av. (Barr.) G78	59	L18
Burnside Ct., Clyde. G81	4	K6
Scott St.		
Burnside Gdns. (Mill.Pk.), John. PA10	42	B15
Burnside Gate (Ruther.) G73	65	Z17
Burnside Gro., John. PA5	43	D15
Quarrelton Rd.		
Burnside Pl., Pais. PA3	29	H12
Burnside Rd. (Ruther.) G73	65	Z17
Burnside Rd. (Elder.), John. PA5	44	F15
Burntbroom Dr. (Bail.) G69	55	DD14
Burntbroom Gdns. (Bail.) G69	55	DD14
Burntbroom St. G33	39	CC12
Burntshields Rd. (Kilb.), John. PA10	42	A15
Burra Gdns. (Bishop.) G64	11	Z6
Solway Rd.		
Burrells La. G4	36	X12
High St.		
Burrelton Rd. G43	63	U17
Burton La. G42	51	V15
Langside Rd.		
Bushes Av., Pais. PA2	46	J15
Busheyhill St. (Camb.) G72	66	BB17
Bute Av., Renf. PA4	31	M11
Bute Cres. (Old Kil.) G60	4	J5
Bute Cres. (Bears.) G61	7	R7
Bute Cres., Pais. PA2	46	J16
Bute Dr. (Old Kil.) G60	4	J5
Bute Dr., John. PA5	43	C15
Bute Gdns. G12	34	T11
Bute Gdns. G44	63	U18
Bute Gdns. (Old Kil.) G60	4	J5
Bute La. G12	34	T11
Great George St.		
Bute Rd. (Abbots.), Pais. PA3	30	J11
Bute Ter. (Udd.) G71	57	HH16
Bute Ter. (Ruther.) G73	65	Y17
Butterbiggins Rd. G42	51	V14
Butterfield Pl. G41	51	U15
Pollokshaws Rd.		
Byrebush Rd. G53	49	Q15
Byres Av., Pais. PA3	31	L13
Byres Cres., Pais. PA3	31	L13
Byres Rd. G11	34	T11
Byres Rd. G12	34	T11
Byres Rd. (Elder.), John. PA5	44	F15
Byron Ct. (Both.) G71	69	HH19
Shelley Dr.		
Byron St. G11	33	R11
Byron St., Clyde. G81	4	K6
Byshot St. G22	22	W10

C

Entry		
Cable Depot Rd., Clyde. G81	4	K7
Cadder Ct. (Bishop.) G64	11	Y5
Cadder Gro. G20	21	U8
Cadder Rd.		
Cadder Pl. G20	21	U8
Cadder Rd. G20	21	U8
Cadder Rd. G23	21	U8
Cadder Rd. (Bishop.) G64	11	Y5
Cadder Way (Bishop.) G64	11	Y5
Cadoc St. (Camb.) G72	66	BB17
Cadogan St. G2	35	V12
Cadzow Dr. (Camb.) G72	66	AA17
Cadzow St. G2	35	V12
Cadogan St.		
Caird Dr. G11	34	S11
Cairn Av., Renf. PA4	32	N11
Cairn Dr. (Linw.), Pais. PA3	28	E13
Cairn La., Pais. PA3	30	J12
Mosslands Rd.		
Cairn St. G21	22	X9
Cairnban St. G51	33	Q13
Cairnbrook Rd. G34	40	FF12
Cairncraig St. G31	53	Z14
Cairndow Av. G44	63	U18
Cairndow Ct. G44	63	U18
Cairngorm Cres. (Bears.) G61	7	R7
Cairngorm Cres. (Barr.) G78	59	M19
Cairngorm Cres., Pais. PA2	46	K15
Cairngorm Rd. G43	62	T17
Cairnhill Circ. G52	48	N14
Cairnhill Dr. G52	48	N14
Cairnhill Pl. G52	48	N14
Cairnhill Circ.		
Cairnhill Rd. (Bears.) G61	7	R7
Cairnlea Dr. G51	34	S13
Cairnoch Hill (Cumb.) G68	70	MM3
Cairns Av. (Camb.) G72	66	BB17
Cairns Rd. (Camb.) G72	66	BB18

Name	Num	Ref
Cairnsmore Rd. G15	6	N7
Cairnswell Av. (Camb.) G72	67	CC18
Cairnswell Pl. (Camb.) G72	67	CC18
Cairntoul Ct. (Cumb.) G68	70	LL3
Cairntoul Dr. G14	18	P9
Cairntoul Pl. G14	18	P9
Caithness St. G20	21	U10
Calcots Path G34	40	FF11
Auchingill Rd.		
Calcots Pl. G34	40	FF11
Caldarvan St. G22	21	V10
Calder Av. (Barr.) G78	59	M19
Calder Dr. (Camb.) G72	66	BB17
Calder Gate (Bishop.) G64	10	X6
Calder Pl. (Bail.) G69	56	EE14
Calder Rd. (Udd.) G71	68	EE17
Calder Rd., Pais. PA3	29	H13
Calder St. G42	51	V15
Calderbank Vw. (Bail.) G69	56	FF14
Calderbraes Av. (Udd.) G71	57	GG16
Caldercuilt Rd. G20	20	T8
Caldercuilt Rd. G23	20	T8
Calderpark Av. (Udd.) G71	56	EE15
Calderpark Cres. (Udd.) G71	56	EE15
Caldervale (Udd.) G71	68	FF17
Calderwood Av. (Bail.) G69	56	EE14
Calderwood Dr. (Bail.) G69	56	EE14
Calderwood Gdns. (Bail.) G69	56	EE14
Calderwood Rd. G43	62	T17
Calderwood Rd. (Ruther.) G73	53	Z16
Caldwell Av. G13	18	P9
Caldwell Av. (Linw.), Pais. PA3	28	E13
Caledon La. G12	34	T11
Highburgh Rd.		
Caledon St. G12	34	T11
Caledonia Av. G5	52	W14
Caledonia Av. (Ruther.) G73	53	Y16
Caledonia Ct., Pais. PA3	30	J13
Mossvale St.		
Caledonia Dr. (Bail.) G69	56	EE14
Caledonia Rd. G5	52	W14
Caledonia Rd. (Bail.) G69	56	EE14
Caledonia St. G5	52	W14
Caledonia St., Clyde. G81	4	K7
Caledonia St., Pais. PA3	30	J13
Caledonia Way E. (Abbots.), Pais. PA3	30	K11
Caledonia Way W. (Abbots.), Pais. PA3	30	J11
Caledonian Cres. G12	35	U11
Caledonian Mans. G12	20	T10
Great Western Rd.		
Caledonian Pl. (Camb.) G72	67	DD17
Caley Brae (Udd.) G71	69	GG17
Calfhill Rd. G53	48	P14
Calfmuir Rd. (Kirk.) G66	14	EE5
Calfmuir Rd. (Chry.) G69	14	EE5
Calgary St. G4	36	W11
Callaghan Wynd (Blan.) G72	68	FF19
Callander St. G20	21	V10
Callender Ct. (Cumb.) G68	70	NN2
Callender Rd. (Cumb.) G68	70	NN2
Callieburn Rd. (Bishop.) G64	23	Y8
Cally Av. G15	6	P6
Calside, Pais. PA2	46	K15
Calside Av., Pais. PA2	46	J14
Calton Entry G40	36	X13
Gallowgate		
Calvay Cres. G33	39	CC12
Calvay Pl. G33	39	DD13
Calvay Rd. G33	39	CC12
Cambourne Rd. (Chry.) G69	15	GG6
Cambridge Av., Clyde. G81	5	L6
Cambridge Dr. G20	20	T9
Glenfinnan Dr.		
Cambridge La. G3	35	V11
Cambridge St.		
Cambridge Rd., Renf. PA4	31	M11
Cambridge St. G2	35	V12
Cambridge St. G3	35	V12
Camburn St. G32	38	AA13
Cambus Pl. G33	39	CC11
Cambusdoon Rd. G33	39	CC11
Cambuskenneth Gdns. G32	39	DD13
Cambuskenneth Pl. G33	39	CC11
Cambuslang Rd. G32	54	AA16
Cambuslang Rd. (Camb.) G72	53	Z16
Cambuslang Rd. (Ruther.) G73	53	Y15
Cambusmore Pl. G33	39	CC11
Camden Ter. G5	52	W14
Camelon St. G32	38	AA13
Cameron Dr. (Bears.) G61	8	S6
Cameron Dr. (Udd.) G71	57	HH16
Cameron Sq., Clyde. G81	5	M5
Glasgow Rd.		
Cameron St. G52	32	N12
Cameron St., Clyde. G81	17	M8
Cameron Way (Blan.) G72	68	FF19
Camlachie St. G31	37	Y13
Camp Rd. (Bail.) G69	40	EE13
Camp Rd. (Ruther.) G73	52	X15
Campbell Cres. (Both.) G71	69	HH18
Campbell Dr. (Bears.) G61	7	Q5
Campbell Dr. (Barr.) G78	59	M19
Campbell St. G20	20	T8
Campbell St., John. PA5	43	D15
Campbell St., Renf. PA4	17	M10
Camperdown St. G20	21	V10
Garscube Rd.		
Camphill, Pais. PA1	46	J14
Camphill Av. G41	51	U16
Camps Cres., Renf. PA4	32	N11
Campsie Av. (Barr.) G78	59	M19
Campsie Ct. (Kirk.) G66	13	CC5
Campsie Dr., Pais. PA2	46	J16
Campsie Dr. (Abbots.), Pais. PA3	30	K11
Campsie Dr., Renf. PA4	31	L12
Campsie Pl. (Chry.) G69	26	FF8
Campsie St. G21	22	X9
Campsie Vw. (Stepps) G33	25	CC10
Campsie Vw. (Cumb.) G67	71	PP2
Campsie Vw. (Bail.) G69	41	GG13
Campsie Vw. (Chry.) G69	26	FF8
Campsie Vw. (Udd.) G71	57	HH16
Campsie Vw. (Camb.) G72	67	DD18
Campston Pl. G33	38	BB11
Camstradden Dr. E. (Bears.) G61	7	Q6
Camstradden Dr. W. (Bears.) G61	7	Q6
Camus Pl. G15	6	N6
Canal Av., John. PA5	44	E15
Canal Rd., John. PA5	43	D15
Canal St. G4	36	W11
Canal St., Clyde. G81	17	L8
Canal St., John. PA5	44	E14
Canal St. (Elder.), John. PA5	44	F14
Canal St., Pais. PA1	46	J14
Canal St., Renf. PA4	17	M10
Canal Ter., Pais. PA1	46	J14
Canberra Av., Clyde. G81	4	J6
Canberra Ct. (Giff.) G46	62	T18
Braidpark Dr.		
Cander Rigg (Bishop.) G64	11	Y6
Candleriggs G1	36	W13
Candren Rd., Pais. PA3	45	H14
Candren Rd. (Linw.), Pais. PA3	28	F13
Canmore Pl. G31	53	Z14
Canmore St. G31	53	Z14
Cannich Dr., Pais. PA2	47	L15
Canniesburn Rd. (Bears.) G61	7	Q6
Canniesburn Sq. (Bears.) G61	7	R7
Switchback Rd.		
Canniesburn Toll (Bears.) G61	7	R6
Canonbie St. G34	40	FF11
Canting Way G51	34	T12
Capelrig St. (Thorn.) G46	61	R18
Caplaw Rd., Pais. PA2	58	J17
Caplethill Rd. (Barr.) G78	46	K16
Caplethill Rd., Pais. PA2	46	K16
Caprington St. G33	38	BB11
Cara Dr. G51	33	R12
Caravelle Way, Renf. PA4	31	M11
Friendship Way		
Carberry Rd. G41	50	T15
Carbeth St. G22	21	V10
Carbisdale St. G22	22	X9
Carbost St. G23	8	T7
Torgyle St.		
Carbrook St. G21	37	Y11
Carbrook St., Pais. PA1	46	J14
Cardarrach St. G21	23	Y10
Cardell Av., Pais. PA2	45	H14
Cardell Dr., Pais. PA2	45	H14
Cardell Rd., Pais. PA2	45	H14
Carding La. G3	35	U12
Argyle St.		
Cardonald Dr. G52	48	P14
Cardonald Gdns. G52	48	P14
Cardonald Pl. Rd. G52	48	P14
Cardow Rd. G21	23	Z10
Cardowan Dr. (Stepps) G33	25	CC9
Cardowan Pk. (Udd.) G71	57	HH15
Cardowan Rd. G32	38	AA13
Cardowan Rd. (Stepps) G33	25	DD9
Cardrona St. G33	24	BB10
Cardross Ct. G31	36	X12
Cardross St. G31	36	X12
Cardwell St. G41	51	V14
Careston Pl. (Bishop.) G64	11	Z7
Carfin St. G42	51	V15
Carfrae St. G3	34	T12
Cargill Sq. (Bishop.) G64	23	Y8
Carham Cres. G52	33	Q13
Carham Dr. G52	33	Q13
Carillon Rd. G51	34	T13
Carisbrooke Cres. (Bishop.) G64	11	Y6
Carlaverock Rd. G43	62	T17
Carleith Av., Clyde. G81	4	K5
Carleith Quad. G51	33	Q12
Carleith Ter., Clyde. G81	4	K5
Carleith Av.		
Carleston St. G21	22	X10
Atlas Rd.		
Carleton Ct. (Giff.) G46	62	T18
Carleton Dr. (Giff.) G46	62	T18
Carleton Gate (Giff.) G46	62	T18
Carlibar Av. G13	18	N9
Carlibar Dr. (Barr.) G78	59	M18
Carlibar Gdns. (Barr.) G78	59	M18
Commercial Rd.		
Carlibar Rd. (Barr.) G78	59	L18
Carlile La., Pais. PA3	30	K13
New Sneddon St.		
Carlile Pl., Pais. PA3	30	K13
Carlisle St. G21	22	W10
Carlisle Ter., Pais. PA3	30	K13
Carlowrie Av. (Blan.) G72	68	FF19
Carlton Ct. G5	35	V13
Carlton Pl. G5	35	V13
Carlton Ter. G20	21	U10
Wilton St.		
Carlyle Av. G52	32	N12
Carlyle St., Pais. PA3	30	K13
Carlyle Ter. (Ruther.) G73	53	Y15
Carmaben Rd. G33	39	DD12
Carment Dr. G41	50	T16
Carment La. G41	50	T16
Carmichael Pl. G42	51	U16
Carmichael St. G51	34	S13
Carmunnock La. G44	63	V17
Madison Av.		
Carmunnock Rd. G44	51	V16
Carmunnock Rd. G45	64	W17
Carmunnock Rd. (Clark.) G76	64	W19
Carmyle Av. G32	54	BB15
Carna Dr. G44	64	W17
Carnarvon St. G3	35	U11
Carnbooth Ct. G45	64	X19
Carnbroe St. G20	35	V11
Carnegie Rd. G52	32	P13
Carnock Cres. (Barr.) G78	59	L19
Carnock Rd. G53	49	Q16
Carnoustie Ct. (Both.) G71	69	GG19
Carnoustie Cres. (Bishop.) G64	11	Z7
Carnoustie St. G5	35	U13
Carntyne Gdns. G32	38	AA12
Abbeyhill St.		
Carntyne Pl. G32	37	Z12
Carntyne Rd. G31	37	Z13
Carntyne Rd. G32	38	AA12
Carntynehall Rd. G32	38	AA12
Carnwadric Rd. (Thorn.) G46	61	R18
Carnwath Av. G43	63	U17
Caroline St. G31	38	AA13
Carolside Dr. G15	6	P6
Carradale Gdns. (Bishop.) G64	11	Z7
Thrums Av.		
Carradale Pl. (Linw.), Pais. PA3	28	E13
Carrbridge Dr. G20	20	T9
Glenfinnan Dr.		
Carresbrook Av. (Kirk.) G66	14	EE5
Carriagehill Av., Pais. PA2	46	K15
Carriagehill Dr., Pais. PA2	46	K15
Carrick Cres. (Giff.) G46	62	T19
Carrick Dr. G32	55	DD14
Carrick Dr. (Ruther.) G73	65	Y17

Carrick Gro. G32 55 DD14
Carrick Rd. (Bishop.) G64 11 Z7
Carrick Rd. (Cumb.) G67 71 PP2
Carrick Rd. (Ruther.) G73 64 X17
Carrick St. G2 35 V13
Carrickarden Rd. (Bears.) G61 7 R6
Carrickstone Rd. (Cumb.) G68 70 NN1
Carrickstone Vw. (Cumb.) G68 70 NN1
Carriden Pl. G33 39 DD12
Carrington St. G4 35 U11
Carroglen Gdns. G32 39 CC13
Carroglen Gro. G32 39 CC13
Carron Ct. (Camb.) G72 67 CC17
Carron Cres. G22 22 W9
Carron Cres. (Bears.) G61 7 Q6
Carron Cres. (Bishop.) G64 11 Y7
Carron Cres. (Lenzie) G66 13 DD6
Carron La., Pais. PA3 31 L12
  Kilearn Rd.
Carron Pl. G22 22 X9
Carron St. G22 22 X9
Carrour Gdns. (Bishop.) G64 10 X7
Carsaig Dr. G52 33 R13
Carse Vw. Dr. (Bears.) G61 8 S5
Carsebrook Av. (Kirk.) G66 14 EE5
  Chryston Rd.
Carsegreen Av., Pais. PA2 45 H16
Carstairs St. G40 53 Y15
Carswell Gdns. G41 51 U15
Cart St., Clyde. G81 17 L8
Cartbank Gdns. G44 63 V18
  Cartbank Rd.
Cartbank Gro. G44 63 V18
Cartbank Rd. G44 63 V18
Cartcraigs Rd. G43 62 S17
Cartha Cres., Pais. PA2 47 L14
Cartha St. G41 51 U16
Cartside Av., John. PA5 43 C15
Cartside Quad. G42 51 V16
Cartside St. G42 51 U16
Cartside Ter. (Mill.Pk.), John. 43 C15
  PA10
  Kilbarchan Rd.
Cartvale La., Pais. PA3 30 K13
Cartvale Rd. G42 51 U16
Caskie Dr. (Blan.) G72 69 GG19
Cassley Av., Renf. PA4 32 N11
Castle Av. (Udd.) G71 69 GG17
Castle Av. (Elder.), John. PA5 44 E15
Castle Chimmins Av. 67 CC18
  (Camb.) G72
Castle Chimmins Rd. 67 CC18
  (Camb.) G72
Castle Cres. N. Ct. G1 36 W12
  Royal Ex. Sq.
Castle Gait, Pais. PA1 46 J14
Castle Gdns. (Chry.) G69 15 GG7
Castle Gdns., Pais. PA2 45 H14
Castle Gate (Udd.) G71 69 GG17
Castle Pl. (Udd.) G71 69 GG17
  Ferry Rd.
Castle Rd. (Elder.), John. PA5 44 F14
Castle Sq., Clyde. G81 4 K6
Castle St. G4 36 X12
Castle St. G11 34 T11
  Benalder St.
Castle St. (Bail.) G69 56 EE14
Castle St. (Ruther.) G73 53 Y16
Castle St., Clyde. G81 4 K6
Castle St., Pais. PA1 46 J14
Castle Vw., Clyde. G81 5 L6
  Granville St.
Castle Way (Cumb.) G67 71 QQ2
Castle Way (Bail.) G69 41 GG13
  Dukes Rd.
Castlebank Ct. G13 19 R9
Castlebank Cres. G11 34 S11
  Meadowside St.
Castlebank Gdns. G13 19 R9
Castlebank St. G11 33 R11
Castlebank Vills. G13 19 R9
Castlebay Dr. G22 10 W7
Castlebay Pl. G22 22 W8
Castlebay St. G22 22 W8
Castlecroft Gdns. (Udd.) G71 69 GG17
Castlefern Rd. (Ruther.) G73 65 Y18
Castlehill Cres., Renf. PA4 17 M10
  Ferry Rd.
Castlehill Rd. (Bears.) G61 6 P5
Castlelaw Gdns. G32 38 BB13
Castlelaw Pl. G32 38 BB13
Castlelaw St. G32 38 BB13

Castlemilk Cres. G44 64 X17
Castlemilk Dr. G45 64 X18
Castlemilk Ms. G44 64 X17
  Castlemilk Rd.
Castlemilk Rd. G44 52 X16
Castleton Av. (Bishop.) G64 22 X8
  Colston Rd.
Castleton Ct. G45 64 X19
Castleview Av., Pais. PA2 45 H16
Castleview Dr., Pais. PA2 45 H16
Castleview Pl., Pais. PA2 45 H16
Cathay St. G22 22 W8
Cathcart Cres., Pais. PA2 47 L14
Cathcart Pl. (Ruther.) G73 52 X16
Cathcart Rd. G42 51 V16
Cathcart Rd. (Ruther.) G73 52 X16
Cathedral Ct. G4 36 W12
  Rottenrow E.
Cathedral La. G4 36 W12
  Cathedral St.
Cathedral Sq. G4 36 X12
Cathedral St. G1 36 W12
Cathedral St. G4 36 W12
Catherine Pl. G3 35 U12
  Hydepark St.
Cathkin Av. (Camb.) G72 66 AA17
Cathkin Av. (Ruther.) G73 53 Z16
Cathkin Bypass (Ruther.) G73 65 Z18
Cathkin Ct. G45 64 X19
Cathkin Cres. (Cumb.) G68 70 NN2
Cathkin Gdns. (Udd.) G71 57 GG15
Cathkin Pl. (Camb.) G72 66 AA17
Cathkin Rd. G42 51 U16
Cathkin Rd. (Udd.) G71 57 GG15
Cathkin Rd. (Ruther.) G73 65 Y19
Cathkin Rd. (Clark.) G76 65 Y19
Cathkin Vw. G32 54 BB16
Cathkinview Pl. G42 51 V16
Cathkinview Rd. G42 51 V16
Catrine Ct. G53 48 P16
Catrine Gdns. G53 48 P16
Catrine Pl. G53 48 P16
Catrine Rd. G53 48 P16
Causewayside Cres. G32 54 BB15
Causewayside St. G32 54 BB15
Causeyside St., Pais. PA1 46 K14
Cavendish Pl. G5 51 V14
Cavendish St. G5 51 V14
Cavin Dr. G45 64 X18
Cavin Rd. G45 64 X18
Cawder Ct. (Cumb.) G68 70 MM1
Cawder Pl. (Cumb.) G68 70 MM1
Cawder Rd. (Cumb.) G68 70 MM2
Cawder Vw. (Cumb.) G68 70 MM1
Cawder Way (Cumb.) G68 70 MM1
Cayton Gdns. (Bail.) G69 55 DD14
Cecil Pl. G51 35 U13
  Paisley Rd. W.
Cecil St. G12 20 T10
Cedar Av., Clyde. G81 4 J6
Cedar Av., John. PA5 44 E16
Cedar Ct. G20 35 V11
Cedar Ct. (Kilb.), John. PA10 42 B14
Cedar Dr. (Lenzie) G66 13 CC5
Cedar Gdns. (Ruther.) G73 65 Z18
Cedar Pl. (Blan.) G72 68 FF19
Cedar Pl. (Barr.) G78 59 M19
Cedar Rd. (Bishop.) G64 23 Y8
Cedar Rd. (Cumb.) G67 71 QQ2
Cedar St. G20 35 V11
Cedar Wk. (Bishop.) G64 23 Y8
Cedric Pl. G13 19 Q8
Cedric Rd. G13 19 Q8
Celtic St. G20 20 T8
Cemetery Rd. G52 49 Q14
  Paisley Rd. W.
Centenary Ct., Clyde. G81 5 L7
  Bruce St.
Central Av. G11 33 R11
  Broomhill Ter.
Central Av. G32 55 CC14
Central Av. (Camb.) G72 66 AA17
Central Av., Clyde. G81 5 L7
Central Chambers G2 35 V12
  Hope St.
Central Gro. G32 55 CC14
Central Gro. (Camb.) G72 66 AA17
Central Path G32 55 DD14
Central Rd., Pais. PA1 30 K13
Central Sta. G1 35 V12
Central Way (Cumb.) G67 70 NN4
Central Way, Pais. PA1 30 K13

Centre, The (Barr.) G78 59 L19
Centre St. G5 35 V13
Centre Way (Barr.) G78 59 L18
Ceres Gdns. (Bishop.) G64 11 Z7
Cessnock Pl. (Camb.) G72 67 CC17
Cessnock Rd. G33 24 BB9
Cessnock St. G51 34 T13
Chachan Dr. G51 33 R12
  Skipness Dr.
Chalmers Ct. G40 36 X13
Chalmers Gate G40 36 X13
  Claythorn St.
Chalmers Pl. G40 36 X13
  Claythorn St.
Chalmers St. G40 36 X13
Chalmers St., Clyde. G81 5 L7
Chamberlain La. G13 19 R9
Chamberlain Rd. G13 19 R9
Chancellor St. G11 34 S11
Chapel Rd., Clyde. G81 5 L5
Chapel St. G20 21 U9
Chapel St. (Ruther.) G73 52 X16
Chapelhill Rd., Pais. PA2 47 L15
Chapelton Av. (Bears.) G61 7 R6
Chapelton Gdns. (Bears.) G61 7 R6
Chapelton St. G22 21 V9
Chaplet Av. G13 19 Q8
Chapman St. G42 51 V15
  Allison St.
Chappell St. (Barr.) G78 59 L18
Charing Cross G2 35 U11
Charing Cross La. G3 35 U12
  Granville St.
Charles Av., Renf. PA4 17 M10
Charles Cres. (Lenzie) G66 13 CC6
Charles St. G21 36 X11
Charlotte La. G1 36 W13
  London Rd.
Charlotte La. S. G1 36 W13
  Charlotte St.
Charlotte La. W. G1 36 W13
  London Rd.
Charlotte Pl., Pais. PA2 46 K15
Charlotte St. G1 36 W13
Charnwood Av., John. PA5 43 C16
Chatelherault Av. (Camb.) 66 AA17
  G72
Chatton St. G23 8 T7
Cheapside St. G3 35 U12
Chelmsford Dr. G12 20 S9
Cherry Bk. (Kirk.) G66 12 BB5
Cherry Cres., Clyde. G81 5 L6
Cherry Pl. (Bishop.) G64 23 Y8
Cherry Pl., John. PA5 44 E15
Cherrybank Rd. G43 63 U17
Cherrytree Dr. (Camb.) G72 67 DD18
Cherrywood Rd. (Elder.), 44 F15
  John. PA5
Chester St. G32 38 BB13
Chesterfield Av. G12 20 S9
Chesters Pl. (Ruther.) G73 53 Y16
Chesters Rd. (Bears.) G61 7 Q6
Chestnut Dr. (Kirk.) G66 12 BB5
Chestnut Dr., Clyde. G81 5 L5
Chestnut Pl., John. PA5 44 E16
Chestnut St. G22 22 W9
Chestnut Way (Camb.) G72 67 DD18
Cheviot Av. (Barr.) G78 59 M19
Cheviot Rd. G43 62 T17
Cheviot Rd., Pais. PA2 46 K16
Chirmorie Pl. G53 48 P15
  Dalmellington Rd.
Chirnside Pl. G52 32 P13
Chirnside Rd. G52 32 P13
Chisholm St. G1 36 W13
Crighton Grn. (Udd.) G71 57 HH16
Christian St. G43 50 T16
Christie La., Pais. PA3 30 K13
  New Sneddon St.
Christie Pl. (Camb.) G72 66 BB17
Christie St., Pais. PA1 30 K13
Christopher St. G21 37 Y11
Chryston Rd. (Kirk.) G66 14 FF5
Chryston Rd. (Chry.) G69 26 FF8
Church Av. (Stepps) G33 25 CC9
Church Av. (Ruther.) G73 65 Z17
Church Dr. (Kirk.) G66 13 CC5
Church Hill, Pais. PA1 30 K13
Church La. G42 51 V15
  Victoria Rd.
Church Rd. (Giff.) G46 62 T19
Church Rd. (Muir.) G69 26 FF8

Street	Page	Ref
Church St. G11	34	T11
Church St. (Bail.) G69	56	FF14
Church St. (Udd.) G71	69	GG17
Church St., Clyde. G81	5	L6
Church St., John. PA5	43	D14
Church St. (Kilb.), John. PA10	42	B14
Church Vw. (Camb.) G72	54	BB16
Churchill Av., John. PA5	43	C16
Churchill Cres. (Both.) G71	69	HH18
Churchill Dr. G11	19	R10
Churchill Pl. (Kilb.), John. PA10	42	B14
Churchill Way (Bishop.) G64	10	X7
Kirkintilloch Rd.		
Circus Dr. G31	36	X12
Circus Pl. G31	36	X12
Circus Pl. La. G31	36	X12
Circus Pl.		
Cityford Cres. (Ruther.) G73	52	X16
Cityford Dr. (Ruther.) G73	52	X16
Clachan Dr. G51	33	R12
Skipness Dr.		
Claddens Pl. (Lenzie) G66	13	DD6
Claddens Quad. G22	22	W9
Claddens St. G22	21	V9
Claddens Wynd (Kirk.) G66	13	DD6
Claddon Vw., Clyde. G81	5	M6
Kirkoswald Dr.		
Clair Rd. (Bishop.) G64	11	Z7
Clairinsh Gdns., Renf. PA4	31	M11
Sandy Rd.		
Clairmont Gdns. G3	35	U11
Clare St. G21	37	Y11
Claremont Pas. G3	35	U11
Claremont Ter.		
Claremont Pl. G3	35	U11
Claremont Ter.		
Claremont St. G3	35	U12
Claremont Ter. G3	35	U11
Claremont Ter. La. G3	35	U11
Clifton St.		
Claremount Av. (Giff.) G46	62	T19
Clarence Dr. G11	20	S10
Clarence Dr. G12	20	S10
Clarence Dr., Pais. PA1	47	L14
Clarence Gdns. G11	20	S10
Clarence La. G12	20	S10
Hyndland Rd.		
Clarence St., Clyde. G81	5	M6
Clarence St., Pais. PA1	31	L13
Clarendon La. G20	35	V11
Clarendon St.		
Clarendon Pl. G20	35	V11
Clarendon Pl. (Stepps) G33	25	CC9
Clarendon St. G20	35	V11
Clarion Cres. G13	18	P8
Clarion Rd. G13	18	P8
Clark St. G41	35	U13
Tower St.		
Clark St., Clyde. G81	4	K6
Clark St., John. PA5	43	D14
Clark St., Pais. PA3	30	J13
Clark St., Renf. PA4	17	L10
Clarkston Av. G44	63	U18
Clarkston Rd. G44	63	U18
Clarkston Rd. (Clark.) G76	63	U19
Clathic Av. (Bears.) G61	8	S6
Claud Rd., Pais. PA3	31	L13
Claude Av. (Camb.) G72	67	DD18
Clavens Rd. G52	32	N13
Claverhouse Pl., Pais. PA2	47	L14
Claverhouse Rd. G52	32	N12
Clavering St. E., Pais. PA1	30	J13
Well St.		
Clavering St. W., Pais. PA1	30	J13
King St.		
Clayhouse Rd. G33	25	DD9
Claypotts Pl. G33	38	BB11
Claypotts Rd. G33	38	BB11
Clayslaps Rd. G3	34	T11
Argyle St.		
Claythorn Av. G40	36	X13
Claythorn Circ. G40	36	X13
Claythorn Av.		
Claythorn Ct. G40	36	X13
Claythorn Pk.		
Claythorn Pk. G40	36	X13
Claythorn St. G40	36	X13
Claythorn Ter. G40	36	X13
Claythorn Pk.		
Clayton Ter. G31	36	X12
Cleddans Cres., Clyde. G81	5	M5
Cleddans Rd., Clyde. G81	5	M5
Cleddens Ct. (Bishop.) G64	11	Y7
Cleeves Pl. G53	60	P17
Cleeves Quad. G53	60	P17
Cleeves Rd. G53	60	P17
Cleghorn St. G22	21	V10
Cleland La. G5	36	W13
Cleland St.		
Cleland St. G5	36	W13
Clelland Av. (Bishop.) G64	23	Y8
Clerwood St. G32	37	Z13
Cleveden Cres. G12	20	S9
Cleveden Cres. La. G12	20	S9
Cleveden Dr.		
Cleveden Dr. G12	20	S9
Cleveden Dr. (Ruther.) G73	65	Z17
Cleveden Gdns. G12	20	T9
Cleveden La. G12	20	S9
Burlington Av.		
Cleveden Pl. G12	20	S9
Cleveden Rd. G12	20	S9
Cleveland St. G3	35	U12
Cliff Rd. G3	35	U11
Clifford Gdns. G51	34	S13
Clifford La. G51	34	T13
North Gower St.		
Clifford Pl. G51	34	T13
Clifford St.		
Clifford St. G51	34	S13
Clifton Pl. G3	35	U11
Clifton St.		
Clifton Rd. (Giff.) G46	62	S18
Clifton St. G3	35	U11
Clifton Ter. (Camb.) G72	66	AA18
Clifton Ter., John. PA5	44	E15
Clincart Rd. G42	51	V16
Clincarthill Rd. (Ruther.) G73	53	Y16
Clippens Rd. (Linw.), Pais. PA3	28	E13
Cloan Av. G15	6	P7
Cloan Cres. (Bishop.) G64	11	Y6
Cloberhill Rd. G13	7	Q7
Cloch St. G33	38	BB12
Clochoderick Av. (Mill.Pk.), John. PA10	42	B15
Mackenzie Dr.		
Clonbeith St. G33	39	DD11
Closeburn St. G22	22	W9
Cloth St. (Barr.) G78	59	M19
Clouden Rd. (Cumb.) G67	71	PP3
Cloudhowe Ter. (Blan.) G72	68	FF19
Clouston Ct. G20	21	U10
Clouston La. G20	20	T10
Clouston St.		
Clouston St. G20	20	T10
Clova Pl. (Udd.) G71	69	GG17
Clova St. (Thorn.) G46	61	R18
Clover Av. (Bishop.) G64	10	X7
Cloverbank St. G21	37	Y11
Clovergate (Bishop.) G64	10	X7
Clunie Rd. G52	49	R14
Cluny Av. (Bears.) G61	8	S7
Cluny Dr. (Bears.) G61	8	S7
Cluny Dr., Pais. PA3	31	L13
Cluny Gdns. G14	19	R10
Cluny Gdns. (Bail.) G69	56	EE14
Cluny Vills. G14	19	Q10
Westland Dr.		
Clutha St. G51	35	U13
Paisley Rd. W.		
Clyde Av. (Both.) G71	69	GG19
Clyde Av. (Barr.) G78	59	M19
Clyde Ct., Clyde. G81	4	K6
Littleholm		
Clyde Pl. G5	35	V13
Clyde Pl. (Camb.) G72	67	CC18
Clyde Pl., John. PA5	43	C16
Clyde Rd., Pais. PA3	31	L12
Clyde St. G1	35	V13
Clyde St., Clyde. G81	17	L8
Clyde St., Renf. PA4	17	M9
Clyde Ter. (Both.) G71	69	HH19
Clyde Tunnel G14	33	R11
Clyde Tunnel G51	33	R11
Clyde Tunnel Expressway G51	33	Q12
Clyde Vale (Both.) G71	69	HH19
Clyde Vw., Pais. PA2	47	L15
Clydebrae Dr. (Both.) G71	69	HH19
Clydebrae St. G51	34	S12
Clydeford Dr. G32	54	AA14
Clydeford Dr. (Udd.) G71	56	FF16
Clydeford Rd. (Camb.) G72	54	BB16
Clydeholm Rd. G14	33	Q11
Clydeholm Ter., Clyde. G81	17	M8
Clydeneuk Dr. (Udd.) G71	56	FF16
Clydesdale Av., Pais. PA3	31	L11
Clydeside Expressway G3	34	T11
Clydeside Expressway G14	19	Q10
Clydeside Rd. (Ruther.) G73	52	X15
Clydesmill Dr. G32	54	BB16
Clydesmill Gro. G32	54	BB16
Clydesmill Pl. G32	54	BB16
Clydesmill Rd. G32	54	BB16
Clydeview G11	34	S11
Dumbarton Rd.		
Clydeview La. G11	33	R11
Broomhill Dr.		
Clydeview Ter. G32	55	CC16
Clydeview Ter. G40	52	X14
Newhall St.		
Clynder St. G51	34	S13
Clyth Dr. (Giff.) G46	62	T19
Coalhill St. G31	37	Y13
Coatbridge Rd. (Bail.) G69	41	GG13
Coatbridge Rd. (Gart.) G69	27	GG10
Coats Cres. (Bail.) G69	40	EE13
Coats Dr., Pais. PA2	45	H14
Coatshill Av. (Blan.) G72	68	FF19
Cobblerigg Way (Udd.) G71	69	GG17
Cobden Rd. G21	36	X11
Cobington Pl. G33	38	BB11
Cobinshaw St. G32	38	BB13
Coburg St. G5	35	V13
Cochno St., Clyde. G81	17	M8
Cochran St., Pais. PA1	46	K14
Cochrane Sq. (Linw.), Pais. PA3	28	E13
Cochrane St. G1	36	W12
Cochrane St. (Barr.) G78	59	L19
Cochranemill Rd., John. PA5	43	C15
Cockels Ln., Renf. PA4	31	L11
Cockenzie St. G32	38	BB13
Cockmuir St. G21	23	Y10
Cogan Pl. (Barr.) G78	59	L19
Cogan Rd. G43	62	T17
Cogan St. G43	50	T16
Cogan St. (Barr.) G78	59	L19
Colbert St. G40	52	X14
Colbreggan Ct., Clyde. G81	5	M5
St. Helena Cres.		
Colbreggan Gdns., Clyde. G81	5	M5
Colchester Dr. G12	20	S9
Coldingham Av. G14	18	N9
Coldstream Dr. (Ruther.) G73	65	Z17
Coldstream Dr., Pais. PA2	45	H15
Coldstream Pl. G21	22	W10
Keppochhill Rd.		
Coldstream Rd., Clyde. G81	5	L7
Colebrook St. (Camb.) G72	66	BB17
Colebrooke La. G12	21	U10
Colebrooke St.		
Colebrooke Pl. G12	21	U10
Belmont St.		
Colebrooke St. G12	21	U10
Colebrooke Ter. G12	21	U10
Colebrooke St.		
Coleridge (Both.) G71	69	HH18
Colfin St. G34	40	FF11
Colgrain St. G20	21	V9
Colgrave Cres. G32	54	AA14
Colinbar Circle (Barr.) G78	59	L19
Colinslee Av., Pais. PA2	46	K15
Colinslee Cres., Pais. PA2	46	K15
Colinslee Dr., Pais. PA2	46	K15
Colinslie Rd. G53	49	Q16
Colinton Pl. G32	38	BB12
Colintraive Av. G33	24	AA10
Colintraive Cres. G33	24	AA10
Coll Av., Renf. PA4	31	M11
Coll Pl. G21	37	Y11
Coll St. G21	37	Y11
Colla Gdns. (Bishop.) G64	11	Z7
College La. G1	36	W13
High St.		
College La., Pais. PA1	46	J14
College St. G1	36	W12
Collessie Dr. G33	39	CC11
Collier St., John. PA5	43	D14
Collina St. G20	20	T9
Collins St. G4	36	X12
Collylin Rd. (Bears.) G61	7	R6
Colmonell Av. G13	18	N8

Name		
Colonsay Av., Renf. PA4	31	M11
Colonsay Rd. G52	33	R13
Colonsay Rd., Pais. PA2	46	J16
Colquhoun Av. G52	32	P12
Colquhoun Dr. (Bears.) G61	7	Q5
Colston Av. (Bishop.) G64	22	X8
Colston Dr. (Bishop.) G64	22	X8
Colston Gdns. (Bishop.) G64	22	X8
Colston Path (Bishop.) G64	22	X8
Colston Gdns.		
Colston Pl. (Bishop.) G64	22	X8
Colston Rd.		
Colston Rd. (Bishop.) G64	22	X8
Coltmuir Av. (Bishop.) G64	22	X8
Coltmuir Dr.		
Coltmuir Cres. (Bishop.) G64	22	X8
Coltmuir Dr. (Bishop.) G64	22	X8
Coltmuir Gdns. (Bishop.) G64	22	X8
Coltmuir Dr.		
Coltmuir St. G22	21	V9
Coltness La. G33	39	CC12
Coltness St. G33	39	CC12
Coltpark Av. (Bishop.) G64	22	X8
Coltpark La. (Bishop.) G64	22	X8
Coltsfoot Dr. G53	60	P18
Columba Path, Clyde. G81	5	M7
Onslow Rd.		
Columba St. G51	34	S12
Colvend Dr. (Ruther.) G73	65	Y18
Colvend St. G40	52	X14
Colville Dr. (Ruther.) G73	65	Z17
Colwood Av. G53	60	P18
Colwood Gdns. G53	60	P18
Colwood Av.		
Colwood Path G53	60	P18
Parkhouse Rd.		
Colwood Pl. G53	60	P18
Colwood Sq. G53	60	P18
Colwood Av.		
Comedie Rd. G33	25	DD10
Comelypark St. G31	37	Y13
Comley Pl. G31	37	Y13
Gallowgate		
Commerce St. G5	35	V13
Commercial Ct. G5	36	W13
Commercial Rd. G5	52	W14
Commercial Rd. (Barr.) G78	59	M18
Commonhead Rd. G34	40	FF12
Commore Av. (Barr.) G78	59	M19
Commore Dr. G13	18	P8
Comrie Rd. G33	25	CC9
Comrie St. G32	54	BB14
Cona St. (Thorn.) G46	61	R18
Conan Ct. (Camb.) G72	67	CC17
Condorrat Ring Rd. (Cumb.) G67	70	MM4
Congleton St. G53	60	N17
Nitshill Rd.		
Congress Rd. G3	35	U12
Congress Way G3	35	U12
Conifer Pl. (Kirk.) G66	12	BB5
Conisborough Path G34	39	DD11
Balfluig St.		
Conisborough Rd. G34	39	DD11
Conistone Cres. (Bail.) G69	55	DD14
Connal St. G40	53	Y14
Conniston St. G32	38	AA12
Connor Rd. (Barr.) G78	59	L18
Conon Av. (Bears.) G61	7	Q6
Consett La. G33	39	CC12
Consett St. G33	39	CC12
Consett La.		
Contin Pl. G12	20	T9
Convair Way, Renf. PA4	31	M11
Lismore Av.		
Conval Way, Pais. PA3	30	J12
Abbotsburn Way		
Cook St. G5	35	V13
Cooperage Ct. G14	17	M9
Coopers Well La. G11	34	T11
Dumbarton Rd.		
Coopers Well St. G11	34	T11
Dumbarton Rd.		
Copland Pl. G51	34	S13
Copland Quad. G51	34	S13
Copland Rd. G51	34	S13
Coplaw St. G42	51	V14
Copperfield La. (Udd.) G71	57	HH16
Hamilton Vw.		
Corbett St. G32	38	BB14
Corbiston Way (Cumb.) G67	71	PP3
Cordiner St. G44	51	V16
Corkerhill Gdns. G52	49	R14
Corkerhill Pl. G52	49	Q15
Corkerhill Rd. G52	49	Q15
Corlaich Av. G42	52	X16
Corlaich Dr. G42	52	X16
Corn St. G4	35	V11
Cornaig Rd. G53	48	P16
Cornalee Gdns. G53	48	P16
Cornalee Pl. G53	48	P16
Cornalee Rd. G53	48	P16
Cornhill St. G21	23	Y9
Cornock St. G23	8	T7
Torrin Rd.		
Cornock Cres., Clyde. G81	5	L6
Cornock St., Clyde. G81	5	L6
Cornwall Av. (Ruther.) G73	65	Z17
Cornwall St. G41	34	T13
Cornwall St. S. G41	34	T13
Coronation Pl. (Gart.) G69	27	GG8
Coronation Way (Bears.) G61	7	Q5
Corpach Pl. G34	40	FF11
Corran St. G33	38	AA12
Corrie Dr., Pais. PA1	48	N14
Corrie Gro. G44	63	U18
Corrie Pl. (Lenzie) G66	13	DD6
Corrour Rd. G43	50	T16
Corse Rd. G52	32	N13
Corsebar Av., Pais. PA2	46	J15
Corsebar Cres., Pais. PA2	46	J15
Corsebar Dr., Pais. PA2	46	J15
Corsebar La., Pais. PA2	45	H15
Balgonie Av.		
Corsebar Rd., Pais. PA2	45	H15
Corsebar Way, Pais. PA2	46	J14
Corseford Av., John. PA5	43	C16
Corsehill Pl. G34	40	FF12
Corsehill St. G34	40	FF12
Corselet Rd. G53	60	P18
Corsewall Av. G32	55	DD14
Corsford Dr. G53	61	Q17
Corsock St. G31	37	Z12
Corston St. G33	37	Z12
Cortachy Pl. (Bishop.) G64	11	Z7
Coruisk Way, Pais. PA2	45	G16
Spencer Dr.		
Corunna St. G3	35	U12
Coshneuk Rd. G33	24	BB9
Cottar St. G20	21	U8
Cotton Av. (Linw.), Pais. PA3	28	E13
Cotton St. G40	53	Y15
Cotton St., Pais. PA1	46	K14
Coulin Gdns. G22	22	W10
Coulters La. G40	36	X13
Countess Way (Bail.) G69	41	HH13
Park Rd.		
Counting Ho., The, Pais. PA1	45	H14
County Av. (Camb.) G72	53	Z16
County Pl., Pais. PA1	30	K13
Moss St.		
County Sq., Pais. PA1	30	K13
Couper St. G4	36	W11
Courthill (Bears.) G61	7	Q5
Courthill Av. G44	63	V17
Coustonhill St. G43	50	T16
Pleasance St.		
Coustonholm Rd. G43	50	T16
Coventry Dr. G31	37	Y12
Cowal Dr. (Linw.), Pais. PA3	28	E13
Cowal Rd. G20	20	T8
Cowal St. G20	20	T8
Cowan Clo. (Barr.) G78	59	M18
Cowan Cres. (Barr.) G78	59	M19
Cowan La. G12	35	U11
Cowan St.		
Cowan Rd. (Cumb.) G68	70	MM3
Cowan St. G12	35	U11
Cowan Wilson Av. (Blan.) G72	68	FF19
Cowan Wynd (Udd.) G71	57	HH16
Cowcaddens Rd. G4	35	V11
Cowcaddens St. G2	35	V12
Renfield St.		
Cowden Dr. (Bishop.) G64	11	Y6
Cowden St. G51	33	Q12
Cowdenhill Circ. G13	19	Q8
Cowdenhill Pl. G13	19	Q8
Cowdenhill Rd. G13	19	Q8
Cowdray Cres., Renf. PA4	17	M10
Cowell Vw., Clyde. G81	5	L6
Granville St.		
Cowglen Pl. G53	49	Q16
Cowglen Rd.		
Cowglen Rd. G53	49	Q16
Cowglen Ter. G53	49	Q16
Cowlairs Rd. G21	22	X10
Coxhill St. G21	22	W10
Coxton Pl. G33	39	CC11
Coylton Rd. G43	63	U17
Craggan Dr. G14	18	N9
Crags Av., Pais. PA2	46	K15
Crags Cres., Pais. PA2	46	K15
Crags Rd., Pais. PA2	46	K15
Craig Rd. G44	63	V17
Craigallian Av. (Camb.) G72	67	CC18
Craiganour La. G43	62	T17
Craiganour Pl. G43	62	T17
Craigard Pl. (Ruther.) G73	66	AA18
Inverclyde Gdns.		
Craigbank Dr. G53	60	P17
Craigbank St. G22	22	W10
Craigbarnet Cres. G33	24	BB10
Craigbo Av. G23	8	T7
Craigbo Ct. G23	20	T8
Craigbo Dr. G23	20	T8
Craigbo Pl. G23	20	T8
Craigbo Rd. G23	20	T8
Craigbo St. G23	8	T7
Craigbog Av., John. PA5	43	C15
Craigdonald Pl., John. PA5	43	D14
Craigellan Rd. G43	62	T17
Craigenbay Cres. (Lenzie) G66	13	CC5
Craigenbay Rd. (Lenzie) G66	13	CC6
Craigenbay St. G21	23	Y10
Craigencart Ct., Clyde. G81	4	K5
Gentle Row		
Craigend Pl. G13	19	R9
Craigend St. G13	19	R9
Craigendmuir Rd. G33	25	DD10
Craigendmuir St. G33	37	Z11
Craigendon Oval, Pais. PA2	58	J17
Craigendon Rd., Pais. PA2	58	J17
Craigends Dr. (Kilb.), John. PA10	42	B14
High Barholm		
Craigenfeoch Av., John. PA5	43	C15
Craigfaulds Av., Pais. PA2	45	H15
Craigflower Gdns. G53	60	P18
Craigflower Rd. G53	60	P18
Craighalbert Rd. (Cumb.) G68	70	MM2
Craighalbert Way (Cumb.) G68	70	MM2
Craighall Rd. G4	35	V11
Craighead Av. G33	23	Z10
Craighead St. (Barr.) G78	59	L19
Craighead Way (Barr.) G78	59	L19
Craighouse St. G33	38	BB11
Craigie Pk. (Lenzie) G66	13	DD5
Craigie St. G42	51	V15
Craigiebar Dr., Pais. PA2	46	J16
Craigieburn Gdns. G20	20	S8
Craigieburn Rd. (Cumb.) G67	70	NN3
Craigiehall Pl. G51	34	T13
Craigiehall St. G51	35	U13
Craigiehall Pl.		
Craigielea Dr., Pais. PA3	29	H13
Craigielea Pk., Renf. PA4	17	L10
Craigielea Rd., Renf. PA4	17	M10
Craigielea St. G31	37	Y12
Craigielinn Av., Pais. PA2	58	J17
Craigievar St. G33	39	DD11
Craigleith St. G32	38	AA13
Craiglockhart St. G33	39	CC11
Craigmaddie Ter. La. G3	35	U12
Derby St.		
Craigmillar Rd. G42	51	V16
Craigmont Dr. G20	21	U9
Craigmont St. G20	21	U9
Craigmore St. G31	37	Z13
Craigmount Av., Pais. PA2	58	J17
Craigmuir Cres. G52	32	N13
Craigmuir Pl. G52	32	N13
Craigmuir Rd.		
Craigmuir Rd. G52	32	N13
Craigneil St. G33	39	DD11
Craignestock Pl. G40	36	X13
London Rd.		
Craignestock St. G40	36	X13
Craignethan Gdns. G11	34	S11
Lawrie St.		
Craignure Rd. (Ruther.) G73	65	Y18
Craigpark G31	37	Y12
Craigpark Dr. G31	37	Y12
Craigpark Ter. G31	37	Y12
Craigpark		

Street		
Craigpark Way (Udd.) G71	57	HH16
Newton Dr.		
Craigs Av., Clyde. G81	5	M5
Craigston Pl., John. PA5	43	D15
Craigston Rd., John. PA5	43	D15
Craigton Av. (Barr.) G78	60	N19
Craigton Dr. G51	33	R13
Craigton Dr. (Barr.) G78	60	N19
Craigton Pl. G51	33	R13
Craigton Dr.		
Craigton Pl. (Blan.) G72	68	FF19
Craigton Rd. G51	33	R13
Craigvicar Gdns. G32	39	CC13
Hailes Av.		
Craigview Av., John. PA5	43	C16
Craigwell Av. (Ruther.) G73	65	Z17
Crail St. G31	37	Z13
Cramond Av., Renf. PA4	32	N11
Cramond St. G5	52	W15
Cramond Ter. G32	38	BB13
Cranborne Rd. G12	20	S9
Cranbrooke Dr. G20	20	T8
Cranston St. G3	35	U12
Cranworth La. G12	20	T10
Great George St.		
Cranworth St. G12	20	T10
Crarae Av. (Bears.) G61	7	R7
Crathes Ct. G44	63	U18
Crathie Dr. G11	34	S11
Crathie La. G11	34	S11
Exeter Dr.		
Craw Rd., Pais. PA2	46	J14
Crawford Av. (Lenzie) G66	13	DD6
Crawford Ct. (Giff.) G46	62	S19
Milverton Rd.		
Crawford Cres. (Udd.) G71	57	GG16
Crawford Cres. (Blan.) G72	68	FF19
Crawford Dr. G15	6	N7
Crawford La. G11	34	S11
Crawford Path G11	34	S11
Crawford St.		
Crawford St. G11	34	S11
Crawford Dr., Pais. PA3	29	H13
Crawfurd Gdns. (Ruther.) G73	65	Y18
Crawfurd Rd. (Ruther.) G73	65	Y18
Crawriggs Av. (Kirk.) G66	13	CC5
Crebar Dr. (Barr.) G78	59	M19
Crebar St. (Thorn.) G46	61	R18
Credon Gdns. (Ruther.) G73	65	Z18
Cree Av. (Bishop.) G64	11	Z7
Cree Gdns. G32	38	AA13
Kilmany Dr.		
Creran Dr., Renf. PA4	17	L10
Creran St. G40	36	X13
Tobago St.		
Crescent Ct., Clyde. G81	4	K6
Swindon St.		
Crescent Rd. G13	18	P9
Crescent Rd. G14	18	P9
Cresswell La. G12	20	T10
Great George St.		
Cresswell St. G12	20	T10
Cressy St. G51	33	R12
Crest Av. G13	18	P8
Crestlea Av., Pais. PA2	46	K16
Creswell Ter. (Udd.) G71	57	GG16
Kylepark Dr.		
Crichton Ct. G45	64	X19
Crichton Pl. G21	22	X10
Crichton St.		
Crichton St. G21	22	X10
Crieff Ct. G3	35	U12
North St.		
Criffell Gdns. G32	55	CC14
Criffell Rd. G32	55	CC14
Crimea St. G2	35	V12
Crinan Gdns. (Bishop.) G64	11	Y7
Crinan Rd. (Bishop.) G64	11	Y7
Crinan St. G31	37	Y12
Cripps Av., Clyde. G81	5	M7
Croft Rd. (Camb.) G72	66	BB17
Croft Way, Renf. PA4	31	M11
Croft Wynd (Udd.) G71	69	HH17
Croftbank Av. (Both.) G71	69	HH19
Croftbank Cres. (Both.) G71	69	HH19
Croftbank Gate (Both.) G71	69	HH19
Croftbank Gro. (Udd.) G71	69	GG17
Croftbank St. G21	22	X10
Croftbank St. (Udd.) G71	69	GG17
Croftburn Dr. G44	64	W18
Croftcroighn Rd. G33	38	BB11
Croftend Av. G44	64	X17
Croftfoot Cotts. (Gart.) G69	27	HH9
Croftfoot Cres. G45	65	Y18
Croftfoot Dr. G45	64	X18
Croftfoot Pl. (Gart.) G69	27	HH9
Inchnock Av.		
Croftfoot Quad. G45	64	X18
Croftfoot Rd. G44	64	W18
Croftfoot Rd. G45	64	W18
Croftfoot St. G45	65	Y18
Croftfoot Ter. G45	64	X18
Crofthead St. (Udd.) G71	69	GG17
Crofthill Av. (Udd.) G71	69	GG17
Crofthill Rd. G44	64	W17
Crofthouse Dr. G44	64	X18
Croftmont Av. G44	64	X18
Croftmoraig Av. (Chry.) G69	15	HH6
Crofton Av. G44	64	W18
Croftpark Av. G44	64	W18
Croftside Av. G44	64	X18
Croftspar Av. G32	39	CC13
Croftspar Ct. G32	39	CC13
Croftspar Gro.		
Croftspar Dr. G32	39	CC13
Croftspar Gate G32	39	CC13
Croftspar Gro.		
Croftspar Gro. G32	39	CC13
Croftspar Pl. G32	39	CC13
Croftwood (Bishop.) G64	11	Y6
Croftwood Av. G44	64	W18
Cromart Pl. (Chry.) G69	14	FF7
Cromarty Av. G43	63	U17
Cromarty Av. (Bishop.) G64	11	Z7
Cromarty Gdns. (Clark.) G76	63	V19
Crombie Gdns. (Bail.) G69	56	EE14
Cromdale St. G51	33	R13
Cromer La., Pais. PA3	30	J12
Abbotsburn Way		
Cromer St. G20	21	U9
Cromer Way, Pais. PA3	30	J12
Mosslands Rd.		
Crompton Av. G44	63	V17
Cromwell La. G20	35	V11
Cromwell St.		
Cromwell St. G20	35	V11
Cronberry Quad. G52	48	N14
Cronberry Ter. G52	48	N14
Crookedshields Rd. (Camb.) G72	66	BB19
Crookston Av. G52	48	P14
Crookston Ct. G52	48	P14
Crookston Dr. G52	48	N14
Crookston Dr., Pais. PA1	48	N14
Crookston Gdns. G52	48	N14
Crookston Gro. G52	48	P14
Crookston Pl. G52	48	N14
Crookston Quad. G52	48	N14
Crookston Rd. G52	48	N15
Crookston Rd. G53	48	P15
Crookston Ter. G52	48	P14
Crookston Rd.		
Crosbie Dr., Pais. PA2	45	G16
Crosbie La. G20	20	T8
Crosbie St. G20	20	T8
Crosbie Wd., Pais. PA2	45	H15
Cross, The G1	36	W13
Cross, The, Pais. PA1	30	K13
Cross Arthurlie St. (Barr.) G78	59	L19
Cross Rd., Pais. PA2	45	H15
Cross St. G32	55	CC15
Cross St., Pais. PA1	46	J14
Crossbank Av. G42	52	X15
Crossbank Dr. G42	52	X15
Crossbank Rd. G42	52	W15
Crossbank Ter. G42	52	W15
Crossdykes (Kirk.) G66	14	EE5
Crossflat Cres., Pais. PA1	31	L13
Crossford Dr. G23	9	U7
Crosshill Av. G42	51	V15
Crosshill Av. (Kirk.) G66	13	CC5
Crosshill Dr. (Ruther.) G73	65	Y17
Crosshill Rd. (Bishop.) G64	11	Z5
Crosshill Rd. (Kirk.) G66	12	BB6
Crosshill Sq. (Bail.) G69	56	FF14
Crosslee St. G52	33	R13
Crosslees Ct. (Thorn.) G46	61	R18
Main St.		
Crosslees Dr. (Thorn.) G46	61	R18
Crosslees Pk. (Thorn.) G46	61	R18
Crosslees Rd. (Thorn.) G46	61	R19
Crosslee Pl. G51	33	R12
Crossloan Rd. G51	33	R12
Crossloan Ter. G51	33	R12
Crossmill Av. (Barr.) G78	59	M18
Crossmyloof Gdns. G41	50	T15
Crosspoint Dr. G23	9	U7
Invershiel Rd.		
Crosstobs Rd. G53	48	P15
Crossview Av. (Bail.) G69	40	FF13
Swinton Av.		
Crossview Pl. (Bail.) G69	40	FF13
Crovie Rd. G53	48	P16
Crow Ct., The (Bishop.) G64	10	X7
Kenmure Av.		
Crow La. G13	19	R9
Crow Rd. G11	19	R10
Crow Rd. G13	19	R10
Crow Wd. Rd. (Chry.) G69	26	EE8
Crow Wd. Ter. (Chry.) G69	26	EE8
Crowflats Rd. (Udd.) G71	69	GG17
Lady Isle Cres.		
Crowhill Rd. (Bishop.) G64	22	X8
Crowhill St. G22	22	W9
Crowlin Cres. G33	38	BB12
Crown Av., Clyde. G81	5	L6
Crown Circ. G12	20	S10
Crown Rd. S.		
Crown Ct. G1	36	W12
Virginia St.		
Crown Gdns. G12	20	S10
Crown Rd. N.		
Crown Mans. G11	20	S10
North Gardner St.		
Crown Rd. N. G12	20	S10
Crown Rd. S. G12	20	S10
Crown St. G5	52	W14
Crown St. (Bail.) G69	55	DD14
Crown Ter. G12	20	S10
Crown Rd. S.		
Crownhall Pl. G32	55	CC14
Crownhall Rd. G32	39	CC13
Crownpoint Rd. G40	36	X13
Crowpoint Rd. G40	37	Y13
Alma St.		
Croy Pl. G21	23	Z9
Croy Rd.		
Croy Rd. G21	23	Z9
Cruachan Av., Pais. PA2	46	K16
Cruachan Av., Renf. PA4	31	M11
Cruachan Dr. (Barr.) G78	59	M19
Cruachan Rd. (Ruther.) G73	65	Z18
Cruachan St. (Thorn.) G46	61	R18
Cruachan Way (Barr.) G78	59	M19
Cruden St. G51	33	R13
Crum Av. (Thorn.) G46	62	S18
Crusader Av. G13	7	Q7
Cubie St. G40	36	X13
Cuilhill Rd. (Bail.) G69	41	GG12
Cuillin Way (Barr.) G78	59	M19
Cuillins, The (Mood.) G69	15	HH6
Cuillins, The (Udd.) G71	56	FF15
Cuillins Rd. (Ruther.) G73	65	Z18
Culbin Dr. G13	18	N8
Cullen Pl. (Udd.) G71	57	HH16
Kingston St.		
Cullen St. G32	54	BB14
Culloden St. G31	37	Y12
Coventry Dr.		
Culrain Gdns. G32	38	BB13
Culrain St. G32	38	BB13
Culross La. G32	55	CC14
Culross St. G32	55	CC14
Cult Rd. (Lenzie) G66	13	DD6
Cults St. G51	33	R13
Culzean Cres. (Bail.) G69	56	EE14
Huntingtower Rd.		
Culzean Dr. G32	39	CC13
Cumberland Ct. G1	36	W13
Gallowgate		
Cumberland La. G5	51	V14
Cumberland St.		
Cumberland Pl. G5	52	W14
Cumberland Pl., Pais. PA1	46	K14
Causeyside St.		
Cumberland St. G5	35	V13
Cumbernauld Rd. G31	37	Z12
Cumbernauld Rd. G33	24	AA10
Cumbernauld Rd. (Chry.) G69	26	EE9
Cumbrae Ct., Clyde. G81	5	L7
Montrose St.		
Cumbrae Rd., Pais. PA2	46	K16
Cumbrae Rd., Renf. PA4	31	M11
Cumbrae St. G33	38	BB12

Cumlodden Dr. G20	20	T8
Cumming Dr. G42	51	V16
Cumnock Dr. (Barr.) G78	59	M19
Cumnock Rd. G33	24	AA9
Cunard St., Clyde. G81	17	L8
Cunningham Dr. (Giff.) G46	63	U18
Cunningham Dr., Clyde. G81	4	K5
Cunningham Rd. G52	32	N12
Cunningham Rd. (Ruther.) G73	53	Z16
Cunninghame Rd. (Kilb.), John. PA10	42	B14
Curfew Rd. G13	7	Q7
Curle St. G14	33	Q11
Curlew Pl., John. PA5	43	C16
Curling Cres. G44	52	W16
Currie St. G20	21	U9
Curtis Av. G44	52	W16
Curtis Av. (Ruther.) G73	52	W16
Curzon St. G20	21	U9
Custom Ho. Quay G1	36	W12
Cut, The (Udd.) G71	69	GG17
Cuthbert St. (Udd.) G71	57	HH16
Cuthbertson St. G42	51	V15
Cuthelton Dr. G31	54	AA14
Cuthelton St.		
Cuthelton St. G31	53	Z14
Cuthelton Ter. G31	53	Z14
Cypress Av. (Udd.) G71	57	HH16
Cypress Av. (Blan.) G72	68	FF19
Cypress Ct. (Kirk.) G66	12	BB5
Cypress St. G22	22	W9
Cypress Way (Camb.) G72	67	DD18
Cyprus Av. (Elder.), John. PA5	44	E15
Cyril St., Pais. PA1	47	L14

D

Daer Av., Renf. PA4	32	N11
Dairsie Ct. G44	63	U18
Dairsie Gdns. (Bishop.) G64	23	Z8
Dairsie St. G44	63	U18
Daisy St. G42	51	V15
Dakota Way, Renf. PA4	31	M11
Friendship Way		
Dalbeth Rd. G32	54	AA15
Dalcharn Path G34	40	EE12
Dalcharn Pl.		
Dalcharn Pl. G34	40	EE12
Dalcraig Cres. (Blan.) G72	68	FF19
Dalcross La. G11	34	T11
Byres Rd.		
Dalcross St. G11	34	T11
Dalcruin Gdns. (Mood.) G69	15	HH6
Daldowie Av. G32	55	CC14
Daldowie Rd. (Udd.) G71	56	EE15
Dale St. G40	52	X14
Dale Way (Ruther.) G73	65	Y18
Daleview Av. G12	20	S9
Dalfoil Ct., Pais. PA1	48	N14
Dalgarroch Av., Clyde. G81	18	N8
Dalgleish Av., Clyde. G81	4	K5
Dalhouse Rd. (Udd.) G71	56	EE15
Dalhousie Gdns. (Bishop.) G64	10	X7
Dalhousie La. G3	35	V11
Scott St.		
Dalhousie La. W. G3	35	V11
Buccleuch St.		
Dalhousie Rd. (Mill.Pk.), John. PA10	42	B15
Dalhousie St. G3	35	V11
Dalilea Dr. G34	40	FF11
Dalilea Path G34	40	FF11
Dalilea Dr.		
Dalilea Pl. G34	40	FF11
Dalintober St. G5	35	V13
Dalkeith Av. G41	50	S14
Dalkeith Av. (Bishop.) G64	11	Y6
Dalkeith Rd. (Bishop.) G64	11	Y6
Dalmahoy St. G32	38	AA12
Dalmally St. G20	21	U10
Dalmarnock Bri. G40	53	Y15
Dalmarnock Bri. (Ruther.) G73	53	Y15
Dalmarnock Ct. G40	53	Y14
Baltic St.		
Dalmarnock Rd. G40	52	X14
Dalmarnock Rd. (Ruther.) G73	53	Y15
Dalmary Dr., Pais. PA1	31	L13

Dalmellington Dr. G53	48	P16
Dalmellington Rd. G53	48	P16
Dalmeny Av. (Giff.) G46	62	T18
Dalmeny Dr. (Barr.) G78	59	L19
Dalmeny St. G5	52	X15
Dalmuir Ct., Clyde. G81	4	K6
Stewart St.		
Dalnair St. G3	34	T11
Dalness Pas. G32	54	BB14
Ochil St.		
Dalness St. G32	54	BB14
Dalreoch Av. (Bail.) G69	40	FF13
Dalriada St. G40	53	Z14
Dalry Rd. (Udd.) G71	57	HH16
Myrtle Rd.		
Dalry St. G32	54	BB14
Dalserf Cres. (Giff.) G46	62	S19
Dalserf St. G31	37	Y13
Dalsetter Av. G15	6	N7
Dalsetter Pl. G15	6	P7
Dalsholm Av. G20	20	S8
Dalsholm Rd. G20	20	S8
Dalskeith Av., Pais. PA3	29	H13
Dalskeith Cres., Pais. PA3	29	H13
Dalskeith Rd., Pais. PA3	45	H14
Dalswinton Pl. G34	40	FF12
Dalswinton St.		
Dalswinton St. G34	40	FF12
Dalton Av., Clyde. G81	5	M7
Dalton St. G31	38	AA13
Dalveen Ct. (Barr.) G78	59	M19
Dalveen Dr. (Udd.) G71	57	GG16
Dalveen St. G32	38	AA13
Dalveen Way (Ruther.) G73	65	Z18
Dalwhinnie Av. (Blan.) G72	68	FF19
Daly Gdns. (Blan.) G72	69	GG19
Dalziel Dr. G41	50	T14
Dalziel Quad. G41	50	T14
Dalziel Dr.		
Dalziel Rd. G52	32	N12
Damshot Cres. G53	49	Q15
Damshot Rd. G53	49	Q16
Danby Rd. (Bail.) G69	55	DD14
Danes Av. G14	19	Q10
Danes Cres. G14	18	P9
Danes Dr. G14	18	P9
Danes La. N. G14	19	Q10
Upland Rd.		
Danes La. S. G14	19	Q10
Dunglass Av.		
Dargarvel Av. G41	50	S14
Darkwood Ct., Pais. PA3	29	H13
Darkwood Cres., Pais. PA3	29	H13
Darkwood Dr., Pais. PA3	29	H13
Darkwood Cres.		
Darleith St. G32	38	AA13
Darley Mains Rd. G53	61	Q18
Darley Rd. (Cumb.) G68	70	NN1
Darnaway Av. G33	39	CC11
Darnaway Dr. G33	39	CC11
Darnaway St. G33	39	CC11
Darnick St. G21	23	Y10
Hobden St.		
Darnley Cres. (Bishop.) G64	10	X6
Darnley Gdns. G41	51	U15
Darnley Path (Thorn.) G46	61	R17
Kennisholm Av.		
Darnley Pl. G41	51	U15
Darnley Rd.		
Darnley Rd. G41	51	U15
Darnley Rd. (Barr.) G78	60	N18
Darnley St. G41	51	U15
Darroch Way (Cumb.) G67	71	PP2
Dartford St. G22	21	V10
Darvel Cres., Pais. PA1	47	M14
Darvel St. G53	60	N17
Darwin Pl., Clyde. G81	4	J6
Dava St. G51	34	S12
Davaar Dr., Pais. PA2	46	K16
Davaar Rd., Renf. PA4	31	M11
Davaar St. G40	53	Y14
Daventry Dr. G12	20	S9
David Pl. (Bail.) G69	55	DD14
David Pl., Pais. PA3	31	L12
Killarn Way		
David St. G40	37	Y13
David Way, Pais. PA3	31	L12
Killarn Way		
Davidson Gdns. G14	19	Q10
Westland Dr.		
Davidson Pl. G32	39	CC13
Davidson St. G40	53	Y15

Davidson St., Clyde. G81	18	N8
Davidston Pl. (Kirk.) G66	13	DD6
Davieland Rd. (Giff.) G46	62	S19
Daviot St. G51	33	Q13
Dawes La. N. G14	19	Q10
Upland Rd.		
Dawson Pl. G4	21	V10
Dawson Rd.		
Dawson Rd. G4	21	V10
Deaconsbank Av. (Thorn.) G46	61	Q19
Deaconsbank Cres. (Thorn.) G46	61	Q19
Deaconsbank Gdns. (Thorn.) G46	61	R19
Deaconsbank Gro. (Thorn.) G46	61	Q19
Deaconsbank Av.		
Deaconsbank Pl. (Thorn.) G46	61	Q19
Dealston Rd. (Barr.) G78	59	L18
Dean Cres. (Muir.) G69	14	FF7
Dean Pk. Dr. (Camb.) G72	67	CC18
Dean Pk. Rd., Renf. PA4	32	N11
Dean St., Clyde. G81	5	M7
Deanbrae St. (Udd.) G71	69	GG17
Deanfield Quad. G52	32	N13
Deans Av. (Camb.) G72	67	CC18
Deanside La. G4	36	W12
Rottenrow		
Deanside Rd. G52	32	P12
Deanston Av. (Barr.) G78	59	L19
Deanston Dr. G41	51	U16
Deanston Gdns. (Barr.) G78	59	L19
Deanston Pk. (Barr.) G78	59	L19
Deanwood Av. G44	63	U18
Deanwood Rd. G44	63	U18
Debdale Cotts. G13	19	R9
Whittingehame Dr.		
Dechmont Av. (Camb.) G72	67	CC18
Dechmont Gdns. (Udd.) G71	57	GG15
Dechmont Gdns. (Blan.) G72	68	FF19
Dechmont Pl. (Camb.) G72	67	CC18
Dechmont Rd. (Udd.) G71	57	GG15
Dechmont St. G31	53	Z14
Dechmont Vw. (Udd.) G71	57	HH16
Hamilton Vw.		
Dee Av., Pais. PA2	45	G15
Dee Av., Renf. PA4	18	N10
Dee Dr., Pais. PA2	45	G15
Dee Pl., John. PA5	43	C16
Dee St. G33	37	Z11
Deepdene Rd. (Bears.) G61	7	Q7
Deepdene Rd. (Chry.) G69	15	HH7
Delburn St. G31	53	Z14
Delhi Av., Clyde. G81	4	J6
Delvin Rd. G44	63	V17
Denbeck St. G32	38	AA13
Denbrae St. G32	38	AA13
Dene Wk. (Bishop.) G64	23	Z8
Denewood Av., Pais. PA2	46	J16
Denham St. G22	21	V10
Denholm Dr. (Giff.) G46	62	T19
Denkenny Sq. G15	6	N6
Denmark St. G22	22	W10
Denmilne Path G34	40	FF12
Denmilne Pl. G34	40	FF12
Denmilne Rd. (Bail.) G69	40	FF12
Denmilne St. G34	40	FF12
Derby St. G3	35	U12
Derby Ter. La. G3	35	U12
Derby St.		
Derwent St. G22	21	V10
Despard Av. G32	55	DD14
Despard Gdns. G32	55	DD14
Deveron Av. (Giff.) G46	62	T19
Deveron Rd. (Bears.) G61	7	Q7
Deveron St. G33	37	Z11
Devol Cres. G53	48	P16
Devon Gdns. G12	20	S10
Hyndland Rd.		
Devon Gdns. (Bishop.) G64	10	X6
Devon Pl. G41	51	V14
Devon St. G5	51	V14
Devondale Av. (Blan.) G72	68	FF19
Devonshire Gdns. G12	20	S10
Devonshire Gdns. La. G12	20	S10
Hyndland Rd.		
Devonshire Ter. G12	20	S10
Devonshire Ter. La. G12	20	S10
Hughenden Rd.		

Street	Page	Grid
Dewar Clo. (Udd.) G71	57	HH15
Diana Av. G13	18	P8
Dick St. G20	21	U10
Henderson St.		
Dickens Av., Clyde. G81	4	K6
Dilwara Av. G14	33	R11
Dimity St., John. PA5	43	D15
Dinard Dr. (Giff.) G46	62	T18
Dinart St. G33	37	Z11
Dinduff St. G34	40	FF11
Dingwall St. G3	34	T12
Kelvinhaugh St.		
Dinmont Pl. G41	51	U15
Norham St.		
Dinmont Rd. G41	50	T15
Dinwiddie St. G21	37	Z11
Dipple Pl. G15	6	P7
Dirleton Dr. G41	51	U16
Dirleton Dr., Pais. PA2	45	H15
Dirleton Gate (Bears.) G61	7	Q7
Dixon Av. G42	51	V15
Dixon Rd. G42	52	W15
Dixon St. G1	35	V13
Dixon St., Pais. PA1	46	K14
Dobbies Ln. G4	35	V11
Dobbies Ln. Pl. G4	36	W12
Dochart Av., Renf. PA4	32	N11
Dochart St. G33	38	AA11
Dock St., Clyde. G81	17	M8
Dodhill Pl. G13	18	P9
Dodside Gdns. G32	55	CC14
Dodside Pl. G32	55	CC14
Dodside St. G32	55	CC14
Dolan St. (Bail.) G69	40	EE13
Dollar Ter. G20	20	T8
Crosbie St.		
Dolphin Rd. G41	50	T15
Don Av., Renf. PA4	32	N11
Don Dr., Pais. PA2	45	G15
Don Pl., John. PA5	43	C16
Don St. G33	37	Z12
Donald Way (Udd.) G71	57	HH16
Donaldson Dr., Renf. PA4	17	M10
Ferguson St.		
Donaldson Grn. (Udd.) G71	57	HH16
Donaldswood Pk., Pais. PA2	46	J16
Donaldswood Rd., Pais. PA2	46	J16
Doncaster St. G20	21	V10
Doon Cres. (Bears.) G61	7	Q6
Doon Side (Cumb.) G67	71	PP3
Doon St., Clyde. G81	5	M6
Doonfoot Rd. G43	62	T17
Dora St. G40	53	Y14
Dorchester Av. G12	20	S9
Dorchester Ct. G12	20	S9
Dorchester Av.		
Dorchester Pl. G12	20	S9
Dorlin Rd. G33	25	DD9
Dormanside Ct. G53	48	P14
Dormanside Gate G53	48	P14
Dormanside Gro. G53	48	P14
Dormanside Rd. G53	48	P14
Dornal Av. G13	18	N8
Dornford Av. G32	55	CC15
Dornford Rd. G32	55	CC15
Dornie Dr. G32	55	CC16
Dornie Dr. (Thorn.) G46	61	R18
Dornoch Av. (Giff.) G46	62	T19
Dornoch Pl. (Bishop.) G64	11	Z7
Dornoch Pl. (Chry.) G69	14	FF7
Dornoch Rd. (Bears.) G61	7	Q7
Dornoch St. G40	36	X13
Dornoch Way (Cumb.) G68	71	PP1
Dorset Sq. G3	35	U12
Dorset St.		
Dorset St. G3	35	U12
Dosk Av. G13	18	N8
Dosk Pl. G13	18	N8
Dougalston Rd. G23	9	U7
Douglas Av. G32	54	BB15
Douglas Av. (Giff.) G46	62	T19
Douglas Av. (Lenzie) G66	13	CC5
Douglas Av. (Ruther.) G73	65	Z17
Douglas Av. (Elder.), John. PA5	44	E15
Douglas Ct. (Lenzie) G66	13	CC5
Douglas Cres. (Udd.) G71	57	HH16
Douglas Dr. G15	6	N7
Douglas Dr. (Bail.) G69	39	DD13
Douglas Dr. (Both.) G71	69	HH19
Douglas Dr. (Camb.) G72	66	AA17
Douglas Gdns. (Giff.) G46	62	T19
Douglas Gdns. (Bears.) G61	7	R6
Douglas Gdns. (Lenzie) G66	13	CC5
Douglas Gdns. (Udd.) G71	69	GG17
Douglas Gate (Camb.) G72	66	BB17
Douglas La. G2	35	V12
West George St.		
Douglas Pk. Cres. (Bears.) G61	8	S5
Douglas Pl. (Bears.) G61	7	R5
Douglas Pl. (Kirk.) G66	13	CC5
Douglas Av.		
Douglas Rd., Renf. PA4	31	L12
Douglas St. G2	35	V12
Douglas St. (Udd.) G71	57	HH16
Douglas St., Pais. PA1	30	J13
Douglas Ter. G41	51	U15
Glencairn Dr.		
Douglas Ter., Pais. PA3	30	K11
Dougray Pl. (Barr.) G78	59	M19
Dougrie Dr. G45	64	W18
Dougrie Gdns. G45	64	W19
Dougrie Pl. G45	64	X18
Dougrie Rd. G45	64	W19
Dougrie St. G45	64	X18
Dougrie Ter. G45	64	W18
Doune Cres. (Bishop.) G64	11	Y6
Doune Gdns. G20	21	U10
Doune Quad. G20	21	U10
Dove St. G53	60	P17
Dovecot G43	50	T16
Shawhill Rd.		
Dovecothall St. (Barr.) G78	59	M18
Dover St. G3	35	U12
Downfield Rd. (Cumb.) G67	70	NN3
Dowanhill St. G11	34	T11
Dowanhill St. G12	34	T11
Dowanside La. G12	20	T10
Byres Rd.		
Dowanside Rd. G12	20	T10
Dowanvale Ter. G11	34	S11
White St.		
Downcraig Dr. G45	64	W19
Downcraig Gro. G45	64	W19
Downcraig Rd. G45	64	W19
Downcraig Ter. G45	64	W19
Downfield Gdns. (Both.) G71	69	GG19
Downfield St. G32	54	AA14
Downie Clo. (Udd.) G71	57	HH16
Downiebrae Rd. (Ruther.) G73	53	Y15
Downs St. G21	22	X10
Dowrie Cres. G53	48	P15
Dows Pl. G4	21	V10
Possil Rd.		
Drainie St. G34	40	EE12
Westerhouse Rd.		
Drake St. G40	36	X13
Drakemire Av. G45	64	W18
Drakemire Dr. G44	64	W18
Drakemire Dr. G45	64	W18
Dreghorn St. G31	37	Z12
Drem Pl. G11	34	S11
Merkland St.		
Drimnin Rd. G33	25	DD9
Drive Rd. G51	33	R12
Drochil St. G34	40	EE11
Drumbeg Dr. G53	60	P17
Drumbeg Pl. G53	60	P17
Drumbottie Rd. G21	23	Y9
Drumby Cres. (Clark.) G76	62	T19
Drumcavel Rd. (Muir.) G69	26	FF8
Drumchapel Gdns. G15	6	P7
Drumchapel Pl. G15	6	P7
Drumchapel Rd. G15	6	P7
Drumclog Gdns. G33	24	AA9
Drumcross Rd. G53	49	Q15
Drumhead La. G32	54	AA15
Drumhead Pl. G32	54	AA15
Drumhead Rd. G32	54	AA15
Drumilaw Rd. (Ruther.) G73	65	Y17
Drumilaw Way (Ruther.) G73	65	Y17
Drumlaken Av. G23	8	T7
Drumlaken Ct. G23	8	T7
Drumlaken St. G23	8	T7
Drumlanrig Av. G34	40	FF11
Drumlanrig Pl. G34	40	FF11
Drumlochy Rd. G33	38	BB11
Drummond Av. (Ruther.) G73	52	X16
Drummond Dr., Pais. PA1	47	M14
Drummond Gdns. G13	19	R9
Crow Rd.		
Drummore Rd. G15	6	P5
Drumover Dr. G31	54	AA14
Drumoyne Av. G51	33	R12
Drumoyne Circ. G51	33	R13
Drumoyne Dr. G51	33	R12
Drumoyne Pl. G51	33	R13
Drumoyne Circ.		
Drumoyne Quad. G51	33	R13
Drumoyne Rd. G51	33	R13
Drumoyne Sq. G51	33	R12
Drumpark St. (Thorn.) G46	61	R18
Drumpark St., Coat. ML5	57	HH14
Dunnachie Dr.		
Drumpellier Av. (Bail.) G69	56	EE14
Drumpellier Pl. (Bail.) G69	56	EE14
Drumpellier Rd. (Bail.) G69	56	EE14
Drumpellier St. G33	37	Z11
Drumreoch Dr. G42	52	X16
Drumreoch Pl. G42	52	X16
Drumry Pl. G15	6	N7
Drumry Rd., Clyde. G81	5	L6
Drumry Rd. E. G15	5	M7
Drums Av., Pais. PA3	29	H13
Drums Cres., Pais. PA3	30	J13
Drums Rd. G53	48	P14
Drumsack Av. (Chry.) G69	26	FF8
Drumsargard Rd. (Ruther.) G73	65	Z17
Drumshaw Dr. G32	55	CC16
Drumvale Dr. (Chry.) G69	15	GG7
Drury St. G2	35	V12
Dryad St. (Thorn.) G46	61	R17
Dryburgh Av. (Ruther.) G73	53	Y16
Dryburgh Av., Pais. PA2	45	H15
Dryburgh Gdns. G20	21	U10
Dryburgh Rd. (Bears.) G61	7	Q5
Dryburgh Wk. (Mood.) G69	15	HH6
Dryburn Av. G52	32	P13
Drygate G4	36	X12
Drygrange Rd. G33	39	CC11
Drymen Pl. (Lenzie) G66	13	CC6
Drymen Rd. (Bears.) G61	7	Q5
Drymen St. G52	33	R13
Morven St.		
Drymen Wynd (Bears.) G61	7	R6
Drynoch Pl. G22	21	V8
Drysdale St. G14	18	N9
Duart Dr. (Elder.), John. PA5	44	E15
Duart St. G20	20	T8
Dubs Rd. (Barr.) G78	60	N18
Dubton Path G34	40	EE11
Dubton St. G34	40	EE11
Duchall Pl. G14	18	P10
Duchess Pl. (Ruther.) G73	53	Z16
Duchess Rd. (Ruther.) G73	53	Z15
Duchess Way (Bail.) G69	41	GG13
Park Rd.		
Duchray Dr., Pais. PA1	48	N14
Duchray La. G33	37	Z11
Duchray St.		
Duchray St. G33	37	Z11
Dudhope St. G33	39	CC11
Dudley Dr. G12	20	S10
Dudley La. G12	20	S10
Clarence Dr.		
Duffus Pl. G32	55	CC16
Duffus St. G34	40	EE11
Duffus Ter. G32	55	CC16
Duich Gdns. G23	9	U7
Duisdale Rd. G32	55	CC16
Duke St. G4	36	X12
Duke St. G31	36	X12
Duke St., Pais. PA2	46	K15
Duke St. (Linw.), Pais. PA3	28	F13
Dukes Gate (Both.) G71	69	GG18
Dukes Rd. (Bail.) G69	41	GG13
Dukes Rd. (Camb.) G72	65	Z17
Dukes Rd. (Ruther.) G73	65	Z17
Dulnain St. (Camb.) G72	67	DD17
Dulsie Rd. G21	23	Z9
Dumbarton Rd. G11	34	S11
Dumbarton Rd. G14	18	P10
Dumbarton Rd. (Old Kil.) G60	4	J6
Dumbarton Rd., Clyde. G81	4	J6
Dumbarton Rd. (Dunt.), Clyde. G81	4	K5
Dumbreck Av. G41	50	S14
Dumbreck Ct. G41	50	S14
Dumbreck Pl. (Kirk.) G66	13	DD6
Dumbreck Rd. G41	50	S14
Dumbreck Sq. G41	50	S14
Dumbreck Av.		

Dunagoil Gdns. G45   64 X19
Dunagoil St.
Dunagoil Pl. G45   64 X19
Dunagoil Rd. G45   64 W19
Dunagoil St. G45   64 X19
Dunagoil Ter. G45   64 X19
Dunalistair Dr. G33   24 BB9
Dunan Pl. G33   39 DD12
Dunard Rd. (Ruther.) G73   53 Y16
Dunard St. G20   21 U10
Dunard Way, Pais. PA3   30 J12
Mosslands Rd.
Dunaskin St. G11   34 T11
Dunbar Av. (Ruther.) G73   53 Z16
Dunbar Av., John. PA5   43 D16
Dunbar Rd., Pais. PA2   45 H15
Dunbeith Pl. G20   20 T9
Dunblane St. G4   35 V11
Dunbrach Rd. (Cumb.) G68   70 MM2
Duncan Av. G14   19 Q10
Duncan La. G14   19 Q10
Duncan Av.
Duncan La. N. G14   19 Q10
Ormiston Av.
Duncan La. S. G14   19 Q10
Duncan Av.
Duncan St., Clyde. G81   5 L6
Duncansby Rd. G33   39 CC13
Dunchattan Pl. G31   36 X12
Duke St.
Dunchattan St. G31   36 X12
Dunchurch Rd., Pais. PA1   31 M13
Dunclutha Dr. (Both.) G71   69 HH19
Dunclutha St. G40   53 Y15
Duncombe St. G20   20 T8
Duncombe Vw., Clyde. G81   5 M6
Kirkoswald Dr.
Duncraig Cres., John. PA5   43 C16
Duncrub Dr. (Bishop.) G64   10 X7
Duncruin St. G20   20 T8
Duncryne Av. G32   55 CC14
Duncryne Gdns. G32   55 DD14
Duncryne Pl. (Bishop.) G64   22 X8
Dundaff Hill (Cumb.) G68   70 MM3
Dundas La. G1   36 W12
Dundas St. G1   36 W12
Dundashill G4   35 V11
Dundasvale Ct. G4   35 V11
Maitland St.
Dundasvale Rd. G4   35 V11
Maitland St.
Dundee Dr. G52   48 P14
Dundee Path G52   49 Q14
Dundee Dr.
Dundonald Av., John. PA5   43 C15
Dundonald Rd. G12   20 T10
Dundonald Rd., Pais. PA3   31 L12
Dundrennan Rd. G42   51 U16
Dunearn Pl., Pais. PA2   47 L14
Dunearn St. G4   35 U11
Dunellan St. G52   33 R13
Dungeonhill Rd. G34   40 FF12
Dunglass Av. G14   19 Q10
Dunglass La. G14   19 Q10
Dunglass Av.
Dunglass La. N. G14   19 Q10
Verona Av.
Dunglass La. S. G14   19 Q10
Dunglass Av.
Dungoil Av. (Cumb.) G68   70 LL2
Dungoil Rd. (Lenzie) G66   13 DD6
Dungoyne St. G20   20 T8
Dunira St. G32   54 AA14
Dunivaig St. G33   39 DD12
Dunkeld Av. (Ruther.) G73   53 Y16
Dunkeld Dr. (Bears.) G61   8 S6
Dunkeld Gdns. (Bishop.) G64   11 Y7
Dunkeld La. (Chry.) G69   15 HH7
Burnbrae Av.
Dunkeld St. G31   53 Z14
Dunkenny Pl. G15   6 N6
Dunkenny Rd. G15   6 N6
Dunkenny Sq. G15   6 N6
Dunlin G12   20 S9
Dunlop Cres. (Both.) G71   69 HH19
Dunlop Cres., Renf. PA4   17 M10
Fulbar St.
Dunlop Gro. (Udd.) G71   57 HH15
Dunlop St. G1   36 W13
Dunlop St. (Camb.) G72   67 DD17
Dunlop St. (Linw.) Pais.   28 F13
PA3

Dunlop St., Renf. PA4   17 M10
Fulbar St.
Dunmore La. G5   35 V13
Norfolk St.
Dunmore St. G5   35 V13
Dunmore St., Clyde. G81   17 M8
Dunn St. G40   53 Y14
Dunn St., Clyde. G81   4 K6
Dunn St. (Dunt.), Clyde. G81   4 K5
Dunn St., Pais. PA1   47 L14
Dunnachie Dr., Coat. ML5   57 HH14
Dunnichen Gdns. (Bishop.)   11 Z7
G64
Dunnottar St. G33   38 BB11
Dunnottar St. (Bishop.) G64   11 Z7
Dunolly St. G21   37 Y11
Dunphail Dr. G34   40 FF12
Dunphail Rd. G34   40 FF12
Dunragit St. G31   37 Z12
Dunrobin Av. (Elder.), John.   44 F15
PA5
Dunrobin St. G31   37 Y13
Dunrod St. G32   54 BB14
Dunside Dr. G53   60 P17
Dunskaith Pl. G34   40 FF12
Dunskaith St. G34   40 FF12
Dunsmuir St. G51   34 S12
Dunster Gdns. (Bishop.) G64   11 Y6
Dunswin Av., Clyde. G81   4 K6
Dunswin Ct., Clyde. G81   4 K6
Dunswin Av.
Dunsyre Pl. G23   9 U7
Dunsyre St. G33   38 AA12
Duntarvie Av. G34   40 FF12
Duntarvie Clo. G34   40 FF12
Duntarvie Cres. G34   40 FF12
Duntarvie Dr. G34   40 EE12
Duntarvie Gdns. G34   40 FF12
Duntarvie Gro. G34   40 FF12
Duntarvie Pl. G34   40 EE12
Duntarvie Quad. G34   40 FF12
Duntarvie Rd. G34   40 EE12
Dunterlie Av. G13   18 P9
Dunterlie Ct. (Barr.) G78   59 M18
Duntiglennan Rd., Clyde. G81   5 L5
Duntocher Rd. (Bears.) G61   6 P5
Duntocher Rd., Clyde. G81   4 K6
Duntocher Rd. (Dunt.), Clyde.   5 L5
G81
Duntocher St. G21   22 X10
Northcroft Rd.
Duntreath Av. G13   18 N8
Duntreath Av. G15   18 N8
Duntreath Dr. G15   6 N7
Duntreath Gdns. G15   6 N7
Duntreath Gro. G15   6 N7
Duntroon St. G31   37 Y12
Dunure Dr. (Ruther.) G73   64 X17
Dunure St. G20   20 T8
Dunvegan Av. (Elder.), John.   44 F15
PA5
Dunvegan Ct. G13   18 P9
Kintillo Dr.
Dunvegan Dr. (Bishop.) G64   11 Y6
Dunvegan Quad., Renf. PA4   17 L10
Kirklandneuk Rd.
Dunwan Av. G13   18 N8
Dunwan Pl. G13   18 N8
Durban Av., Clyde. G81   4 J6
Durham St. G41   34 T13
Durness Av. (Bears.) G61   8 S5
Durno Path G33   39 DD12
Duror St. G32   38 BB13
Durris Gdns. G32   55 CC14
Durrockstock Cres., Pais. PA2   45 G16
Durrockstock Rd., Pais. PA2   45 G16
Durward Av. G41   50 T15
Durward Ct. G41   50 T15
Durward Cres., Pais. PA2   45 G15
Duthil St. G51   33 Q13
Dyce La. G11   34 S11
Dyers La. G1   36 W13
Turnbull St.
Dyers Wynd, Pais. PA1   30 K13
Gilmour St.
Dyke Pl. G13   18 P8
Dyke Rd. G13   18 N9
Dyke Rd. G14   18 N9
Dyke St. (Bail.) G69   40 FF13
Dykebar Av. G13   18 P9
Dykebar Cres., Pais. PA2   47 L15
Dykefoot Dr. G53   49 Q16

Dykehead La. G33   39 CC12
Dykehead Rd. (Bail.) G69   41 GG13
Dykehead St. G33   39 CC12
Dykemuir Pl. G21   23 Y10
Dykemuir Quad. G21   23 Y10
Dykemuir St.
Dykemuir St. G21   23 Y10

E

Eagle Cres. (Bears.) G61   6 P5
Eagle St. G4   36 W11
Eaglesham Ct. G51   35 U13
Blackburn St.
Eaglesham Pl. G51   35 U13
Earl Haig Rd. G52   32 N12
Earl La. G14   19 Q10
Harland St.
Earl Pl. G14   19 Q10
Earl St. G14   18 P10
Earlbank Av. G14   19 Q10
Earlbank La. N. G14   19 Q10
Dunglass Av.
Earlbank La. S. G14   19 Q10
Verona Av.
Earls Gate (Both.) G71   69 GG18
Earls Hill (Cumb.) G68   70 LL2
Earlsburn Rd. (Lenzie) G66   13 DD6
Earlscourt (Mood.) G69   15 GG7
Langdale Rd.
Earlspark Av. G43   51 U16
Earn Av. (Bears.) G61   8 S6
Earn Av., Renf. PA4   32 N11
Almond Av.
Earn St. G33   38 AA11
Earnock St. G33   23 Z10
Earnside St. G32   38 BB13
Easdale Dr. G32   54 BB14
East Av., Renf. PA4   17 M10
East Barns St., Clyde. G81   17 M8
East Bath La. G2   35 V12
Sauchiehall St.
East Buchanan St., Pais. PA1   30 K13
East Campbell St. G1   36 X13
East Greenlees Av. (Camb.)   67 CC18
G72
East Greenlees Cres.   66 BB18
(Camb.) G72
East Greenlees Dr. (Camb.)   66 BB18
G72
East Greenlees Gro. (Camb.)   66 BB18
G72
East Greenlees Rd. (Camb.)   66 BB18
G72
East Hallhill Rd. (Bail.) G69   40 EE13
East Kilbride Expressway   66 BB19
(Camb.) G72
East Kilbride Rd. (Ruther.)   65 Z17
G73
East La., Pais. PA1   47 L14
East Reid St. (Ruther.) G73   53 Z16
East Rd. (Kilb.), John. PA10   42 B14
East Springfield Ter.   23 Y8
(Bishop.) G64
East Thomson St., Clyde. G81   5 L6
East Wellington St. G31   37 Z13
East Whitby St. G31   53 Z14
Eastbank Dr. G12   20 T10
Eastbank Dr. G32   39 CC13
Eastbank Pl. G12   20 T10
Eastbank Pl. G32   39 CC13
Eastbank Ri. G12   20 T9
Eastbank Ri. G32   39 CC13
Eastburn Cres. G21   23 Y9
Eastburn Pl. G21   23 Y9
Eastburn Rd. G21   23 Y9
Eastcote Av. G14   19 R10
Eastcroft (Ruther.) G73   53 Y16
Eastcroft Ter. G21   23 Y10
Easter Av. (Udd.) G71   69 GG17
Easter Garngaber Rd.   13 DD5
(Lenzie) G66
Easter Ms. (Udd.) G71   69 GG17
Church St.
Easter Queenslie Rd. G33   39 DD12
Eastercraigs G31   37 Y12
Easterhill Pl. G32   54 AA14
Easterhill St. G32   54 AA14
Easterhouse Pl. G34   40 FF12
Easterhouse Rd.
Easterhouse Quad. G34   40 FF12
Easterhouse Rd.

Easterhouse Rd. G34 — 40 FF12
Easterhouse Rd. (Bail.) G69 — 40 FF12
Eastfield Av. (Camb.) G72 — 66 AA17
Eastfield Rd. G21 — 22 X10
Eastfield Rd. (Cumb.) G68 — 70 MM2
Eastgate (Gart.) G69 — 27 HH9
Easthall Pl. G33 — 39 DD12
Eastmuir St. G32 — 38 BB13
Eastvale Pl. G3 — 34 T12
Eastwood Av. G41 — 50 T16
Eastwood Av. (Giff.) G46 — 62 T19
Eastwood Ct. (Thorn.) G46 — 61 R18
  Main St.
Eastwood Cres. (Thorn.) G46 — 61 R18
Eastwood Rd. (Chry.) G69 — 15 GG7
Eastwood Vw. (Camb.) G72 — 67 DD17
Eastwoodmains Rd. (Giff.) G46 — 62 S19
Eastwoodmains Rd. (Clark.) G76 — 62 S19
Easwald Bk. (Mill.Pk.), John. PA10 — 42 B15
Eccles St. G22 — 22 X9
Eckford St. G32 — 54 BB14
Eday St. G22 — 22 W9
Edderton Pl. G34 — 40 EE12
Eddleston Pl. (Camb.) G72 — 67 DD17
Eddlewood Path G33 — 39 DD12
Eddlewood Pl. G33 — 39 DD12
Eddlewood Rd. G33 — 39 DD12
Edelweiss Ter. G11 — 34 S11
  Gardner St.
Eden La. G33 — 37 Z11
Eden Pk. (Both.) G71 — 69 GG19
Eden Pl. (Camb.) G72 — 67 CC17
Eden Pl., Renf. PA4 — 32 N11
Eden St. G33 — 37 Z11
Edenwood St. G31 — 38 AA13
Edgam Dr. G52 — 33 Q13
Edgefauld Av. G21 — 22 X10
Edgefauld Dr. G21 — 22 X10
Edgefauld Pl. G21 — 22 X9
  Balgrayhill Rd.
Edgefauld Rd. G21 — 22 X10
Edgehill La. G11 — 20 S10
  Marlborough Av.
Edgehill Rd. G11 — 20 S10
Edgehill Rd. (Bears.) G61 — 7 R5
Edgemont St. G41 — 51 U16
Edinbeg Av. G42 — 52 X16
Edinbeg Pl. G42 — 52 X16
Edinburgh Rd. G33 — 37 Z12
Edinburgh Rd. (Bail.) G69 — 39 DD12
Edington Gdns. (Chry.) G69 — 15 GG6
Edington St. G4 — 35 V11
Edison St. G52 — 32 N12
Edmiston Dr. G51 — 33 R13
Edmiston Dr. (Linw.), Pais. PA3 — 28 E13
Edmiston St. G31 — 53 Z14
Edmondstone Ct., Clyde. G81 — 17 M8
  Yokerburn Ter.
Edrom Path G32 — 38 AA13
  Edrom St.
Edrom St. G32 — 38 AA13
Edward Av., Renf. PA4 — 18 N10
Edward St. G3 — 34 T12
  Lumsden St.
Edward St. (Bail.) G69 — 41 GG13
Edward St., Clyde. G81 — 17 M8
Edwin St. G51 — 34 T13
Edzell Ct. G14 — 33 Q11
Edzell Dr. (Elder.), John. PA5 — 44 F15
Edzell Gdns. (Bishop.) G64 — 23 Z8
Edzell Pl. G14 — 33 Q11
Edzell St. G14 — 33 Q11
Egidia Av. (Giff.) G46 — 62 S19
Egilsay Cres. G22 — 22 W8
Egilsay Pl. G22 — 22 W8
Egilsay St. G22 — 22 W8
Egilsay Ter. G22 — 22 W8
Eglinton Av. (Udd.) G71 — 69 GG17
Eglinton Ct. G5 — 35 V13
Eglinton Dr. (Giff.) G46 — 62 T19
Eglinton La. G5 — 51 V14
  Eglinton St.
Eglinton St. G5 — 51 V14
Eider G12 — 20 S8
Eighth St. (Udd.) G71 — 57 GG15
Eildon Dr. (Barr.) G78 — 59 M19
Eileen Gdns. (Bishop.) G64 — 11 Y7
Elba La. G31 — 37 Z13

Elcho St. G40 — 36 X13
Elder Cres. (Camb.) G72 — 67 DD18
Elder Gro. (Udd.) G71 — 57 HH16
Elder St. G51 — 33 R12
Elderbank (Bears.) G61 — 7 R6
Elderpark Gdns. G51 — 33 R12
Elderpark Gro. G51 — 33 R12
Elderpark St. G51 — 33 R12
Elderslie St. G3 — 35 U11
Eldin Pl. (Elder.), John. PA5 — 44 E15
Eldon Gdns. (Bishop.) G64 — 10 X7
Eldon St. G3 — 35 U11
Eldon Ter. G11 — 34 S11
  Caird Dr.
Elgin St. G40 — 37 Y13
Elibank St. G33 — 38 BB11
Elie St. G11 — 34 T11
Elizabeth Cres. (Thorn.) G46 — 62 S18
Elizabeth St. G51 — 34 T13
Elizabethan Way, Renf. PA4 — 31 M11
  Cockels Ln.
Ellangowan Rd. G41 — 50 T16
Ellergreen Rd. (Bears.) G61 — 7 R6
Ellerslie St., John. PA5 — 44 E14
Ellesmere St. G22 — 21 V10
Ellinger Ct., Clyde. G81 — 4 K6
  Scott St.
Elliot Av. (Giff.) G46 — 62 T19
Elliot Av., Pais. PA2 — 45 G16
Elliot Dr. (Giff.) G46 — 62 T18
Elliot La. G3 — 35 U12
  Elliot St.
Elliot Pl. G3 — 35 U12
Elliot St. G3 — 35 U12
Ellisland Av., Clyde. G81 — 5 M6
Ellisland Cres. (Ruther.) G73 — 64 X17
Ellisland Rd. G43 — 62 T17
Ellisland Rd. (Cumb.) G67 — 71 PP3
Ellismuir Fm. Rd. (Bail.) G69 — 56 FF14
Ellismuir Pl. (Bail.) G69 — 56 FF14
Ellismuir Rd. (Bail.) G69 — 56 FF14
Ellismuir Way (Udd.) G71 — 57 HH15
Elliston Av. G53 — 61 Q17
Elliston Cres. G53 — 61 Q17
Elliston Dr. G53 — 61 Q17
Elliston Pl. G53 — 61 Q17
  Ravenscraig Dr.
Ellon Dr. (Linw.), Pais. PA3 — 28 E13
Ellon Way, Pais. PA3 — 31 L12
Elm Av. (Lenzie) G66 — 13 CC5
Elm Av., Renf. PA4 — 17 M10
Elm Bk. (Bishop.) G64 — 11 Y7
Elm Dr. (Camb.) G72 — 67 CC17
Elm Dr., John. PA5 — 43 D16
Elm Gdns. (Bears.) G61 — 7 R5
Elm La. E. G14 — 19 Q10
  Elm St.
Elm La. W. G14 — 19 Q10
  Elm St.
Elm Rd. (Ruther.) G73 — 65 Y18
Elm Rd., Clyde. G81 — 5 L5
Elm Rd., Pais. PA2 — 47 L15
Elm St. G14 — 19 Q10
Elm Wk. (Bears.) G61 — 7 R5
Elm Way (Camb.) G72 — 67 DD18
Elmbank Av. (Udd.) G71 — 57 HH16
Elmbank Cres. G2 — 35 V12
  Elmbank St.
Elmbank La. G3 — 35 U12
  North St.
Elmbank St. G2 — 35 V12
Elmbank St. La. G2 — 35 V12
  Elmbank St.
Elmfoot St. G5 — 52 W15
Elmira Rd. (Muir.) G69 — 26 FF8
Elmore Av. G44 — 63 V17
Elmore La. G44 — 63 V17
Elmslie Ct. (Bail.) G69 — 56 EE14
Elmvale Row G21 — 22 X10
Elmvale Row E. G21 — 22 X10
  Elmvale Row
Elmvale Row W. G21 — 22 X10
  Elmvale Row
Elmvale St. G21 — 22 X9
Elmwood Av. G11 — 19 R10
Elmwood Ct. (Both.) G71 — 69 HH19
Elmwood Gdns. G11 — 19 R10
  Randolph Rd.
Elmwood Gdns. (Kirk.) G66 — 12 BB5
Elmwood La. G11 — 19 R10
  Elmwood Av.

Elmwood Ter. G11 — 19 R10
  Crow Rd.
Elphin St. G23 — 8 T7
  Invershiel Rd.
Elphinstone Pl. G51 — 34 T12
Elrig Rd. G44 — 63 V17
Elspeth Gdns. (Bishop.) G64 — 11 Y7
Eltham St. G22 — 21 V10
Elvan Ct. G32 — 38 AA13
  Edrom St.
Elvan St. G32 — 38 AA13
Embo Dr. G13 — 18 P9
Emerson Rd. (Bishop.) G64 — 11 Y7
Emerson St. G20 — 21 V9
Emily Pl. G31 — 36 X13
Endfield Av. G12 — 20 S9
Endrick Bk. (Bishop.) G64 — 11 Y6
Endrick Dr. (Bears.) G61 — 7 R6
Endrick Dr., Pais. PA1 — 31 L13
Endrick St. G21 — 22 W10
Endsleigh Gdns. G11 — 20 S10
  Partickhill Rd.
Ensay St. G22 — 22 W8
Enterkin St. G32 — 54 AA14
Ericht Rd. G43 — 62 T17
Eriska Av. G14 — 18 P9
Eriskay Dr. (Old Kil.) G60 — 4 J5
Eriskay Pl. (Old Kil.) G60 — 4 J5
Erradale St. G22 — 21 V8
Erriboll Pl. G22 — 21 V8
Erriboll St. G22 — 21 V8
Errogie St. G34 — 40 EE12
Errol Gdns. G5 — 52 W14
Erskine Av. G41 — 50 S14
Erskine Sq. G52 — 32 N12
Erskine Vw., Clyde. G81 — 5 L6
  Singer St.
Erskinefauld Rd. (Linw.), Pais. PA3 — 28 E13
Ervie St. G34 — 40 FF12
Esk Av., Renf. PA4 — 32 N11
Esk Dr., Pais. PA2 — 45 G15
Esk St. G14 — 18 N9
Esk Way, Pais. PA2 — 45 G15
Eskbank St. G32 — 38 BB13
Eskdale Dr. (Ruther.) G73 — 53 Z16
Eskdale Rd. (Bears.) G61 — 7 Q7
Eskdale St. G42 — 51 V15
Esmond St. G3 — 34 T11
Espedair St., Pais. PA2 — 46 K14
Essenside Av. G15 — 7 Q7
Essex Dr. G14 — 19 R10
Essex La. G14 — 19 R10
Esslemont Av. G14 — 18 P9
Estate Quad. G32 — 55 CC16
Estate Rd. G32 — 55 CC16
Etive Av. (Bears.) G61 — 8 S6
Etive Ct., Clyde. G81 — 5 M5
Etive Cres. (Bishop.) G64 — 11 Y7
Etive Dr. (Giff.) G46 — 62 T19
Etive St. G32 — 38 BB13
Eton Gdns. G12 — 35 U11
  Oakfield Av.
Eton La. G12 — 35 U11
  Great George St.
Eton Pl. G12 — 35 U11
  Oakfield Av.
Eton Ter. G12 — 35 U11
  Oakfield Av.
Ettrick Av., Renf. PA4 — 32 N11
Ettrick Ct. (Camb.) G72 — 67 DD18
  Gateside Av.
Ettrick Cres. (Ruther.) G73 — 53 Z16
Ettrick Oval, Pais. PA2 — 45 G16
Ettrick Pl. G43 — 50 T16
Ettrick Ter., John. PA5 — 43 C16
Ettrick Way, Renf. PA4 — 32 N11
Eure Point Ct. G33 — 38 BB12
  Sutherness Dr.
Evan Cres. (Giff.) G46 — 62 T19
Evan Dr. (Giff.) G46 — 62 T19
Evanton Dr. (Thorn.) G46 — 61 R18
Evanton Pl. (Thorn.) G46 — 61 R18
  Evanton Dr.
Everard Ct. G21 — 22 X8
Everard Dr. G21 — 22 X8
Everard Pl. G21 — 22 X8
Everard Quad. G21 — 22 X8
Everglades, The (Chry.) G69 — 26 EE8
Eversley St. G32 — 54 BB14
Everton Rd. G53 — 49 Q15

Ewart Pl. G3   34   T12
Kelvinhaugh St.
Ewing Pl. G31   37   Z13
Ewing St. (Ruther.) G73   53   Y16
Ewing St. (Kilb.), John. PA10   42   B14
Exchange Pl. G1   36   W12
Buchanan St.
Exeter Dr. G11   34   S11
Exeter La. G11   34   S11
Exeter Dr.
Eynort St. G22   21   V8

F

Fagan Ct. (Blan.) G72   69   GG19
Faifley Rd., Clyde. G81   5   L5
Fairbairn Cres. (Thorn.) G46   62   S19
Fairbairn Path G40   53   Y14
Ruby St.
Fairbairn St. G40   53   Y14
Dalmarnock Rd.
Fairburn St. G32   54   AA14
Fairfax Av. G44   64   W17
Fairfield Gdns. G51   33   R12
Fairfield Pl. G51   33   R12
Fairfield Pl. (Both.) G71   69   HH19
Fairfield St. G51   33   R12
Fairhaven Dr. G23   20   T8
Fairhill Av. G53   49   Q16
Fairholm St. G32   54   AA14
Fairley St. G51   34   S13
Fairlie Pk. Dr. G11   34   S11
Fairway Av., Pais. PA2   46   J16
Fairways (Bears.) G61   6   P5
Fairways Vw., Clyde. G81   5   M5
Fairyknowe Gdns. (Both.) G71   69   HH19
Falcon Cres., Pais. PA3   29   H13
Falcon Rd., John. PA5   43   C16
Falcon Ter. G20   20   T8
Falcon Ter. La. G20   20   T8
Falfield St. G5   51   V14
Falkland Cres. (Bishop.) G64   23   Z8
Falkland La. G12   20   S10
Clarence Dr.
Falkland Mans. G12   20   S10
Clarence Dr.
Falkland St. G12   20   S10
Falloch Rd. G42   51   V16
Falloch Rd. (Bears.) G61   7   Q7
Fallside Rd. (Both.) G71   69   HH19
Falside Av., Pais. PA2   46   K15
Falside Rd. G32   54   BB14
Falside Rd., Pais. PA2   46   J15
Fara St. G23   21   U8
Farie St. (Ruther.) G73   53   Y16
Farm Castle Ct. (Ruther.) G73   53   Z15
Farm Ct. (Both.) G71   69   HH18
Farm La. (Udd.) G71   69   HH17
Myers Cres.
Farm Pk. (Lenzie) G66   13   CC6
Farm Rd. G41   50   S14
Farm Rd. (Blan.) G72   68   FF19
Farm Rd. (Dalmuir), Clyde. G81   4   J6
Farm Rd. (Dunt.), Clyde. G81   5   L5
Farme Cross (Ruther.) G73   53   Y15
Farmeloan Rd. (Ruther.) G73   53   Y16
Farmington Av. G32   39   CC13
Farmington Gdns. G32   39   CC13
Farmington Gate G32   39   CC13
Farmington Gro. G32   39   CC13
Farne Dr. G44   63   V18
Farnell St. G4   35   V11
Farrier Ct., John. PA5   43   D14
Faskally Av. (Bishop.) G64   10   X6
Faskin Cres. G53   48   N16
Faskin Pl. G53   48   N16
Faskin Rd. G53   48   N16
Fasque Pl. G15   6   N6
Fastnet St. G33   38   BB12
Fauldhouse St. G5   52   W14
Faulds (Bail.) G69   40   FF13
Faulds Gdns. (Bail.) G69   40   FF13
Fauldshead Rd., Renf. PA4   17   M10
Fauldspark Cres. (Bail.) G69   40   FF13
Fauldswood Cres., Pais. PA2   45   H15
Fauldswood Dr., Pais. PA2   45   H15
Fearnmore Rd. G20   20   T8

Felton Pl. G13   18   N8
Fendoch St. G32   54   BB14
Fenella St. G32   38   BB13
Fennsbank Av. (Ruther.) G73   65   Z18
Fenwick Dr. (Barr.) G78   59   M19
Fenwick Pl. (Giff.) G46   62   S19
Fenwick Rd. (Giff.) G46   62   T18
Fereneze Av. (Barr.) G78   59   L18
Fereneze Av., Renf. PA4   31   L12
Fereneze Cres. G13   18   P8
Fereneze Dr., Pais. PA2   46   J16
Fereneze Gro. (Barr.) G78   59   L18
Fereneze Rd. (Barr.) G78   58   J19
Fergus Av., Pais. PA3   29   H13
Westburn Av.
Fergus Ct. G20   21   U10
Fergus Dr. G20   21   U10
Fergus Dr., Pais. PA3   29   H13
Woodvale Dr.
Ferguslie, Pais. PA1   45   H14
Ferguslie Pk. Av., Pais. PA3   29   H13
Ferguslie Pk. Cres., Pais. PA3   45   H14
Ferguslie Pk. Av.
Ferguslie Wk., Pais. PA1   45   H14
Ferguson Av., Renf. PA4   17   M10
Ferguson St., John. PA5   43   D14
Ferguson St., Renf. PA4   17   M10
Fergusson Rd. (Cumb.) G67   70   NN3
Ferguston Rd. (Bears.) G61   7   R6
Fern Av. (Bishop.) G64   23   Y8
Fern Av. (Lenzie) G66   13   CC5
Fern Dr. (Barr.) G78   59   L18
Fern Gro. (Gart.) G69   27   HH9
Inchnock Av.
Fern La. G13   19   R9
Whittingehame Dr.
Fernan St. G32   38   AA13
Fernbank Av. (Camb.) G72   67   CC18
Fernbank St. G21   22   X9
Fernbank St. G22   22   X9
Fernbrae Av. (Ruther.) G73   65   Z18
Fernbrae Way (Ruther.) G73   65   Y18
Ferncroft Dr. G44   64   W17
Ferndale Ct. G23   20   T8
Ferndale Dr. G23   20   T8
Ferndale Gdns. G23   20   T8
Ferndale Pl. G23   20   T8
Ferness Oval G21   23   Z8
Ferness Pl. G21   23   Z8
Ferness Rd. G21   23   Z9
Ferngrove Av. G12   20   S9
Fernhill Gra. (Both.) G71   69   HH19
Fernhill Rd. (Ruther.) G73   65   Y18
Fernie Gdns. G20   21   U8
Fernlea (Bears.) G61   7   R6
Fernleigh Pl. (Chry.) G69   15   GG7
Fernleigh Rd. G43   62   T17
Ferry Rd. G3   34   S12
Ferry Rd. (Both.) G71   69   HH19
Ferry Rd. (Udd.) G71   68   FF17
Ferry Rd., Renf. PA4   17   M10
Ferryden St. G14   33   R11
Fersit St. G43   62   T17
Fetlar Dr. G44   64   W17
Fettercairn Av. G15   6   N6
Fettercairn Gdns. (Bishop.) G64   11   Z7
Fettes St. G33   38   AA12
Fidra St. G33   38   AA12
Fielden Pl. G40   37   Y13
Fielden St. G40   37   Y13
Fieldhead Dr. G43   62   S17
Fieldhead Sq. G43   62   S17
Fife Av. G52   48   P14
Fife Cres. (Both.) G71   69   HH19
Fife Way (Bishop.) G64   23   Z8
Fifth Av. G12   19   R9
Fifth Av. (Stepps) G33   24   BB9
Fourth Av.
Fifth Av. (Kirk.) G66   13   CC7
Fifth Av., Renf. PA4   31   M11
Fifty Pitches Pl. G51   33   Q12
Fifty Pitches Rd. G51   33   Q13
Finch Dr. G13   18   N8
Finch Pl., John. PA5   43   C16
Findhorn Av., Pais. PA2   45   G15
Findhorn Av., Renf. PA4   18   N10
Findhorn St. G33   37   Z12
Findochty St. G33   39   CC11
Fingal La. G20   20   T8
Fingal St.

Fingal St. G20   20   T8
Fingask St. G32   55   CC14
Finglas Av., Pais. PA2   47   L15
Fingleton Av. (Barr.) G78   59   M19
Finhaven St. G32   54   AA14
Finlarig St. G34   40   FF12
Finlas St. G22   22   W10
Finlay Dr. G31   37   Y12
Finnart Dr., Pais. PA2   47   L15
Finnart Sq. G40   52   X14
Finnart St. G40   52   X14
Finnieston Pl. G3   35   U12
Finnieston St.
Finnieston Quay G3   35   U12
Finnieston Sq. G3   35   U12
Houldsworth St.
Finnieston St. G3   35   U12
Finsbay St. G51   33   R13
Fintry Av., Pais. PA2   46   K16
Fintry Cres. (Bishop.) G64   11   Z7
Fintry Cres. (Barr.) G78   59   M19
Fintry Dr. G44   52   W16
Fir Ct. (Camb.) G72   67   DD18
Fir Pl. (Bail.) G69   56   EE14
Fir Pl. (Camb.) G72   67   CC17
Birch Dr.
Fir Pl., John. PA5   44   E15
Firbank Ter. (Barr.) G78   60   N19
Firdon Cres. G15   6   P7
Firhill Rd. G20   21   V10
Firhill St. G20   21   V10
Firpark Pl. G31   36   X12
Firpark St.
Firpark Rd. (Bishop.) G64   23   Y8
Firpark St. G31   36   X12
Firpark Ter. G31   36   X12
Ark La.
First Av. (Millerston) G33   24   BB10
First Av. G44   63   U19
First Av. (Bears.) G61   8   S6
First Av. (Kirk.) G66   13   CC7
First Av. (Udd.) G71   57   GG16
First Av., Renf. PA4   31   M11
First Gdns. G41   50   S14
First St. (Udd.) G71   57   GG16
First Ter., Clyde. G81   5   L6
Firwood Dr. G44   64   W17
Fischer Gdns., Pais. PA1   29   G13
Fisher Av., Pais. PA1   45   G14
Fisher Ct. G31   36   X12
Fisher Cres., Clyde. G81   5   L5
Fisher Dr., Pais. PA1   45   G14
Fisher Way, Pais. PA1   45   G14
Fisher Dr.
Fishers Rd., Renf. PA4   17   M9
Fishescoates Av. (Ruther.) G73   65   Z18
Fishescoates Gdns. (Ruther.) G73   65   Z17
Fishescoates Rd.
Fishescoates Rd. (Ruther.) G73   65   Z17
Fitzalan Dr., Pais. PA3   31   L13
Fitzalan Rd., Renf. PA4   31   L11
Fitzroy La. G3   35   U12
North Claremont St.
Fitzroy Pl. G3   35   U12
North Claremont St.
Flax Rd. (Udd.) G71   69   HH17
Fleet Av., Renf. PA4   32   N11
Fleet St. G32   54   BB14
Fleming Av. (Chry.) G69   26   FF8
Fleming Av., Clyde. G81   17   M8
Fleming Rd. (Cumb.) G67   70   NN3
Fleming St. G31   37   Y13
Fleming St., Pais. PA3   30   K12
Flemington Rd. (Camb.) G72   67   DD19
Flemington St. G21   22   X10
Fleurs Av. G41   50   S14
Fleurs Rd. G41   50   S14
Floors St., John. PA5   43   D15
Floorsburn Cres., John. PA5   43   D15
Flora Gdns. (Bishop.) G64   11   Z7
Florence Dr. (Giff.) G46   62   T19
Florence Gdns. (Ruther.) G73   65   Z18
Florence St. G5   36   W13
Florentine Pl. G12   35   U11
Gibson St.
Florentine Ter. G12   35   U11
Southpark Av.
Florida Av. G42   51   V16
Florida Cres. G42   51   V16

Street	Page	Grid
Florida Dr. G42	51	V16
Florida Gdns. (Bail.) G69	40	EE13
Florida Sq. G42	51	V16
Florida St. G42	51	V16
Flowerdale Pl. G53	60	P19
Waukglen Dr.		
Flures Av., Ersk. PA8	16	K8
Flures Cres., Ersk. PA8	16	K8
Flures Dr., Ersk. PA8	16	K8
Flures Pl., Ersk. PA8	16	K8
Fochabers Dr. G52	33	Q13
Fogo Pl. G20	20	T9
Foinaven Dr. (Thorn.) G46	62	S17
Foinaven Gdns. (Thorn.) G46	62	S17
Foinaven Way (Thorn.) G46	62	S17
Forbes Dr. G40	36	X13
Forbes Pl., Pais. PA1	46	K14
Forbes St. G40	36	X13
Ford Rd. G12	20	T10
Fordneuk St. G40	37	Y13
Fordoun St. G34	40	FF12
Fordyce St. G11	34	S11
Fore St. G14	19	Q10
Forehouse Rd. (Kilb.), John. PA10	42	A14
Foremount Ter. La. G12	20	T10
Hyndland Rd.		
Forest Dr. (Both.) G71	69	HH18
Forest Gdns. (Kirk.) G66	12	BB6
Forest Pl. (Kirk.) G66	12	BB6
Forest Pl., Pais. PA2	46	K15
Brodie Pk. Av.		
Forest Rd. (Cumb.) G67	71	QQ3
Forest Vw. (Cumb.) G67	71	QQ2
Foresthall Cres. G21	23	Y10
Foresthall Dr. G21	23	Y10
Forfar Av. G52	48	P14
Forfar Cres. (Bishop.) G64	23	Z8
Forgan Gdns. (Bishop.) G64	23	Z8
Forge, The (Giff.) G46	62	T18
Braidpark Dr.		
Forge Pl. G21	37	Y11
Forge St. G21	37	Y11
Forglen St. G34	40	EE11
Formby Dr. G23	8	T7
Forres Av. (Giff.) G46	62	T18
Forres Gate (Giff.) G46	62	T19
Forres Av.		
Forres St. G23	9	U7
Tolsta St.		
Forrest Gate (Udd.) G71	57	HH15
Forrest St. G40	37	Y13
Forrester Ct. (Bishop.) G64	22	X8
Crowhill Rd.		
Forrestfield St. G21	37	Y11
Forteviot Av. (Bail.) G69	40	FF13
Forteviot Pl. (Bail.) G69	40	FF13
Forth Av., Pais. PA2	45	G15
Forth Pl., John. PA5	43	C16
Forth Rd. (Bears.) G61	7	Q7
Forth St. G41	51	U14
Forth St., Clyde. G81	17	M8
Forties Cres. (Thorn.) G46	61	R17
Forties Way (Thorn.) G46	62	S17
Fortingall Av. G12	20	T9
Grandtully Dr.		
Fortingall Pl. G12	20	T9
Fortrose St. G11	34	S11
Foswell Pl. G15	6	N5
Fotheringay La. G41	51	U15
Beaton Rd.		
Fotheringay Rd. G41	50	T15
Foulis La. G13	19	R9
Herschell St.		
Foulis St. G13	19	R9
Herschell St.		
Foundry La. (Barr.) G78	59	L19
Main St.		
Foundry St. G21	22	X10
Fountain Cres. (Inch.), Renf. PA4	16	J9
Fountain Dr. (Inch.), Renf. PA4	16	J9
Fountain St. G31	36	X13
Fountainwell Av. G21	36	W11
Fountainwell Dr. G21	36	W11
Fountainwell Pl. G21	36	W11
Fountainwell Rd. G21	36	W11
Fountainwell Sq. G21	36	X11
Fountainwell Ter. G21	36	X11
Fourth Av. G33	24	BB9
Fourth Av. (Kirk.) G66	13	CC7
Fourth Av., Renf. PA4	31	M11
Third Av.		
Fourth Gdns. G41	50	S14
Fourth St. (Udd.) G71	57	GG15
Fox La. G1	36	W13
Fox St. G1	35	V13
Foxbar Cres., Pais. PA2	45	G16
Foxbar Dr. G13	18	P9
Foxbar Dr., Pais. PA2	45	G16
Foxbar Rd. (Elder.), John. PA5	45	G16
Foxbar Rd., Pais. PA2	45	G16
Foxes Gro. (Lenzie) G66	13	DD5
Foxglove Pl. G53	60	P18
Foxhills Pl. G23	9	U7
Foxley St. G32	55	CC15
Foyers Ct. G13	18	P9
Kirkton Av.		
Foyers Ter. G21	23	Y10
Francis St. G5	51	V14
Frankfield Rd. G33	25	DD9
Frankfield St. G33	37	Z11
Frankfort St. G41	51	U15
Franklin St. G40	52	X14
Fraser Av. (Ruther.) G73	53	Z16
Fraser Av., John. PA5	44	E15
Fraser St. (Camb.) G72	66	AA17
Fraserbank St. G21	22	W10
Keppochhill Rd.		
Frazer St. G40	37	Y13
Freeland Ct. G53	60	P17
Freeland Dr. G53	60	P17
Freeland Dr. (Inch.), Renf. PA4	16	J9
Freelands Ct. (Old Kil.) G60	4	J5
Freelands Pl. (Old Kil.) G60	4	J6
Freelands Rd. (Old Kil.) G60	4	J5
French St. G40	52	X14
French St., Clyde. G81	4	K6
French St., Renf. PA4	31	L11
Freuchie St. G34	40	EE12
Friar Av. (Bishop.) G64	11	Y6
Friars Pl. G13	19	Q8
Friarscourt Av. G13	7	Q7
Friarscourt La. G13	19	Q8
Arrowsmith Av.		
Friarscourt Rd. (Chry.) G69	14	EE7
Friarton Rd. G43	63	U17
Friendship Way, Renf. PA4	31	M11
Fruin Pl. G22	22	W10
Fruin Rd. G15	6	N7
Fruin St. G22	22	W10
Fulbar Av., Renf. PA4	17	M10
Fulbar Ct., Renf. PA4	17	M10
Fulbar Av.		
Fulbar Cres., Pais. PA2	45	G15
Fulbar Gdns., Pais. PA2	45	G15
Peacock Dr.		
Fulbar La., Renf. PA4	17	M10
Fulbar Rd. G51	33	Q12
Fulbar Rd., Pais. PA2	45	G15
Fulbar St., Renf. PA4	17	M10
Fullarton Av. G32	54	BB15
Fullarton Dr. G32	54	BB15
Fullarton La. G32	54	BB15
Fullarton Rd. G32	54	BB16
Fullarton Rd. (Cumb.) G68	70	NN1
Fullerton St., Pais. PA3	30	J12
Fullerton Ter., Pais. PA3	30	K12
Fulmar Ct. (Bishop.) G64	22	X8
Fulmar Pl., John. PA5	43	C16
Fulton Cres. (Kilb.), John. PA10	42	B14
Fulton St. G13	19	Q8
Fulwood Av. G13	18	N8
Fulwood Av. (Linw.), Pais. PA3	28	E13
Fulwood Pl. G13	18	N8
Fyvie Av. G43	62	S17

G

Street	Page	Grid
Gadie Av., Renf. PA4	32	N11
Gadie St. G33	37	Z12
Gadloch Av. (Kirk.) G66	13	CC7
Gadloch Gdns. (Kirk.) G66	13	CC6
Gadloch St. G22	22	W9
Gadloch Vw. (Kirk.) G66	13	CC7
Gadsburn Ct. G21	23	Z9
Wallacewell Quad.		
Gadshill St. G21	36	X11
Gailes Pk. (Both.) G71	69	GG19
Gailes Rd. (Cumb.) G68	70	NN1
Gailes St. G40	53	Y14
Gairbraid Av. G20	20	T9
Gairbraid Ct. G20	20	T9
Gairbraid Pl. G20	20	T9
Gairbraid Ter. (Bail.) G69	41	HH13
Gairn St. G11	34	S11
Castlebank St.		
Gala Av., Renf. PA4	32	N11
Gala St. G33	38	AA11
Galbraith Av. G51	33	R12
Burghead Dr.		
Galbraith St. G51	33	Q12
Moss Rd.		
Galdenoch St. G33	38	BB11
Gallacher Av., Pais. PA2	45	H15
Gallan Av. G23	9	U7
Galloway Dr. (Ruther.) G73	65	Y18
Galloway St. G21	22	X9
Gallowflat St. (Ruther.) G73	53	Y16
Reid St.		
Gallowgate G1	36	W13
Gallowgate G4	36	W13
Gallowgate G31	37	Y13
Gallowgate G40	37	Y13
Gallowhill Av. (Lenzie) G66	13	CC5
Gallowhill Gro. (Kirk.) G66	13	CC5
Gallowhill Rd. (Kirk.) G66	13	CC5
Gallowhill Rd., Pais. PA3	30	K13
Galston St. G53	60	N17
Gamrie Dr. G53	48	P16
Gamrie Gdns. G53	48	P16
Gamrie Rd. G53	48	P16
Gannochy Dr. (Bishop.) G64	11	Z7
Gantock Cres. G33	38	BB12
Gardenside Av. G32	54	BB16
Gardenside Av. (Udd.) G71	69	GG17
Gardenside Cres. G32	54	BB16
Gardenside Gro. G32	54	BB16
Gardenside Pl. G32	54	BB16
Gardenside St. (Udd.) G71	69	GG17
Gardner La. (Bail.) G69	56	FF14
Church St.		
Gardner St. G11	34	S11
Gardyne St. G34	40	EE11
Garfield St. G31	37	Y13
Garforth Rd. (Bail.) G69	55	DD14
Gargrave Av. (Bail.) G69	55	DD14
Garion Dr. G13	18	P9
Talbot Dr.		
Garlieston Rd. G33	39	DD13
Garmouth Ct. G51	33	R12
Garmouth Dr.		
Garmouth Gdns. G51	33	R12
Garmouth St. G51	33	R12
Garnet La. G3	35	V11
Garnet St.		
Garnet St. G3	35	V11
Garnethill St. G3	35	V11
Garngaber Av. (Lenzie) G66	13	CC5
Garngaber Ct. (Kirk.) G66	13	DD5
Woodilee Rd.		
Garnie Av., Ersk. PA8	4	J7
Garnie Cres., Ersk. PA8	4	J7
Garnie La., Ersk. PA8	4	J7
Garnie Oval, Ersk. PA8	4	J7
Garnie Pl., Ersk. PA8	4	J7
Garnieland Rd., Ersk. PA8	4	J7
Garnkirk La. G33	25	DD9
Garnkirk St. G21	36	X11
Garnock St. G21	36	X11
Garrell Way (Cumb.) G67	70	NN3
Garrioch Cres. G20	20	T9
Garrioch Dr. G20	20	T9
Garrioch Gate G20	20	T9
Garrioch Quad. G20	20	T9
Garrioch Rd. G20	20	T10
Garriochmill Rd. G20	21	U10
Raeberry St.		
Garriochmill Way G20	21	U10
Woodside Rd.		
Garrowhill Dr. (Bail.) G69	55	DD14
Garry Av. (Bears.) G61	8	S7
Garry Dr., Pais. PA2	45	H15
Garry St. G44	51	V16
Garscadden Rd. G15	6	P7
Garscadden Rd. S. G13	18	P8
Garscadden Rd., Clyde. G81	5	M6
Kirkoswald Dr.		
Garscube Cross G4	35	V11

Street	Page	Grid
Garscube Mill (Bears.) G61	8	S7
Maryhill Rd.		
Garscube Rd. G4	21	V10
Garscube Rd. G20	21	V10
Gartartan Rd., Pais. PA1	32	N13
Gartcarron Hill (Cumb.) G68	70	MM2
Dunbrach Rd.		
Gartconnell Dr. (Bears.) G61	7	R5
Gartconnell Gdns. (Bears.) G61	7	R5
Gartconnell Rd. (Bears.) G61	7	R5
Gartcosh Rd. (Gart.) G69	41	HH12
Gartcraig Path G33	38	AA11
Gartcraig Pl.		
Gartcraig Pl. G33	38	AA11
Gartcraig Rd. G33	38	AA12
Gartferry Av. (Chry.) G69	15	GG7
Gartferry Rd. (Mood.) G69	15	GG7
Gartferry St. G21	23	Y10
Garth St. G1	36	W12
Garthamlock Rd. G33	39	DD11
Garthland Dr. G31	37	Y12
Garthland La., Pais. PA1	30	K13
Gartliston Ter. (Bail.) G69	41	HH13
Gartloch Cotts. (Gart.) G69	27	GG10
Gartloch Cotts. (Muir.) G69	26	EE9
Gartloch Rd. G33	38	AA11
Gartloch Rd. G34	39	CC11
Gartloch Rd. (Gart.) G69	26	EE10
Gartly St. G44	63	U18
Clarkston Rd.		
Gartmore Gdns. (Udd.) G71	57	GG16
Gartmore La. (Chry.) G69	15	HH7
Gartmore Rd., Pais. PA1	47	L14
Gartmore Ter. (Camb.) G72	66	AA18
Gartness St. G31	37	Y12
Gartocher Dr. G32	39	CC13
Gartocher Rd. G32	39	CC13
Gartocher Ter. G32	39	CC13
Gartochmill Rd. G20	21	U10
Gartons Rd. G21	23	Z10
Gartshore Rd. (Kirk.) G66	15	GG5
Gartshore Rd. (Chry.) G69	15	GG5
Garturk St. G42	51	V15
Garvald Ct. G40	53	Y14
Baltic St.		
Garvald St. G40	53	Y14
Garve Av. G44	63	V18
Garvel Cres. G33	39	DD13
Garvel Rd. G33	39	DD13
Garvock Dr. G43	62	S17
Gas St., John. PA5	44	E14
Gask Pl. G13	18	N8
Gaskin Path G33	25	DD9
Clayhouse Rd.		
Gatehouse St. G32	38	BB13
Gateside Av. (Camb.) G72	67	CC17
Gateside Cres. (Barr.) G78	59	L19
Gateside Pl. (Kilb.), John. PA10	42	B14
Gateside Rd. (Barr.) G78	59	L19
Gateside St. G31	37	Y13
Gauldry Av. G52	49	Q14
Gauze St., Pais. PA1	30	K13
Gavins Rd., Clyde. G81	5	L5
Gavinton St. G44	63	U18
Gear Ter. G40	53	Y15
Geary St. G23	8	T7
Torrin Rd.		
Geddes Rd. G21	23	Z8
Gelston St. G32	54	BB14
General Terminus Quay G51	35	U13
Generals Gate (Udd.) G71	69	GG17
Cobblerigg Way		
Gentle Row, Clyde. G81	4	K5
George Av., Clyde. G81	5	M6
Robert Burns Av.		
George Cres., Clyde. G81	5	M6
George Gray St. (Ruther.) G73	53	Z16
George La., Pais. PA1	46	K14
George St.		
George Mann Ter. (Ruther.) G73	65	Y17
George Pl., Pais. PA1	46	K14
George Reith Av. G12	19	R9
George Sq. G2	36	W12
George St. G1	36	W12
George St. (Bail.) G69	56	EE14
George St. (Barr.) G78	59	L18
George St., John. PA5	43	D14
George St., Pais. PA1	46	J14
Gertrude Pl. (Barr.) G78	59	L19
Gibb St. G21	36	X11
Royston Rd.		
Gibson Cres., John. PA5	43	D15
Gibson Rd., Renf. PA4	31	L11
Gibson St. G12	34	T11
Gibson St. G40	36	X13
Giffnock Pk. Av. (Giff.) G46	62	T18
Gifford Dr. G52	32	P13
Gifford Wynd, Pais. PA2	45	G15
Gilbert St. G3	34	T12
Gilbertfield Pl. G33	38	BB11
Gilbertfield Rd. (Camb.) G72	67	CC18
Gilbertfield St. G33	38	BB11
Gilfillan Way, Pais. PA2	45	G16
Gilhill St. G20	20	T8
Gilia St. (Camb.) G72	66	AA17
Gillies La. (Bail.) G69	56	FF14
Bredisholm Rd.		
Gilmerton St. G32	54	BB14
Gilmour Av., Clyde. G81	5	L5
Gilmour Cres. (Ruther.) G73	52	X16
Gilmour Pl. G5	52	W14
Gilmour St., Clyde. G81	5	M6
Gilmour St., Pais. PA1	30	K13
Girthon St. G32	55	CC14
Girvan St. G33	37	Z11
Gladney Av. G13	18	N8
Gladsmuir Rd. G52	32	P13
Gladstone Av. (Barr.) G78	59	L19
Gladstone Av., John. PA5	43	C16
Gladstone St. G4	35	V11
Gladstone St., Clyde. G81	4	K7
Glaive Rd. G13	7	Q7
Glamis Av. (Elder.), John. PA5	44	E15
Glamis Gdns. (Bishop.) G64	11	Y6
Glamis Pl. G31	53	Z14
Glamis Rd.		
Glamis Rd. G31	53	Z14
Glanderston Av. (Barr.) G78	60	N19
Glanderston Dr. G13	18	P8
Glaselune St. G34	40	FF12
Lochdochart Rd.		
Glasgow Airport (Abbots.), Pais. PA3	30	J11
Glasgow Bri. G1	35	V13
Glasgow Bri. G5	35	V13
Glasgow Grn. G1	36	W13
Glasgow Grn. G40	36	W13
Glasgow Rd. G53	60	N18
Glasgow Rd. (Cumb.) G67	70	MM4
Glasgow Rd. (Cumb.V.) G67	71	PP2
Glasgow Rd. (Bail.) G69	55	DD14
Glasgow Rd. (Udd.) G71	56	FF16
Glasgow Rd. (Blan.) G72	68	FF19
Glasgow Rd. (Camb.) G72	54	AA16
Glasgow Rd. (Turnlaw) G72	66	BB19
Glasgow Rd. (Ruther.) G73	52	X15
Glasgow Rd. (Barr.) G78	59	M18
Glasgow Rd., Clyde. G81	17	L8
Glasgow Rd. (Hardgate), Clyde. G81	5	L5
Glasgow Rd., Pais. PA1	31	L13
Glasgow Rd., Renf. PA4	18	N10
Glasgow St. G12	21	U10
Glassel Rd. G34	40	FF11
Glasserton Pl. G43	63	U17
Glasserton Rd. G43	63	U17
Glassford St. G1	36	W12
Glaudhall Av. (Gart.) G69	27	GG8
Glebe, The (Both.) G71	69	HH19
Green St.		
Glebe Av. (Both.) G71	69	HH19
Glebe Ct. G4	36	W12
Glebe Hollow (Both.) G71	69	HH19
Glebe Wynd		
Glebe Pl. (Camb.) G72	66	BB17
Glebe Pl. (Ruther.) G73	52	X16
Glebe St. G4	36	W11
Glebe St., Renf. PA4	17	M10
Glebe Wynd (Both.) G71	69	HH19
Gleddoch Rd. G52	32	N13
Glen Affric Dr. G53	61	Q18
Glen Alby Pl. G53	61	Q18
Glen Av. G32	38	BB13
Glen Av. (Chry.) G69	15	GG7
Glen Clova Dr. (Cumb.) G68	70	MM2
Glen Clunie Av. G53	61	Q18
Glen Clunie Dr. G53	61	Q18
Glen Clunie Pl. G53	61	Q18
Glen Cona Dr. G53	61	Q18
Glen Cres. G13	18	N8
Glen Douglas Dr. (Cumb.) G68	70	MM2
Glen Esk Cres. G53	61	Q18
Glen Esk Dr. G53	61	Q18
Glen Esk Pl. G53	61	Q18
Glen Etive Pl. (Ruther.) G73	66	AA19
Glen Fyne Rd. (Cumb.) G68	70	LL2
Glen Gdns. (Elder.), John. PA5	44	F14
Glen La., Pais. PA3	30	K13
Glen Lednock Dr. (Cumb.) G68	70	LL2
Glen Livet Pl. G53	61	Q18
Glen Loy Pl. G53	61	Q18
Glen Luss Gdns. (Cumb.) G68	70	MM2
Glen Markie Dr. G53	61	Q18
Glen Moriston Rd. G53	61	Q18
Glen Moriston Rd. (Cumb.) G68	70	LL2
Glen Nevis Pl. (Ruther.) G73	65	Z19
Glen Ogle St. G32	55	CC14
Glen Orchy Ct. (Cumb.) G68	70	MM1
Glen Orchy Dr. G53	61	Q18
Glen Orchy Dr. (Cumb.) G68	70	LL2
Glen Orchy Pl. G53	61	Q18
Glen Orchy Pl. (Cumb.) G68	70	LL2
Glen Rd. G32	38	BB12
Glen Rosa Gdns. (Cumb.) G68	70	LL2
Glen Sannox Dr. (Cumb.) G68	70	LL2
Glen Sannox Vw. (Cumb.) G68	70	LL2
Glen Sax Dr., Renf. PA4	32	N11
Glen St. (Camb.) G72	67	CC18
Glen St. (Barr.) G78	59	M18
Glen St., Pais. PA3	30	J13
Glen Vw. (Cumb.) G67	71	QQ2
Glenacre Cres. (Udd.) G71	57	GG16
Glenacre Dr. G45	64	W18
Glenacre Rd. (Cumb.) G67	70	NN4
Glenacre St. G45	64	W18
Glenacre Ter. G45	64	W18
Glenallan Way, Pais. PA2	45	G16
Glenalmond Rd. (Ruther.) G73	65	Z18
Glenalmond St. G32	54	BB14
Glenapp Av., Pais. PA2	47	L15
Glenapp Pl. (Mood.) G69	15	GG6
Whithorn Cres.		
Glenapp Rd., Pais. PA2	47	L15
Glenapp St. G41	51	U14
Glenarklet Dr., Pais. PA2	47	L15
Glenartney Row (Chry.) G69	14	FF7
Glenashdale Way, Pais. PA2	47	L15
Glenbrittle Dr.		
Glenavon Av. (Ruther.) G73	65	Z18
Glenavon Rd. G20	20	T8
Thornton St.		
Glenavon Ter. G11	34	S11
Crow Rd.		
Glenbank Av. (Lenzie) G66	13	CC6
Glenbank Ct. (Thorn.) G46	61	R19
Glenbank Dr.		
Glenbank Dr. (Thorn.) G46	61	R19
Glenbank Rd. (Lenzie) G66	13	CC6
Glenbarr St. G21	36	X11
Glenbervie Cres. (Cumb.) G68	70	NN2
Glenbervie Pl. G23	8	T7
Glenbrittle Dr., Pais. PA2	47	L15
Glenbrittle Way, Pais. PA2	47	L15
Glenbuck Av. G33	24	AA9
Glenbuck Dr. G33	24	AA9
Glenburn Av. (Bail.) G69	40	FF13
Glenburn Av. (Chry.) G69	15	GG7
Glenburn Av. (Camb.) G72	65	Z17
Glenburn Cres., Pais. PA2	46	J16
Glenburn Gdns. (Bishop.) G64	10	X7
Glenburn La. G20	21	U8
Thornton St.		
Glenburn Rd. (Giff.) G46	62	S19
Glenburn Rd. (Bears.) G61	7	Q5
Glenburn Rd., Pais. PA2	45	H16
Glenburn St. G20	21	U8
Glenburnie Pl. G34	40	EE12
Glencairn Dr. G41	50	T15
Glencairn Dr. (Chry.) G69	15	GG7

Name	Map	Grid
Glencairn Dr. (Ruther.) G73	52	X16
Glencairn Gdns. G41	51	U15
Glencairn Dr.		
Glencairn Gdns. (Camb.) G72	67	CC17
Glencairn La. G41	51	U15
Shields Rd.		
Glencairn Rd. (Cumb.) G67	71	QQ3
Glencairn Rd., Pais. PA3	31	L12
Glencally Av., Pais. PA2	47	L15
Glencart Gro. (Mill.Pk.), John. PA10	43	C15
Milliken Pk. Rd.		
Glenclora Dr., Pais. PA2	47	L15
Glencloy St. G20	20	T8
Glencoats Cres., Pais. PA3	29	H13
Glencoats Dr., Pais. PA3	29	H13
Glencoe Pl. G13	19	R8
Glencoe Rd. (Ruther.) G73	65	Z18
Glencoe St. G13	19	R8
Glencorse Rd., Pais. PA2	46	J15
Glencorse St. G32	38	AA12
Glencroft Av. (Udd.) G71	57	GG16
Glencroft Rd. G44	64	W17
Glencryan Rd. (Cumb.) G67	71	PP4
Glendale Cres. (Bishop.) G64	23	Z8
Glendale Dr. (Bishop.) G64	23	Z8
Glendale Pl. G31	37	Y13
Glendale St.		
Glendale Pl. (Bishop.) G64	23	Z8
Glendale St. G31	37	Y13
Glendaruel Av. (Bears.) G61	8	S6
Glendaruel Rd. (Ruther.) G73	66	AA19
Glendarvel Gdns. G22	22	W10
Glendee Gdns., Renf. PA4	31	M11
Glendee Rd., Renf. PA4	31	M11
Glendevon Pl., Clyde. G81	4	K6
Glendevon Sq. G33	38	BB11
Glendinning Rd. G13	7	R7
Glendore St. G14	33	R11
Glendower Way, Pais. PA2	45	G16
Spencer Dr.		
Glenduffhill Rd. (Bail.) G69	39	DD13
Gleneagles Av. (Cumb.) G67	71	PP1
Gleneagles Cotts. G14	19	Q10
Dumbarton Rd.		
Gleneagles Dr. (Bishop.) G64	11	Y6
Gleneagles Gdns. (Bishop.) G64	11	Y6
Gleneagles La. N. G14	19	Q10
Dunglass Av.		
Gleneagles La. S. G14	19	Q10
Harland St.		
Gleneagles Pk. (Both.) G71	69	GG19
Gleneagles Ter. G14	19	Q10
Dumbarton Rd.		
Glenelg Quad. G34	40	FF11
Glenfarg Cres. (Bears.) G61	8	S6
Glenfarg Rd. (Ruther.) G73	65	Y18
Glenfarg St. G20	35	V11
Glenfield Cres., Pais. PA2	58	J17
Glenfield Gdns., Pais. PA2	58	J17
Glenfield Rd., Pais. PA2	46	J16
Glenfinnan Dr. G20	20	T9
Glenfinnan Dr. (Bears.) G61	8	T6
Glenfinnan Pl. G20	20	T9
Glenfinnan Rd. G20	20	T9
Glenfruin Cres., Pais. PA2	47	L15
Glengarry Dr. G52	33	Q13
Glengavel Cres. G33	24	AA9
Glengyre St. G34	40	FF11
Glenhead Cres. G22	22	W9
Glenhead Rd. (Lenzie) G66	13	CC6
Glenhead Rd., Clyde. G81	5	L5
Glenhead St. G22	22	W9
Glenholme Av., Pais. PA2	45	H15
Glenhove Rd. (Cumb.) G67	71	PP3
Gleniffer Av. G13	18	P9
Gleniffer Cres. (Elder.), John. PA5	44	F15
Gleniffer Dr. (Barr.) G78	59	L17
Gleniffer Rd., Pais. PA2	45	H16
Gleniffer Rd., Renf. PA4	31	L11
Gleniffer Vw., Clyde. G81	5	M6
Kirkoswald Dr.		
Glenisla Av. (Mood.) G69	15	HH6
Glenisla St. G31	53	Z14
Glenkirk Dr. G15	6	P7
Glenlee Cres. G52	48	N14
Glenlora Dr. G53	48	P16
Glenlora Ter. G53	48	P16
Glenluce Dr. G32	55	CC14
Glenluce Gdns. (Mood.) G69	15	HH6
Brady Cres.		
Glenlui Av. (Ruther.) G73	65	Y17
Glenlyon Pl. (Ruther.) G73	65	Z18
Glenmalloch Pl. (Elder.), John. PA5	44	F14
Glenmanor Av. (Chry.) G69	15	GG7
Glenmavis St. G4	35	V11
Maitland St.		
Glenmore Av. G42	52	X16
Glenmuir Dr. G53	60	P17
Glenpark Av. (Thorn.) G46	61	R19
Glenpark Rd. G31	37	Y13
Glenpark St. G31	37	Y13
Glenpark Ter. (Camb.) G72	54	AA16
Glenpatrick Bldgs. (Elder.), John. PA5	44	F15
Glenpatrick Rd. (Elder.), John. PA5	44	F15
Glenraith Rd. G33	24	BB10
Glenraith Sq. G33	24	BB10
Glenraith Wk. G33	25	CC10
Glenshee Ct. G31	53	Z14
Glenshee Gdns. G31	54	AA14
Glenshee St. G31	53	Z14
Glenshiel Av., Pais. PA2	47	L15
Glenshira Av., Pais. PA2	47	L15
Glenside Av. G53	48	P15
Glenside Dr. (Ruther.) G73	65	Z17
Glenspean Pl. G43	62	T17
Glenspean St.		
Glenspean St. G43	62	T17
Glentanar Dr. (Mood.) G69	15	HH7
Glentanar Pl. G22	21	V8
Glentanar Rd. G22	21	V8
Glentarbert Rd. (Ruther.) G73	65	Z18
Glentrool Gdns. G22	22	W10
Glenturret St. G32	54	BB14
Glentyan Av. (Kilb.), John. PA10	42	B14
Glentyan Dr. G53	60	P17
Glentyan Ter. G53	48	P16
Glenview Cres. (Chry.) G69	15	GG6
Glenview Pl. (Blan.) G72	68	FF19
Glenville Av. (Giff.) G46	62	S18
Glenwood Ct. (Kirk.) G66	12	BB5
Glenwood Dr. (Thorn.) G46	61	R19
Glenwood Gdns. (Kirk.) G66	12	BB5
Glenwood Path G45	64	X18
Glenwood Pl. G45	64	X18
Glenwood Pl. (Kirk.) G66	12	BB5
Glenwood Rd. (Kirk.) G66	12	BB5
Gloucester Av. (Ruther.) G73	65	Z17
Gloucester St. G5	35	V13
Gockston Rd., Pais. PA3	30	J12
Gogar Pl. G33	38	AA12
Gogar St. G33	38	AA12
Goldberry Av. G14	18	P9
Goldie Rd. (Udd.) G71	69	HH18
Golf Ct. G44	63	U19
Golf Dr. G15	6	N7
Golf Dr., Pais. PA1	47	M14
Golf Rd. (Ruther.) G73	65	Y18
Golf Vw. (Bears.) G61	6	P5
Golf Vw., Clyde. G81	4	K6
Golfhill Dr. G31	37	Y12
Golfhill La. G31	37	Y12
Whitehill St.		
Golfhill Ter. G31	36	X12
Firpark St.		
Golspie St. G51	34	S12
Goosedubbs G1	36	W13
Stockwell St.		
Gopher Av. (Udd.) G71	57	HH16
Gorbals Cross G5	36	W13
Gorbals La. G5	35	V13
Oxford St.		
Gorbals St. G5	35	V13
Gordon Av. G44	63	U19
Gordon Av. (Bail.) G69	39	DD13
Gordon Dr. G44	63	U18
Gordon La. G1	35	V12
Gordon St.		
Gordon Rd. G44	63	U19
Gordon St. G1	35	V12
Gordon St., Pais. PA1	46	K14
Gordon Ter. (Blan.) G72	68	FF19
Gorebridge St. G32	38	AA12
Gorget Av. G13	7	Q7
Gorget Pl. G13	7	Q7
Gorget Quad. G13	6	P7
Gorget Av.		
Gorse Dr. (Barr.) G78	59	L18
Gorse Pl. (Udd.) G71	57	HH16
Gorsewood (Bishop.) G64	10	X7
Gorstan Pl. G20	20	T9
Wyndford Rd.		
Gorstan St. G23	20	T8
Gosford La. G14	18	P10
Dumbarton Rd.		
Goudie St., Pais. PA3	30	J12
Gough St. G33	37	Z12
Gourlay Path G21	22	W10
Endrick St.		
Gourlay St. G21	22	X10
Crichton St.		
Gourock St. G5	51	V14
Govan Cross G51	34	S12
Govan Rd. G51	33	R12
Govanhill St. G42	51	V15
Gowan Brae (Kirk.) G66	13	CC5
Marguerite Av.		
Gowanbank Gdns., John. PA5	43	D15
Floors St.		
Gowanlea Av. G15	6	P7
Gowanlea Dr. (Giff.) G46	62	T18
Gowanlea Ter. (Udd.) G71	57	HH16
Gower La. G51	34	T13
North Gower St.		
Gower St. G41	50	T14
Gower Ter. G41	34	T13
Goyle Av. G15	7	Q6
Grace Av. (Bail.) G69	41	GG13
Grace St. G3	35	U12
Graffham Av. (Giff.) G46	62	T18
Grafton Pl. G1	36	W12
Graham Av. (Camb.) G72	67	CC17
Graham Av., Clyde. G81	5	L6
Graham Sq. G31	36	X13
Graham St. (Barr.) G78	59	L18
Graham St., John. PA5	43	D15
Graham Ter. (Bishop.) G64	23	Y8
Grahamston Ct., Pais. PA2	47	M16
Grahamston Cres., Pais. PA2	47	M16
Grahamston Pk. (Barr.) G78	59	L17
Grahamston Pl., Pais. PA2	47	M16
Grahamston Rd.		
Grahamston Rd. (Barr.) G78	59	L17
Grahamston Rd., Pais. PA2	47	M16
Grainger Rd. (Bishop.) G64	11	Z7
Grampian Av., Pais. PA2	46	J16
Grampian Cres. G32	54	BB14
Grampian Pl. G32	54	BB14
Grampian St. G32	54	BB14
Grampian Way (Barr.) G78	59	M19
Gran St., Clyde. G81	18	N8
Granby La. G12	20	T10
Great George St.		
Granby Pl. G12	20	T10
Great George St.		
Grandtully Dr. G12	20	T9
Grange (Both.) G71	69	HH19
Blairston Av.		
Grange Rd. G42	51	V16
Grange Rd. (Bears.) G61	7	R5
Grangeneuk Gdns. (Cumb.) G68	70	MM3
Grant St. G3	35	U11
Grantlea Gro. G32	55	CC14
Grantlea Ter. G32	55	CC14
Grantley Gdns. G41	50	T16
Grantley St. G41	50	T16
Granton St. G5	52	X15
Grants Av., Pais. PA2	46	J15
Grants Way, Pais. PA2	46	J15
Granville St. G3	35	U12
Granville St., Clyde. G81	5	L6
Gray Dr. (Bears.) G61	7	R6
Gray St. G3	34	T11
Great Dovehill G1	36	W13
Great George La. G12	20	T10
Great George St.		
Great George St. G12	20	T10
Great Hamilton St., Pais. PA2	46	K15
Great Kelvin La. G12	21	U10
Glasgow St.		
Great Western Rd. G4	20	S9
Great Western Rd. G12	20	T10
Great Western Rd. G13	6	P7
Great Western Rd. G15	6	P7

Name	Page	Grid
Great Western Rd., Clyde. G81	4	J5
Great Western Ter. G12	20	T10
Green, The G40	36	X13
Green Lo. Ter. G40	52	X14
Greenhead St.		
Green Pk. (Both.) G71	69	HH19
Green St.		
Green Rd. (Ruther.) G73	53	Y16
Green Rd., Pais. PA2	45	G14
Green St. G40	36	X13
Green St. (Both.) G71	69	HH19
Green St., Clyde. G81	5	L6
Greenan Av. G42	52	X16
Greenbank Dr., Pais. PA2	46	J16
Greenbank Rd. (Cumb.) G68	70	MM3
Greenbank St. (Ruther.) G73	53	Y16
Greendyke St. G1	36	W13
Greenend Av., John. PA5	43	C15
Greenend Pl. G32	39	CC12
Greenfarm Rd. (Linw.), Pais. PA3	28	E13
Greenfaulds Cres. (Cumb.) G67	71	PP4
Greenfaulds Rd. (Cumb.) G67	70	NN4
Greenfield Av. G32	38	BB12
Greenfield Pl. G32	38	BB13
Budhill Av.		
Greenfield Rd. G32	39	CC13
Greenfield St. G51	33	R12
Greengairs Av. G51	33	Q12
Greenhead Rd. (Bears.) G61	7	R6
Greenhead Rd. (Inch.), Renf. PA4	16	J8
Greenhead St. G40	52	X14
Greenhill (Bishop.) G64	11	Y7
Greenhill Av. (Giff.) G46	62	S19
Greenhill Av. (Gart.) G69	27	GG8
Greenhill Ct. (Ruther.) G73	53	Y16
Greenhill Cres. (Elder.), John. PA5	44	F15
Greenhill Cres. (Linw.), Pais. PA3	28	E13
Greenhill Dr. (Linw.), Pais. PA3	28	F13
Greenhill Rd. (Ruther.) G73	53	Y16
Greenhill Rd., Pais. PA3	30	J13
Greenhill St. (Ruther.) G73	53	Y16
Greenholm Av. (Udd.) G71	57	GG16
Greenholme St. G44	63	V17
Greenknowe Rd. G43	62	S17
Greenlaw Av., Pais. PA1	31	L13
Greenlaw Cres., Pais. PA1	31	L13
Greenlaw Dr., Pais. PA1	31	L13
Greenlaw Rd. G14	17	M9
Greenlaw Ter., Pais. PA1	31	L13
Greenlaw Av.		
Greenlea Rd. (Chry.) G69	26	EE8
Greenlea St. G13	19	R9
Greenlees Gdns. (Camb.) G72	66	AA18
Greenlees Pk. (Camb.) G72	66	BB18
Greenlees Rd. (Camb.) G72	66	BB17
Greenloan Av. G51	33	Q12
Greenmount G22	21	V8
Greenock Av. G44	63	V17
Greenock Rd., Pais. PA3	30	J12
Greenock Rd. (Inch.), Renf. PA4	16	J9
Greenrig St. G33	23	Z10
Greenrig St. (Udd.) G71	69	GG17
Greenrigg (Udd.) G71	69	GG17
Greenrigg Rd. (Cumb.) G67	71	PP3
Greenshields Rd. (Bail.) G69	40	EE13
Greenside Cres. G33	24	AA10
Greenside St. G33	24	AA10
Greentree Dr. (Bail.) G69	55	DD14
Greenview St. G43	50	T16
Greenways Av., Pais. PA2	45	H15
Greenways Ct., Pais. PA2	45	H15
Greenwell Pl. G51	34	S12
Greenwell St. G51	34	S12
Govan Rd.		
Greenwood Av. (Chry.) G69	15	GG7
Greenwood Av. (Camb.) G72	67	DD17
Greenwood Dr. (Bears.) G61	8	S6
Greenwood Dr., John. PA5	43	C16
Greenwood Quad., Clyde. G81	5	M7
Greer Quad., Clyde. G81	5	L6
Grenville Dr. (Camb.) G72	66	AA18
Gretna St. G40	53	Y14
Greyfriars Rd. (Udd.) G71	56	FF16
Greyfriars St. G32	38	AA12
Greystone Av. (Ruther.) G73	65	Z17
Greywood St. G13	19	R8
Grierson La. G33	37	Z12
Lomax St.		
Grierson St. G33	37	Z12
Grieve Cft. (Both.) G71	69	HH19
Grieve Rd. (Cumb.) G67	71	PP2
Griqua Ter. (Both.) G71	69	HH19
Grogarry Rd. G15	6	P6
Springside Pl.		
Grosvenor Cres. G12	20	T10
Observatory Rd.		
Grosvenor Cres. La. G12	20	T10
Byres Rd.		
Grosvenor La. G12	20	T10
Byres Rd.		
Grosvenor Mans. G12	20	T10
Observatory Rd.		
Grosvenor Ter. G12	20	T10
Grove, The (Kilb.), John. PA10	42	B14
Grove Pk. (Lenzie) G66	13	CC6
Groveburn Av. (Thorn.) G46	62	S18
Grovepark Ct. G20	35	V11
Grovepark Gdns. G20	35	V11
Grovepark Pl. G20	21	V10
Grovepark St. G20	21	V10
Groves, The (Bishop.) G64	23	Z8
Woodhill Rd.		
Grudie St. G34	40	EE12
Gryffe Av., Renf. PA4	17	L9
Gryffe Cres., Pais. PA2	45	G15
Gryffe St. G44	63	V17
Guildford St. G33	39	CC11
Gullane Cres. (Cumb.) G68	70	NN1
Gullane St. G11	34	S11
Purdon St.		
Guthrie Dr. (Udd.) G71	57	HH15
Guthrie St. G20	20	T9

H

Name	Page	Grid
Haberlea Av. G53	61	Q18
Haberlea Gdns. G53	61	Q19
Haddow Gro. (Udd.) G71	57	HH16
Hagg Cres., John. PA5	43	D14
Hagg Pl., John. PA5	43	D14
Hagg Rd., John. PA5	43	D15
Haggs Rd. G41	50	T15
Haggswood Av. G41	50	S15
Haghill Rd. G31	37	Z12
Haig Dr. (Bail.) G69	55	DD14
Haig St. G21	23	Y10
Hailes Av. G32	39	CC13
Haining, The, Renf. PA4	31	M11
Haining Rd., Renf. PA4	17	M10
Hairmyres St. G42	51	V15
Govanhill St.		
Hairst St., Renf. PA4	17	M10
Halbeath Av. G15	6	N6
Halbert St. G41	51	U15
Haldane La. G14	19	Q10
Haldane St.		
Haldane St. G14	19	Q10
Halgreen Av. G15	5	M6
Halifax Way, Renf. PA4	31	M11
Britannia Way		
Hall St., Clyde. G81	5	L7
Hallbrae St. G33	38	AA11
Halley Dr. G13	18	N8
Halley Pl. G13	18	N9
Halley Sq. G13	18	N8
Halley St. G13	18	N8
Hallforest St. G33	38	BB11
Gartloch Rd.		
Hallhill Cres. G33	39	DD13
Hallhill Rd. G32	38	BB13
Hallhill Rd. G33	39	DD13
Hallhill Rd., John. PA5	43	C16
Halliburton Cres. G34	40	EE12
Ware Rd.		
Hallidale Cres., Renf. PA4	32	N11
Hallrule Dr. G52	33	Q13
Hallside Av. (Camb.) G72	67	DD17
Hallside Boul. (Camb.) G72	67	DD18
Hallside Cres. (Camb.) G72	67	DD17
Hallside Dr. (Camb.) G72	67	DD17
Hallside Pl. G5	52	W14
Hallside Rd. (Camb.) G72	67	DD18
Hallside St. G5	52	W14
Hallydown Dr. G13	19	Q9
Halton Gdns. (Bail.) G69	55	DD14
Hamilton Av. G41	50	S14
Hamilton Cres. (Camb.) G72	67	CC18
Hamilton Cres., Renf. PA4	17	M9
Hamilton Dr. G12	21	U10
Hamilton Dr. (Giff.) G46	62	T19
Hamilton Dr. (Both.) G71	69	HH19
Hamilton Dr. (Camb.) G72	66	BB17
Hamilton Pk. Av. G12	21	U10
Hamilton Rd. G32	55	CC15
Hamilton Rd. (Both.) G71	69	HH19
Hamilton Rd. (Camb.) G72	66	BB17
Hamilton Rd. (Ruther.) G73	53	Y16
Hamilton St. G42	52	W15
Hamilton St., Clyde. G81	17	M8
Hamilton St., Pais. PA3	30	K13
Hamilton Ter., Clyde. G81	17	M8
Hamilton Vw. (Udd.) G71	57	HH16
Hamiltonhill Cres. G22	21	V10
Hamiltonhill Rd.		
Hamiltonhill Rd. G22	21	V10
Hampden Dr. G42	51	V16
Cathcart Rd.		
Hampden La. G42	51	V16
Cathcart Rd.		
Hampden Ter. G42	51	V16
Cathcart Rd.		
Hampden Way, Renf. PA4	31	M11
Lewis Av.		
Hangingshaw Pl. G42	52	W16
Hanover Clo. G42	51	V16
Battlefield Gdns.		
Hanover Ct., Pais. PA1	31	L13
Kelburne Gdns.		
Hanover Gdns., Pais. PA1	46	J14
Broomlands St.		
Hanover St. G1	36	W12
Hanson St. G31	36	X12
Hapland Av. G53	49	Q15
Hapland Rd. G53	49	Q15
Harbour La., Pais. PA3	30	K13
Harbour Rd., Pais. PA3	30	K12
Harburn Pl. G23	9	U7
Harbury Pl. G14	18	N9
Harcourt Dr. G31	37	Y12
Roebank St.		
Hardgate Dr. G51	33	Q12
Hardgate Gdns. G51	33	Q12
Hardgate Pl. G51	33	Q12
Hardgate Rd. G51	33	Q12
Hardie Av. (Ruther.) G73	53	Z16
Hardridge Av. G52	49	Q15
Hardridge Rd.		
Hardridge Pl. G52	49	R15
Hardridge Rd. G52	49	Q15
Harefield Dr. G14	18	P9
Harelaw Av. G44	63	U18
Harelaw Av. (Barr.) G78	59	M19
Harelaw Cres., Pais. PA2	46	J16
Harhill St. G51	33	R12
Harland Cotts. G14	33	Q11
South St.		
Harland St. G14	19	Q10
Harlaw Gdns. (Bishop.) G64	11	Z7
Harley St. G51	34	T13
Harmetray St. G22	22	W9
Harmony Ct. G52	34	S12
Helen St.		
Harmony Pl. G51	34	S12
Harmony Row G51	34	S12
Harmony Sq. G51	34	S12
Harmsworth St. G11	33	R11
Harport St. (Thorn.) G46	61	R18
Harriet Pl. G43	62	S17
Harriet St. (Ruther.) G73	53	Y16
Harris Rd. G23	9	U7
Harris Rd. (Old Kil.) G60	4	J5
Harrison Dr. G51	34	S13
Harrow Ct. G15	6	N6
Linkwood Dr.		
Harrow Pl. G15	6	N6
Hart St. G31	38	AA13
Hart St. (Linw.), Pais. PA3	28	E13
Hartfield Ter., Pais. PA2	47	L15
Hartlaw Cres. G52	32	P13
Hartree Av. G13	18	N8
Hartstone Pl. G53	48	P16
Hartstone Rd. G53	48	P16
Hartstone Ter. G53	48	P16
Harvey St. G4	36	W11
Harvie St. G51	34	T13

Name	No.	Ref.
Harwood Gdns. (Mood.) G69	15	HH6
Dryburgh Wk.		
Harwood St. G32	38	AA12
Hastie St. G3	34	T11
Old Dumbarton Rd.		
Hatfield Dr. G12	19	R9
Hathaway Dr. (Giff.) G46	62	S19
Hathaway La. G20	21	U9
Avenuepark St.		
Hathaway St. G20	21	U9
Hathersage Av. (Bail.) G69	40	EE13
Hathersage Dr. (Bail.) G69	40	EE13
Hathersage Gdns. (Bail.)	40	EE13
G69		
Hatters Row G40	52	X14
Dalmarnock Rd.		
Hatton Dr. G52	48	P14
Hatton Gdns. G52	48	P14
Haugh Rd. G3	34	T12
Haughburn Pl. G53	48	P16
Haughburn Rd. G53	48	P16
Haughburn Ter. G53	49	Q16
Havelock La. G11	34	T11
Dowanhill St.		
Havelock St. G11	34	T11
Hawick Av., Pais. PA2	45	H15
Hawick St. G13	18	N8
Hawkhead Av., Pais. PA2	47	L15
Hawkhead Rd., Pais. PA1	47	L14
Hawkhead Rd., Pais. PA2	47	L14
Hawthorn Av. (Bishop.) G64	23	Y8
Hawthorn Av. (Lenzie) G66	13	CC5
Hawthorn Av., Ersk. PA8	16	K8
Hawthorn Av., John. PA5	44	E15
Hawthorn Cres., Ersk. PA8	4	K7
Hawthorn Gdns. (Camb.) G72	67	DD18
Elder Cres.		
Hawthorn Quad. G22	22	W9
Hawthorn Rd., Ersk. PA8	16	K8
Hawthorn St. G22	22	W9
Hawthorn St., Clyde. G81	5	L6
Hawthorn Ter. (Udd.) G71	57	HH16
Douglas St.		
Hawthorn Wk. (Bishop.) G64	23	Z8
Letham Dr.		
Hawthorn Wk. (Camb.) G72	65	Z17
Hawthornden Gdns. G23	9	U7
Hay Dr., John. PA5	44	E14
Hayburn Cres. G11	20	S10
Hayburn Gate G11	34	S11
Fortrose St.		
Hayburn La. G11	20	S10
Queensborough Gdns.		
Hayburn St. G11	34	S11
Hayfield St. G5	52	W14
Hayhill Cotts. (Gart.) G69	27	HH9
Hayle Gdns. (Chry.) G69	15	GG6
Haylynn St. G14	33	R11
Haymarket St. G32	38	AA12
Haystack Pl. (Lenzie) G66	13	CC6
Hayston Cres. G22	21	V9
Hayston Rd. (Cumb.) G68	70	NN2
Hayston St. G22	21	V9
Haywood St. G22	21	V9
Hazel Av. G44	63	U18
Clarkston Rd.		
Hazel Av. (Lenzie) G66	13	CC5
Hazel Av., John. PA5	44	E15
Hazel Dene (Bishop.) G64	11	Y7
Hazel Gro. (Kirk.) G66	13	CC5
Hazel Rd. (Cumb.) G67	71	QQ2
Hazel Ter. (Udd.) G71	57	HH16
Douglas St.		
Hazelden Gdns. G44	63	U18
Hazellea Dr. (Giff.) G46	62	T18
Hazelwood Av., Pais. PA2	45	G16
Hazelwood Gdns. (Ruther.)	65	Z18
G73		
Hazelwood Rd. G41	50	T14
Hazlitt Gdns. G20	21	V9
Bilsland Dr.		
Hazlitt Pl. G20	21	V9
Bilsland Dr.		
Hazlitt St. G20	21	V9
Heath Av. (Bishop.) G64	23	Y8
Heath Av. (Lenzie) G66	13	CC6
Heathcliff Av. (Blan.) G72	68	FF19
Heathcot Av. G15	6	N7
Heathcot Pl. G15	6	N7
Heathcot Av.		
Heather Av. (Barr.) G78	59	L17
Heather Dr. (Kirk.) G66	12	BB6
Heather Gdns. (Kirk.) G66	12	BB6
Heather Pl. (Kirk.) G66	12	BB5
Heather Pl., John. PA5	44	E15
Heather St. G41	35	U13
Scotland St.		
Heatherbrae (Bishop.) G64	10	X7
Heatheryknowe Rd. (Bail.)	41	GG12
G69		
Heathfield Av. (Mood.) G69	15	GG7
Heathfield St. G33	39	CC12
Heathfield Ter. G21	22	X9
Broomfield Rd.		
Heathside Rd. (Giff.) G46	62	T18
Heathwood Dr. (Thorn.) G46	62	S18
Hecla Av. G15	6	N6
Hecla Pl. G15	6	N6
Hecla Sq. G15	6	N7
Hector Rd. G41	50	T16
Heddle Pl. G2	35	V12
Cadogan St.		
Heggie Ter. G14	19	Q10
Dumbarton Rd.		
Helen St. G51	34	S12
Helen St. G52	33	R13
Helensburgh Dr. G13	19	Q9
Helenslea (Camb.) G72	67	CC18
Helenvale Ct. G31	37	Z13
Helenvale St. G31	53	Z14
Helmsdale Av. (Blan.) G72	68	FF18
Helmsdale Ct. (Camb.) G72	67	CC17
Helmsdale Dr., Pais. PA2	45	G15
Hemlock St. G13	19	R8
Henderland Dr. (Bears.) G61	7	R7
Henderland Rd. (Bears.) G61	7	R7
Henderson Av. (Camb.) G72	67	CC17
Henderson St. G20	21	U10
Henderson St., Clyde. G81	18	N8
Henderson St., Pais. PA1	30	J13
Henrietta St. G14	19	Q10
Henry St. (Barr.) G78	59	L18
Hepburn Rd. G52	32	P12
Herald Av. G13	7	Q7
Herald Way, Renf. PA4	31	M11
Viscount Av.		
Herbert St. G20	21	U10
Herbertson Gro. (Blan.) G72	68	FF19
Herbertson St. G5	35	V13
Eglinton St.		
Hercla Av. G15	6	N6
Hercla Pl. G15	6	N6
Hercla Sq. G15	6	N7
Hercules Way, Renf. PA4	31	M11
Friendship Way		
Heriot Av., Pais. PA2	45	G16
Heriot Cres. (Bishop.) G64	11	Y6
Heriot Rd. (Lenzie) G66	13	CC6
Herma St. G23	21	U8
Hermiston Av. G32	39	CC13
Hermiston Pl. G32	39	CC13
Hermiston Rd. G32	38	BB12
Hermitage Av. G13	19	Q9
Heron Ct., Clyde. G81	5	L5
Heron Pl., John. PA5	43	C16
Heron Way, Renf. PA4	31	M11
Britannia Way		
Herries Rd. G41	50	T15
Herriet St. G41	51	U14
Herschell St. G13	19	R9
Hertford Av. G12	20	S9
Hexham Gdns. G41	50	T15
Heys St. (Barr.) G78	59	M19
Hickman St. G42	51	V15
Hickman Ter. G42	52	W15
Hickory St. G22	22	X9
High Barholm (Kilb.), John.	42	B14
PA10		
High Calside, Pais. PA2	46	J14
High Craighall Rd. G4	35	V11
High Parksail, Ersk. PA8	16	J8
High Rd. (Castlehead), Pais.	46	J14
PA2		
High St. G1	36	W13
High St. G4	36	W13
High St. (Ruther.) G73	53	Y16
High St., John. PA5	43	D14
High St., Pais. PA1	46	J14
High St., Renf. PA4	17	M10
Highburgh Dr. (Ruther.) G73	65	Y17
Highburgh Rd. G12	34	T11
Highburgh Ter. G12	34	T11
Highburgh Rd.		
Highcraig Av., John. PA5	43	C15
Highcroft Av. G44	64	W17
Highfield Av., Pais. PA2	46	J16
Highfield Cres., Pais. PA2	46	J16
Highfield Dr. G12	20	S9
Highfield Dr. (Ruther.) G73	65	Z18
Highfield Pl. G12	20	S9
Highkirk Vw., John. PA5	43	D15
Highland La. G51	34	T12
Hilary Av. (Ruther.) G73	65	Z17
Hilary Dr. (Bail.) G69	39	DD13
Hilda Cres. G33	24	AA10
Hill Pk., Clyde. G81	5	L5
Hill Path G52	32	P13
Hill Pl. G52	32	P13
Hill Rd. (Cumb.) G67	70	NN3
Hill St. G3	35	V11
Hillcrest (Chry.) G69	26	FF8
Hillcrest Av. G32	54	BB16
Hillcrest Av. G44	63	U18
Hillcrest Av. (Cumb.) G67	70	NN3
Hillcrest Av., Pais. PA2	58	J17
Hillcrest Ct. (Cumb.) G67	70	NN3
Hillcrest Rd. G32	55	CC16
Hillcrest Rd. (Bears.) G61	7	R6
Hillcrest Rd. (Udd.) G71	57	HH16
Hillcrest Ter. (Both.) G71	69	HH18
Churchill Cres.		
Hillcroft Ter. (Bishop.) G64	22	X8
Hillend Cres., Clyde. G81	4	K5
Hillend Rd. G22	21	V8
Hillend Rd. (Ruther.) G73	65	Y17
Hillfoot Av. (Bears.) G61	7	R5
Hillfoot Av. (Ruther.) G73	53	Y16
Hillfoot Dr. (Bears.) G61	7	R5
Hillfoot Gdns. (Udd.) G71	57	GG16
Hillfoot St. G31	37	Y12
Hillfoot Ter. (Bears.) G61	8	S5
Milngavie Rd.		
Hillhead Av. (Chry.) G69	15	GG7
Hillhead Av. (Ruther.) G73	65	Y18
Hillhead Gdns. G12	34	T11
Hillhead St.		
Hillhead Pl. G12	35	U11
Bank St.		
Hillhead Rd. G21	23	Z8
Hillhead St. G12	34	T11
Hillhouse St. G21	23	Y10
Hillington Gdns. G52	49	Q14
Hillington Ind. Est. G52	32	N12
Hillington Pk. Circ. G52	33	Q13
Hillington Quad. G52	32	P13
Hillington Rd. G52	32	N11
Hillington Rd. S. G52	32	P13
Hillington Ter. G52	32	P13
Hillkirk Pl. G21	22	X10
Hillkirk St. G21	22	X10
Hillkirk St. La. G21	22	X10
Hillkirk St.		
Hillneuk Av. (Bears.) G61	7	R5
Hillneuk Dr. (Bears.) G61	8	S5
Hillpark Av., Pais. PA2	46	J15
Hillpark Dr. G43	62	T17
Hillsborough Rd. (Bail.) G69	39	DD13
Hillsborough Sq. G12	34	T11
Hillsborough St.		
Hillsborough Ter. G12	21	U10
Bower St.		
Hillside Av. (Bears.) G61	7	R5
Hillside Ct. (Thorn.) G46	61	R18
Hillside Dr. (Bears.) G61	8	S5
Hillside Dr. (Bishop.) G64	11	Y7
Hillside Dr. (Barr.) G78	59	L18
Hillside Gdns. G11	20	S10
Turnberry Rd.		
Hillside Gdns. La. G11	20	S10
North Gardner St.		
Hillside Gro. (Bishop.) G64	23	Z8
Hillside Gro. (Barr.) G78	59	L19
Hillside Quad. G43	62	S17
Hillside Rd. G43	62	S17
Hillside Rd. (Barr.) G78	59	L18
Hillside Rd., Pais. PA2	47	L15
Hillswick Cres. G22	21	V8
Hilltop Rd. (Chry.) G69	15	GG7
Eastwood Av.		
Hillview Cres. (Udd.) G71	57	GG16
Hillview Dr. (Blan.) G72	68	FF19
Hillview Rd. (Elder.), John.	44	F15
PA5		
Hillview St. G32	38	AA13
Hilton Dr. (Bishop.) G64	10	X6
Hilton Gdns. G13	19	R8

117

Name	Page	Grid
Invercanny Pl. G15	6	P6
Inverclyde Gdns. G11	19	R10
Broomhill Dr.		
Inverclyde Gdns. (Ruther.) G73	66	AA18
Inveresk Quad. G32	38	BB13
Inveresk St. G32	38	BB13
Inverewe Av. (Thorn.) G46	61	Q18
Inverewe Dr. (Thorn.) G46	61	Q19
Inverewe Gdns. (Thorn.) G46	61	Q19
Inverewe Pl. (Thorn.) G46	61	Q18
Invergarry Av. (Thorn.) G46	61	Q19
Invergarry Ct. (Thorn.) G46	61	R19
Invergarry Dr. (Thorn.) G46	61	R19
Invergarry Gdns. (Thorn.) G46	61	Q19
Invergarry Gro. (Thorn.) G46	61	Q19
Invergarry Pl. (Thorn.) G46	61	Q19
Invergarry Quad. (Thorn.) G46	61	R19
Invergarry Vw. (Thorn.) G46	61	R19
Morriston Cres.		
Invergordon Av. G43	51	U16
Invergyle Dr. G52	32	P13
Inverkar Dr., Pais. PA2	45	H15
Inverkip St. G5	36	W13
Inverlair Av. G43	63	U17
Inverlair Av. G44	63	U17
Inverleith St. G32	37	Z13
Inverlochy St. G33	39	CC11
Inverness St. G51	33	Q13
Inveroran Dr. (Bears.) G61	8	S6
Invershiel Rd. G23	8	T7
Invershin Dr. G20	20	T9
Wyndford Rd.		
Inverurie St. G21	22	W10
Inzievar Ter. G32	54	BB15
Iona Cres. (Old Kil.) G60	4	J5
Iona Dr. (Old Kil.) G60	4	J5
Iona Dr., Pais. PA2	46	J16
Iona Gdns. (Old Kil.) G60	4	J5
Iona La. (Chry.) G69	15	HH7
Heathfield Av.		
Iona Pl. (Old Kil.) G60	4	J5
Iona Rd. (Ruther.) G73	66	AA18
Iona Rd., Renf. PA4	31	M11
Iona St. G51	34	S12
Iona Way (Stepps) G33	25	CC10
Iris Av. G45	65	Y18
Irongray St. G31	37	Z12
Irvine Dr. (Linw.), Pais. PA3	28	E13
Irvine St. G40	53	Y14
Irving Av., Clyde. G81	5	L5
Stewart Dr.		
Irving Quad., Clyde. G81	5	L5
Stewart Dr.		
Iser La. G41	51	U16
Island Rd. (Cumb.) G67	70	MM4
Islay Av. (Ruther.) G73	66	AA18
Islay Cres. (Old Kil.) G60	4	J5
Islay Cres., Pais. PA2	46	J16
Islay Dr. (Old Kil.) G60	4	J5
Ivanhoe Rd. G13	19	Q8
Ivanhoe Rd. (Cumb.) G67	70	NN4
Ivanhoe Rd., Pais. PA2	45	G15
Ivanhoe Way, Pais. PA2	45	G15
Ivanhoe Rd.		
Ivybank Av. (Camb.) G72	67	CC18

J

Name	Page	Grid
Jacks Rd. (Udd.) G71	69	HH17
Jagger Gdns. (Bail.) G69	55	DD14
Jamaica St. G1	35	V13
James Dunlop Gdns. (Bishop.) G64	23	Y8
Graham Ter.		
James Gray St. G41	51	U16
James Morrison St. G1	36	W13
St. Andrews Sq.		
James Nisbet St. G21	36	X11
James St. G40	52	X14
James Watt La. G2	35	V12
James Watt St.		
James Watt St. G2	35	V12
Jamieson Ct. G42	51	V15
Jamieson Path G42	51	V15
Jamieson St.		
Jamieson St. G42	51	V15
Janebank Av. (Camb.) G72	67	CC18
Janefield Av., John. PA5	43	D15
Janefield St. G31	37	Y13
Janes Brae (Cumb.) G67	70	NN4
Janetta St., Clyde. G81	5	L6
Jardine St. G20	21	U10
Jardine Ter. (Gart.) G69	27	GG9
Jasgray St. G42	51	U15
Jean Armour Dr., Clyde. G81	5	M6
Jean Maclean Pl. (Bishop.) G64	11	Y5
Jedburgh Av. (Ruther.) G73	53	Y16
Jedburgh Dr., Pais. PA2	45	H15
Jedburgh Gdns. G20	21	U10
Jedworth Av. G15	6	P6
Jedworth Pl. G15	6	P6
Tallant Rd.		
Jedworth Rd. G15	6	P6
Jellicoe St., Clyde. G81	4	K6
Jenny's Well Ct., Pais. PA2	47	L15
Jenny's Well Rd.		
Jenny's Well Rd., Pais. PA2	47	L15
Jerviston Rd. G33	39	CC11
Jessie St. G42	52	W15
Jessiman Sq., Renf. PA4	31	L11
Jocelyn Sq. G1	36	W13
John Brown Pl. (Chry.) G69	26	FF8
John Hendry Rd. (Udd.) G71	69	HH18
John Knox La. G4	36	X12
Drygate		
John Knox St. G4	36	X12
John Knox St., Clyde. G81	17	M8
John Lang St., John. PA5	44	E14
John Marshall Dr. (Bishop.) G64	22	X8
John Smith Gate (Barr.) G78	59	M18
John St. G1	36	W12
John St. (Barr.) G78	59	L18
John St., Pais. PA1	46	J14
Johnsburn Dr. G53	60	P17
Johnsburn Rd. G53	60	P17
Johnshaven St. G43	50	T16
Shawbridge St.		
Johnston Av., Clyde. G81	17	M8
Johnston Rd. (Gart.) G69	27	HH9
Johnston St., Pais. PA1	46	K14
Gordon St.		
Johnstone Av. G52	32	P13
Johnstone Dr. (Camb.) G72	66	BB17
Johnstone Dr. (Ruther.) G73	53	Y16
Joppa St. G33	38	AA12
Jordan St. G14	33	Q11
Jordanhill Cres. G13	19	Q9
Jordanhill Dr. G13	19	Q9
Jordanhill La. G13	19	R9
Austen Rd.		
Jordanvale Av. G14	33	Q11
Jowitt Av., Clyde. G81	5	M7
Jubilee Bk. (Kirk.) G66	13	CC6
Heriot Rd.		
Jubilee Ct. G52	32	N12
Jubilee Path (Bears.) G61	7	R6
Jubilee Ter., John. PA5	43	C15
Julian Av. G12	20	T10
Julian La. G12	20	T10
Julian Av.		
Juniper Ct. (Kirk.) G66	12	BB5
Juniper Pl. G32	55	DD14
Juniper Pl., John. PA5	44	E16
Juniper Ter. G32	55	DD14
Jura Av., Renf. PA4	31	M11
Jura Ct. G52	33	R13
Jura Dr. (Old Kil.) G60	4	J5
Jura Rd.		
Jura Dr. (Blan.) G72	68	FF18
Jura Dr. (Old Kil.) G60	4	J5
Jura Rd.		
Jura Pl. (Old Kil.) G60	4	J5
Jura Rd.		
Jura Rd. (Old Kil.) G60	4	J5
Jura Rd., Pais. PA2	46	J16
Jura St. G52	33	R13

K

Name	Page	Grid
Kaim Dr. G53	61	Q17
Karol Path G4	35	V11
St. Peters St.		
Katewell Av. G15	6	N6
Katewell Pl. G15	6	N6
Katrine Av. (Bishop.) G64	11	Y7
Katrine Dr., Pais. PA2	45	G15
Katrine Pl. (Camb.) G72	66	BB17
Kay St. G21	22	X10
Kaystone Rd. G15	6	P7
Keal Av. G15	18	P8
Keal Cres. G15	18	P8
Keal Dr. G15	18	P8
Keal Pl. G15	18	P8
Kearn Av. G15	6	P7
Kearn Pl. G15	6	P7
Keats Pk. (Both.) G71	69	HH18
Keir Dr. (Bishop.) G64	10	X7
Keir St. G41	51	U14
Keirhill Rd. (Cumb.) G68	70	MM3
Woodburn Way		
Keirs Wk. (Camb.) G72	66	BB17
Keith Av. (Giff.) G46	62	T18
Keith Ct. G11	34	T12
Keith St.		
Keith St. G11	34	T11
Kelbourne St. G20	21	U10
Kelburn St. (Barr.) G78	59	L19
Kelburne Dr., Pais. PA1	31	L13
Kelburne Gdns. (Bail.) G69	56	EE14
Kelburne Gdns., Pais. PA1	31	L13
Kelburne Oval, Pais. PA1	31	L13
Kelhead Av. G52	32	N13
Kelhead Dr. G52	32	N13
Kelhead Path G52	32	P13
Kelhead Pl. G52	32	N13
Kellas St. G51	34	S13
Kells Pl. G15	6	N6
Kelso Av. (Ruther.) G73	53	Y16
Kelso Av., Pais. PA2	45	H15
Kelso Gdns. (Mood.) G69	15	GG6
Whithorn Cres.		
Kelso Pl. G14	18	N9
Kelso St. G13	18	N9
Kelso St. G14	18	N9
Kelton St. G32	54	BB14
Kelty Pl. G5	35	V13
Bedford St.		
Kelty St. G5	51	V14
Eglinton St.		
Kelvin Av. G52	32	N11
Kelvin Ct. G12	19	R9
Kelvin Cres. (Bears.) G61	7	R7
Kelvin Dr. G20	20	T10
Kelvin Dr. (Bishop.) G64	11	Y7
Kelvin Dr. (Chry.) G69	15	GG7
Kelvin Dr. (Barr.) G78	59	M19
Kelvin Rd. (Cumb.) G67	71	PP4
Kelvin Rd. (Udd.) G71	57	GG16
Kelvin Way G3	34	T11
Kelvin Way (Both.) G71	69	HH18
Bracken Ter.		
Kelvindale Bldgs. G12	20	T9
Kelvindale Rd.		
Kelvindale Cotts. G12	20	T9
Kelvindale Rd.		
Kelvindale Gdns. G20	20	T9
Kelvindale Glen G12	20	T9
Kelvindale Rd.		
Kelvindale Pl. G20	20	T9
Kelvindale Rd. G12	20	T9
Kelvindale Rd. G20	20	T9
Kelvingrove St. G3	35	U12
Kelvingrove Ter. G3	35	U12
Kelvingrove St.		
Kelvinhaugh Pl. G3	34	T12
Kelvinhaugh St.		
Kelvinhaugh St. G3	34	T12
Kelvinside Av. G20	21	U10
Queen Margaret Dr.		
Kelvinside Dr. G20	21	U10
Kelvinside Gdns. G20	21	U10
Kelvinside Gdns. E. G20	21	U10
Kelvinside Gdns. La. G20	21	U10
Kelvinside Gdns.		
Kelvinside Ter. S. G20	21	U10
Kelvinside Ter. W. G20	21	U10
Kemp Av., Pais. PA3	31	L11
Kemp St. G21	22	X10
Kempock St. G31	53	Z14
Kempsthorn Cres. G53	48	P15
Kempsthorn Path G53	48	P15
Kempsthorn Rd. G53	48	P15
Kendal Av. G12	20	S9
Kendal Av. (Giff.) G46	62	T18
Kendal Dr. G12	20	S9
Kendal Ter. G12	20	S9
Kendoon Av. G15	6	N6
Kenilworth Av. G41	50	T16
Kenilworth Cres. (Bears.) G61	7	Q5
Kenilworth Way, Pais. PA2	45	G16

Street	Page	Grid
Kenmar Gdns. (Udd.) G71	56	FF16
Kenmore Gdns. (Bears.) G61	8	S5
Kenmore Rd. (Cumb.) G67	71	PP3
Kenmore St. G32	38	BB13
Kenmuir Av. (Bishop.) G64	10	X7
Kenmuir Rd. G32	55	DD14
Kenmuirhill Rd. G32	55	CC15
Kenmure Av. (Bishop.) G64	10	X7
Kenmure Cres. (Bishop.) G64	10	X7
Kenmure Dr. (Bishop.) G64	10	X7
Kenmure Gdns. (Bishop.) G64	10	X7
Kenmure Row G22	9	V7
Kenmure St. G41	51	U14
Kenmure Way (Ruther.) G73	65	Y18
Kennedar Dr. G51	33	R12
Kennedy Ct. (Giff.) G46	62	T18
Braidholm Cres.		
Kennedy St. G4	36	W12
Kennet St. G21	37	Y11
Kennishead Av. (Thorn.) G46	61	R17
Kennishead Path (Thorn.) G46	61	R17
Kennishead Pl.		
Kennishead Pl. (Thorn.) G46	61	R17
Kennishead Rd. G43	61	R17
Kennishead Rd. (Thorn.) G46	61	R17
Kennishead Rd. G53	61	Q18
Kennisholm Av. (Thorn.) G46	61	R17
Kennisholm Path (Thorn.) G46	61	R18
Kennisholm Av.		
Kennisholm Pl. (Thorn.) G46	61	R17
Kennoway Dr. G11	33	R11
Kennoway La. G11	33	R11
Thornwood Dr.		
Kennyhill Sq. G31	37	Y12
Kensington Dr. (Giff.) G46	62	T19
Kensington Gate G12	20	T10
Kensington Rd. G12	20	T10
Kent Dr. (Ruther.) G73	65	Z17
Kent Rd. G3	35	U12
Kent St. G40	36	X13
Kentallen Rd. G33	39	DD13
Kentigern Ter. (Bishop.) G64	23	Y8
Keppel Dr. G44	52	X16
Keppoch St. G21	22	W10
Keppochhill Dr. G21	22	W10
Keppochhill Pl. G21	36	W11
Keppochhill Rd. G21	22	X10
Keppochhill Rd. G22	22	W10
Keppochhill Way G21	36	W11
Kerfield La. G15	6	N6
Kerfield Pl. G15	6	N6
Kerr Dr. G40	36	X13
Kerr Gdns. (Udd.) G71	57	HH16
Kerr Pl. G40	36	X13
Kerr St. G40	36	X13
Kerr St. (Barr.) G78	59	L19
Kerr St., Pais. PA3	30	J13
Kerrera Pl. G33	39	CC13
Kerrera Rd. G33	39	CC13
Kerry Pl. G15	6	N6
Kerrycroy Av. G42	52	W16
Kerrycroy Pl. G42	52	W16
Kerrycroy.		
Kerrycroy St. G42	52	W16
Kerrydale St. G40	53	Y14
Kerrylamont Av. G42	52	X16
Kersland La. G12	20	T10
Kersland St.		
Kersland St. G12	20	T10
Kessington Dr. (Bears.) G61	8	S6
Kessington Rd. (Bears.) G61	8	S6
Kessock Dr. G22	21	V10
Kessock Pl. G22	21	V10
Kestrel Ct., Clyde. G81	5	L5
Kestrel Pl., John. PA5	43	C16
Kestrel Rd. G13	19	Q9
Kew Gdns. G12	20	T10
Ruthven St.		
Kew Gdns. (Udd.) G71	57	HH16
Kew La. G12	20	T10
Saltoun St.		
Kew Ter. G12	20	T10
Keyden St. G41	35	U13
Kibbleston Rd. (Kilb.), John. PA10	42	B14
Kierhill Rd. (Cumb.) G68	70	MM3
Kilbarchan Rd., John. PA5	43	C15
Kilbarchan Rd. (Mill.Pk.), John. PA10	43	C15
Kilbarchan St. G5	35	V13
Bedford St.		
Kilbeg Ter. (Thorn.) G46	61	Q18
Kilberry St. G21	37	Y11
Kilbirnie Pl. G5	51	V14
Kilbirnie St. G5	51	V14
Kilbowie Ct., Clyde. G81	5	L6
Crown Av.		
Kilbowie Rd. (Cumb.) G67	71	PP3
Kilbowie Rd., Clyde. G81	5	L5
Kilbrennan Rd. (Linw.), Pais. PA3	28	E13
Kilbride St. G5	52	W15
Kilbride Vw. (Udd.) G71	57	HH16
Hamilton Vw.		
Kilburn Gro. (Blan.) G72	68	FF19
Kilburn Pl. G13	18	P9
Kilchattan Dr. G44	52	W16
Kilchoan Rd. G33	39	CC11
Kilcloy Av. G15	6	P6
Kildale St. (Ruther.) G73	52	X16
Kildale Way (Ruther.) G73	52	X16
Kildary Av. G44	63	V17
Kildary Rd. G44	63	V17
Kildermorie Rd. G34	40	EE12
Kildonan Dr. G11	34	S11
Kildonan Ter. G51	34	S13
Copland Rd.		
Kildrostan St. G41	51	U15
Terregles Av.		
Kildrum Rd. (Cumb.) G67	71	PP2
Kilearn Rd., Pais. PA3	31	L12
Kilearn Way, Pais. PA3	31	L12
Clyde Rd.		
Kilfinan St. G22	21	V8
Kilkerran Dr. G33	24	AA9
Killarn Way, Pais. PA3	31	L12
Killearn Dr., Pais. PA1	48	N14
Killearn St. G22	21	V10
Killermont Av. (Bears.) G61	8	S7
Killermont Ct. (Bears.) G61	8	S6
Killermont Meadows (Both.) G71	69	GG19
Killermont Rd. (Bears.) G61	8	S6
Killermont St. G2	36	W12
Killermont Vw. G20	8	S7
Killiegrew Rd. G41	50	T15
Killin St. G32	54	BB14
Killoch Av., Pais. PA3	29	H13
Killoch Dr. G13	18	P8
Killoch Dr. (Barr.) G78	59	M19
Killoch Rd., Pais. PA3	29	H13
Kilmailing Rd. G44	63	V17
Kilmair Pl. G20	20	T9
Wyndford Rd.		
Kilmaluag Ter. (Thorn.) G46	61	Q18
Kilmany Dr. G32	38	AA13
Kilmany Gdns. G32	38	AA13
St. Mark St.		
Kilmardinny Av. (Bears.) G61	7	R5
Kilmardinny Cres. (Bears.) G61	7	R5
Kilmardinny Dr. (Bears.) G61	7	R5
Kilmardinny Gate (Bears.) G61	7	R5
Kilmardinny Av.		
Kilmardinny Gro. (Bears.) G61	7	R5
Kilmarnock Rd. G41	62	T17
Kilmarnock Rd. G43	62	T17
Kilmartin Pl. (Thorn.) G46	61	R18
Kilmaurs Dr. (Giff.) G46	63	U18
Kilmaurs St. G51	33	R13
Kilmorie Dr. (Ruther.) G73	52	X16
Kilmory Av. (Udd.) G71	57	HH16
Spindlehowe Rd.		
Kilmuir Cres. (Thorn.) G46	61	Q18
Kilmuir Dr. (Thorn.) G46	61	R18
Kilmuir Rd. (Thorn.) G46	61	R18
Kilmuir Rd. (Udd.) G71	57	GG15
Kilmun La. G20	20	T8
Kilmun St.		
Kilmun Pl. G20	20	T8
Kilmun St.		
Kilmun St. G20	20	T8
Kilnside Rd., Pais. PA1	30	K13
Kiloran St. (Thorn.) G46	61	R18
Kilpatrick Av., Pais. PA2	45	H15
Kilpatrick Cres., Pais. PA2	46	J15
Kilpatrick Dr., Renf. PA4	31	L12
Campsie Dr.		
Kilpatrick Way (Udd.) G71	57	HH16
Kiltearn Rd. G33	39	DD12
Kilvaxter Dr. (Thorn.) G46	61	R18
Kilwynet Way, Pais. PA3	31	L12
Kimberley St., Clyde. G81	4	J5
Kinalty Rd. G44	63	V17
Kinarvie Cres. G53	48	N16
Kinarvie Gdns. G53	48	N16
Kinarvie Rd.		
Kinarvie Pl. G53	48	N16
Kinarvie Rd. G53	48	N16
Kinarvie Ter. G53	48	N16
Kinbuck St. G22	22	W10
Kincaid Gdns. (Camb.) G72	66	BB17
Kincardine Cres. (Bishop.) G64	23	Y8
Graham Ter.		
Kincardine Dr. (Bishop.) G64	23	Y8
Kincardine Pl. (Bishop.) G64	23	Z8
Kincardine Sq. G33	39	CC11
Kincath Av. (Ruther.) G73	65	Z18
Kinclaven Av. G15	6	P6
Kincraig St. G51	33	Q13
Kinellan Rd. (Bears.) G61	7	R7
Kinellar Dr. G14	18	P9
Kinfauns Dr. G15	6	N6
Kinfauns Ter. G51	34	S13
Copland Rd.		
King Edward La. G13	19	R9
King Edward Rd.		
King Edward Rd. G13	19	R9
King George Ct., Renf. PA4	32	N11
King George V Bri. G1	35	V13
King George V Bri. G5	35	V13
King George V Dock G51	32	P11
King George Gdns., Renf. PA4	32	N11
King George Pk. Av.		
King George Pk. Av., Renf. PA4	31	M11
King George Pl., Renf. PA4	32	N11
King George Pk. Av.		
King George Way, Renf. PA4	31	M11
King George Pk. Av.		
King Pl. (Bail.) G69	41	HH13
King St. G1	36	W13
King St. (Ruther.) G73	53	Y16
King St., Clyde. G81	17	M8
King St., Pais. PA1	30	J13
Kingarth La. G42	51	V15
Kingarth St.		
Kingarth St. G42	51	V15
Kingfisher Dr. G13	18	N8
Kingfisher Gdns. G13	18	P8
Kinghorn Dr. G44	52	W16
Kinglas Rd. (Bears.) G61	7	Q7
King's Bri. G5	52	W14
King's Bri. G40	52	W14
Kings Cres. (Camb.) G72	66	BB17
Kings Cres. (Elder.), John. PA5	44	F14
Kings Cross G31	36	X12
King's Dr. G40	52	X14
Kings Dr. (Cumb.) G68	70	NN1
Kings Inch Dr., Renf. PA4	32	N11
Kings Inch Pl., Renf. PA4	32	N11
Kings Inch Rd., Renf. PA4	17	M9
Kings La. W., Renf. PA4	17	M10
Bell St.		
King's Pk. Av. G44	63	V17
King's Pk. Av. (Ruther.) G73	63	V17
Kings Pk. Rd. G44	51	V16
Kings Pl. G22	21	V8
Kings Rd., John. PA5	44	E15
King's Vw. (Cumb.) G68	70	NN1
Kings Vw. (Ruther.) G73	52	X16
Kingsacre Rd. G44	52	W16
Kingsacre Rd. (Ruther.) G73	52	W16
Kingsbarns Dr. G44	51	V16
Kingsborough Gdns. G12	20	S10
Kingsborough Gate G12	20	S10
Prince Albert Rd.		
Kingsborough La. G12	20	S10
Prince Albert Rd.		
Kingsborough La. E. G12	20	S10
Kingsborough Gdns.		

Street		
Kingsborough Ter. G12	20	S10
Hyndland Rd.		
Kingsbrae Av. G44	52	W16
Kingsbridge Cres. G44	64	W17
Kingsbridge Dr. G44	64	W17
Kingsbridge Dr. (Ruther.) G73	64	W17
Kingsburgh Dr., Pais. PA1	31	L13
Kingsburn Dr. (Ruther.) G73	65	Y17
Kingsburn Gro. (Ruther.) G73	65	Y17
Kingscliffe Av. G44	64	W17
Kingscourt Av. G44	64	W17
Kingsdale Av. G44	52	W16
Kingsdyke Av. G44	52	W16
Kingsford Av. G44	63	U18
Kingsheath Av. (Ruther.) G73	64	X17
Kingshill Dr. G44	64	W17
Kingshouse Av. G44	64	W17
Kingshurst Av. G44	52	W16
Kingsknowe Dr. (Ruther.) G73	64	X17
Kingsland Cres. G52	32	P13
Kingsland Dr. G52	32	P13
Kingsland La. G52	33	Q13
Berryknowes Rd.		
Kingsley Av. G42	51	V15
Kingsley Ct. (Udd.) G71	57	HH16
Kingslynn Dr. G44	64	W17
Kingslynn La. G44	64	W17
Kingslynn Dr.		
Kingsmuir Dr. (Ruther.) G73	64	X17
Kingston Av. (Udd.) G71	57	HH16
Kingston Bri. G3	35	U13
Kingston Bri. G5	35	U13
Kingston Pl., Clyde. G81	4	J6
Kingston St. G5	35	V13
Kingsway G14	18	P9
Kingsway Ct. G14	18	P9
Kingswood Dr. G44	64	W17
Kingussie Dr. G44	64	W17
Kiniver Dr. G15	6	P7
Kinloch Av. (Camb.) G72	66	BB18
Kinloch Av. (Linw.), Pais. PA3	28	E13
Pentland Av.		
Kinloch Rd., Renf. PA4	31	L11
Kinloch St. G40	53	Z14
Kinmount Av. G44	51	V16
Kinmount La. G44	51	V16
Kinmount Av.		
Kinnaird Cres. (Bears.) G61	8	S6
Kinnaird Dr. (Linw.), Pais. PA3	28	E13
Kinnaird Pl. (Bishop.) G64	23	Y8
Kinnear Rd. G40	53	Y14
Kinnell Av. G52	49	Q14
Kinnell Cres. G52	49	Q14
Kinnell Path G52	49	Q14
Kinnell Cres.		
Kinnell Pl. G52	49	R15
Mosspark Dr.		
Kinnell Sq. G52	49	Q14
Kinning St. G5	35	U13
Kinnoul La. G12	20	T10
Dowanhill St.		
Kinpurnie Rd., Pais. PA1	31	M13
Kinross Av. G52	48	P14
Kinsail Dr. G52	32	N13
Kinstone Av. G14	18	P9
Kintessack Pl. (Bishop.) G64	11	Z7
Kintillo Dr. G13	18	P9
Kintore Rd. G43	63	U17
Kintra St. G51	34	S13
Kintyre Av. (Linw.), Pais. PA3	28	E13
Kintyre St. G21	37	Y11
Kippen St. G22	22	W9
Kippford St. G32	55	CC14
Kirk La. G43	50	T16
Riverbank St.		
Kirk Pl. (Udd.) G71	69	GG16
Kirk Rd. (Bears.) G61	7	R5
Kirkaig Av., Renf. PA4	32	N11
Kirkbean Av. (Ruther.) G73	65	Y18
Kirkburn Av. (Camb.) G72	66	BB18
Kirkcaldy Rd. G41	50	T15
Kirkconnel Av. G13	18	N9
Kirkconnel Dr. (Ruther.) G73	64	X17
Kirkdale Dr. G52	49	R14
Kirkfield Rd. (Both.) G71	69	HH18
Kirkford Rd. (Chry.) G69	15	GG7
Bridgeburn Dr.		
Kirkhill Av. (Camb.) G72	66	BB18
Kirkhill Dr. G20	20	T9
Kirkhill Gdns. (Camb.) G72	66	BB18
Kirkhill Gro. (Camb.) G72	66	BB18
Kirkhill Pl. G20	20	T9
Kirkhill Rd. (Gart.) G69	27	GG9
Kirkhill Rd. (Udd.) G71	57	GG16
Kirkhill Ter. (Camb.) G72	66	BB18
Kirkhope Dr. G15	6	P7
Kirkinner Rd. G32	55	CC14
Kirkintilloch Rd. (Bishop.) G64	22	X8
Kirkintilloch Rd. (Kirk.) G66	13	CC5
Kirkland Gro., John. PA5	43	D14
Kirkland St. G20	21	U10
Kirklandneuk Cres., Renf. PA4	17	L10
Kirklandneuk Rd.		
Kirklandneuk Rd., Renf. PA4	17	L10
Kirklands Cres. (Both.) G71	69	HH18
Kirklea Av., Pais. PA3	29	H13
Kirklee Circ. G12	20	T10
Kirklee Gdns. G12	20	T9
Bellshaugh Rd.		
Kirklee Gdns. La. G12	20	T9
Bellshaugh Rd.		
Kirklee Pl. G12	20	T10
Kirklee Quad. G12	20	T10
Kirklee Quad. La. G12	20	T10
Kirklee Quad.		
Kirklee Rd. G12	20	T10
Kirklee Ter. G12	20	T10
Kirklee Ter. La. G12	20	T10
Kirklee Ter.		
Kirkles Gdns., Pais. PA3	29	H13
Kirkliston St. G32	38	AA13
Kirkmichael Gdns. G11	20	S10
Blairatholl Av.		
Kirkmuir Dr. (Ruther.) G73	65	Y18
Kirknewton St. G32	38	BB13
Kirkoswald Dr., Clyde. G81	5	M6
Kirkoswald Rd. G43	62	T17
Kirkpatrick St. G40	37	Y13
Kirkriggs Av. (Ruther.) G73	65	Y17
Kirkriggs Gdns. (Ruther.) G73	65	Y17
Kirkriggs Way (Ruther.) G73	65	Y17
Kirkstall Gdns. (Bishop.) G64	11	Y6
Kirkton Av. G13	18	P9
Kirkton Av. (Barr.) G78	59	L19
Kirkton Cres. G13	18	P9
Kirkton Rd. (Camb.) G72	66	BB17
Kirktonside (Barr.) G78	59	L19
Kirkview Gdns. (Udd.) G71	57	GG16
Glencroft Av.		
Kirkville Pl. G15	6	P7
Kirkwall (Cumb.) G67	71	PP1
Kirkwall Av. (Blan.) G72	68	FF18
Kirkwell Rd. G44	63	V17
Kirkwood Av., Clyde. G81	5	M7
Kirkwood Quad., Clyde. G81	5	M7
Kirkwood Av.		
Kirkwood Rd. (Udd.) G71	57	GG15
Newlands Rd.		
Kirkwood St. G51	34	T13
Kirkwood St. (Ruther.) G73	53	Y16
Kirn St. G20	20	T8
Kirriemuir Av. G52	49	Q14
Kirriemuir Gdns. (Bishop.) G64	11	Z7
Kirriemuir Pl. G52	49	Q14
Kirriemuir Rd. (Bishop.) G64	11	Z7
Kirtle Dr., Renf. PA4	32	N11
Kishorn Pl. G33	39	CC11
Knapdale St. G22	21	V8
Knights Gate (Both.) G71	69	GG17
Knight's Gate (Udd.) G71	69	GG17
Knightsbridge Rd. G13	19	Q9
Knightsbridge St. G13	19	Q9
Knightscliffe Av. G13	19	Q8
Knightswood Ct. G13	19	Q8
Knightswood Cross G13	19	Q8
Knightswood Rd. G13	7	Q7
Knightswood Ter. (Blan.) G72	69	GG19
Knock Way, Pais. PA3	31	L12
Knockburnie Rd. (Both.) G71	69	HH18
Knockhall St. G33	39	CC11
Knockhill Dr. G44	51	V16
Knockhill La. G44	51	V16
Mount Annan Dr.		
Knockhill Rd., Renf. PA4	31	L11
Knockside Av., Pais. PA2	46	J16
Knowe Rd. (Chry.) G69	26	FF8
Knowe Rd., Pais. PA3	31	L12
Knowe Ter. G22	21	V8
Hillend Rd.		
Knowehead Dr. (Udd.) G71	69	GG17
Knowehead Gdns. G41	51	U14
Knowehead Ter.		
Knowehead Gdns. (Udd.) G71	69	GG17
Knowehead Ter. G41	51	U14
Knowetap St. G20	21	U8
Knox St., Pais. PA1	45	H14
Kyle Dr. (Giff.) G46	62	T18
Kyle Rd. (Cumb.) G67	71	PP2
Kyle Sq. (Ruther.) G73	65	Y17
Kyle St. G4	36	W11
Kyleaken Gdns. (Blan.) G72	68	EE19
Kyleakin Rd. (Thorn.) G46	61	Q18
Kyleakin Ter. (Thorn.) G46	61	Q18
Kylepark Av. (Udd.) G71	68	FF17
Kylepark Cres. (Udd.) G71	56	FF16
Kylepark Dr. (Udd.) G71	56	FF16
Kylerhea Rd. (Thorn.) G46	61	Q18

L

Street		
La Belle Allee G3	35	U11
Clifton St.		
La Belle Pl. G3	35	U11
La Crosse Ter. G12	21	U10
Laburnum Gdns. (Kirk.) G66	12	BB5
Laburnum Gro.		
Laburnum Gro. (Kirk.) G66	12	BB5
Laburnum Pl., John. PA5	44	E16
Laburnum Rd. G41	50	T14
Gower St.		
Laburnum Rd. (Cumb.) G67	71	QQ3
Lacy St., Pais. PA1	31	L13
Lade Ter. G52	48	P14
Ladeside Dr., John. PA5	43	C15
Ladhope Pl. G13	18	N8
Lady Anne St. G14	18	N9
Lady Isle Cres. (Udd.) G71	69	GG17
Lady Jane Gate (Both.) G71	69	GG18
Lady La., Pais. PA1	46	J14
Ladyacres (Inch.), Renf. PA4	16	J9
Ladyacres Way (Inch.), Renf. PA4	16	J9
Ladybank Dr. G52	49	R14
Ladyburn St., Pais. PA1	47	L14
Ladyhill Dr. (Bail.) G69	56	EE14
Ladykirk Cres. G52	32	P13
Ladykirk Cres., Pais. PA2	46	K14
Ladykirk Dr. G52	32	P13
Ladyloan Av. G15	6	N6
Ladyloan Ct. G15	6	N6
Ladyloan Gdns. G15	6	N6
Ladyloan Pl. G15	6	N6
Ladymuir Cres. G53	49	Q15
Ladysmith Av. (Mill.Pk.), John. PA10	42	B15
Ladywell St. G4	36	X12
Laggan Rd. G43	63	U17
Laggan Rd. (Bishop.) G64	11	Y7
Laggan Ter., Renf. PA4	17	L10
Laidlaw Gdns. (Udd.) G71	57	GG15
Laidlaw St. G5	35	V13
Laigh Kirk La., Pais. PA1	46	K14
Causeyside St.		
Laigh Possil Rd. G23	21	V8
Balmore Rd.		
Laighcartside St., John. PA5	44	E14
Laighlands Rd. (Both.) G71	69	HH19
Laighmuir St. (Udd.) G71	69	GG17
Laighpark Harbour, Pais. PA3	30	K12
Laighpark Vw., Pais. PA3	30	K12
Lainshaw Dr. G45	63	V19
Laird Gro. (Udd.) G71	57	HH16
Laird Pl. G40	52	X14
Lairds Gate (Udd.) G71	69	GG17
Lairds Hill (Cumb.) G67	70	NN3
Lairg Dr. (Blan.) G72	68	FF19
Lamb St. G22	21	V9
Lamberton Dr. G52	32	P13
Lambhill St. G41	34	T13
Lamerton Rd. (Cumb.) G67	71	QQ3
Lamington Rd. G52	48	P14
Lamlash Cres. G33	38	BB12
Lammermoor Av. G52	49	Q14
Lammermoor Rd. (Cumb.) G67	70	NN4

Lammermuir Ct., Pais. PA2   46   K16
Lammermuir Dr., Pais. PA2   46   J15
Lamont Rd. G21   23   Y9
Lanark St. G1   36   W13
Lancaster Cres. G12   20   T10
Lancaster Cres. La. G12   20   S9
  Cleveden Rd.
Lancaster Rd. (Bishop.)   11   Y6
  G64
Lancaster Ter. G12   20   T10
  Westbourne Gdns. W.
Lancaster Ter. La. G12   20   T10
  Westbourne Gdns. W.
Lancefield Quay G3   35   U12
Lancefield St. G3   35   U12
Landemer Dr. (Ruther.) G73   64   X17
Landressy Pl. G40   52   X14
Landressy St. G40   52   X14
Lane Gdns. G11   20   S10
  North Gardner St.
Lanfine Rd., Pais. PA1   47   L14
Lang Av., Renf. PA4   31   M11
Lang Pl., John. PA5   43   D14
Lang St., Pais. PA1   47   L14
Langa St. G20   21   U8
Langbank St. G5   51   V14
  Eglinton St.
Langbar Cres. G33   39   DD12
Langbar Path G33   39   CC12
Langcraigs Dr., Pais. PA2   58   J17
Langcraigs Ter., Pais. PA2   58   J17
Langcroft Dr. (Camb.) G72   67   CC18
Langcroft Pl. G51   33   Q12
Langcroft Rd. G51   33   Q12
Langcroft Ter. G51   33   Q12
Langdale Av. G33   24   AA10
Langdale Rd. (Chry.) G69   15   GG7
Langdale St. G33   24   AA10
Langdale's Av. (Cumb.) G68   70   MM3
Langford Dr. G53   60   P18
Langford Dr. G53   60   P18
Langford Pl. G53   60   P18
  Langford Dr.
Langhaul Rd. G53   48   N15
Langhill Dr. (Cumb.) G68   70   MM2
Langholm Ct. (Chry.) G69   15   HH7
  Heathfield Av.
Langholm Dr. (Linw.), Pais.   28   F13
  PA3
Langlands Av. G51   33   Q12
Langlands Dr. G51   33   Q12
Langlands Rd. G51   33   Q12
Langlea Av. (Camb.) G72   65   Z18
Langlea Ct. (Camb.) G72   66   AA18
Langlea Dr. (Camb.) G72   66   AA17
Langlea Gdns. (Camb.) G72   66   AA17
Langlea Gro. (Camb.) G72   66   AA18
Langlea Rd. (Camb.) G72   66   AA18
Langlea Way (Camb.) G72   66   AA17
Langley Av. G13   18   P8
Langmuir Rd. (Bail.) G69   41   HH13
Langmuir Way (Bail.) G69   41   HH13
Langmuirhead Rd. (Kirk.)   24   BB8
  G66
Langness Rd. G33   38   BB12
Langrig Rd. G21   23   Y10
Langshot St. G51   34   T13
Langside Av. G41   51   U15
Langside Dr. G43   63   U17
Langside Dr. (Kilb.), John.   42   B15
  PA10
Langside Gdns. G42   51   V16
Langside La. G42   51   V15
Langside Pk. (Kilb.), John.   42   B15
  PA10
Langside Pl. G41   51   U16
Langside Rd. G42   51   V16
Langside Rd. (Both.) G71   69   HH19
Langside St., Clyde. G81   5   M5
Langstile Pl. G52   32   N13
Langstile Rd. G52   32   N13
Langton Cres. G53   49   Q15
Langton Cres. (Barr.) G78   59   M19
Langton Gdns. (Bail.) G69   55   DD14
Langton Rd. G53   49   Q15
Langtree Av. (Giff.) G46   62   S19
Lanrig Pl. (Chry.) G69   26   FF8
Lanrig Rd. (Chry.) G69   26   FF8
Lansbury Gdns., Pais. PA3   30   J12
Lansdowne Cres. G20   35   U11
Lansdowne Cres. La. G20   35   U11
  Napiershall St.

Lansdowne Dr. (Cumb.)   70   NN2
  G68
Lanton Dr. G52   32   P13
Lanton Rd. G43   63   U17
Lappin St., Clyde. G81   17   M8
Larbert St. G4   35   V11
  Milton St.
Larch Av. (Bishop.) G64   23   Y8
Larch Av. (Lenzie) G66   13   CC5
Larch Ct. (Cumb.) G67   71   QQ2
Larch Cres. (Kirk.) G66   13   CC5
Larch Gro. (Cumb.) G67   71   RR2
Larch Pl., John. PA5   44   E16
Larch Rd. G41   50   S14
Larch Rd. (Cumb.) G67   71   QQ2
Larches, The (Mood.) G69   15   HH6
Larchfield Av. G14   18   P10
Larchfield Dr. (Ruther.) G73   65   Y18
Larchfield Pl. G14   18   P10
Larchfield Rd. (Bears.) G61   7   R7
Larchfield Rd. (Chry.) G69   15   GG7
  Larchgrove Rd.
Larchgrove Av. G32   39   CC13
Larchgrove Pl. G32   39   CC12
  Larchgrove Rd.
Larchgrove Rd. G32   39   CC12
Larchwood Ter. (Barr.) G78   60   N19
Largie Rd. G43   63   U17
Largo Pl. G51   33   R12
Largs St. G31   37   Y12
Larkfield Rd. (Lenzie) G66   13   DD5
Larkfield St. G42   51   V14
  Inglefield St.
Larkin Gdns., Pais. PA3   30   J12
Lasswade St. G14   17   M9
Latherton Dr. G20   20   T9
Latherton Pl. G20   20   T9
  Latherton Dr.
Latimer Gdns. G52   48   P14
Laudedale La. G12   20   S10
  Clarence Dr.
Lauder Dr. (Ruther.) G73   65   Z17
Lauder Dr. (Linw.), Pais. PA3   28   E13
Lauder Gdns. (Blan.) G72   68   FF19
Lauder St. G5   51   V14
  Eglinton St.
Lauderdale Gdns. G12   20   S10
Laundry La. G33   25   CC9
Laurel Av. (Lenzie) G66   13   CC5
Laurel Av., Clyde. G81   4   J6
Laurel Bk. Rd. (Chry.) G69   26   EE8
Laurel Gdns. (Udd.) G71   57   GG16
Laurel Pk. Gdns. G13   19   Q9
Laurel Pl. G11   34   S11
Laurel St. G11   34   S11
Laurel Wk. (Ruther.) G73   65   Z18
Laurel Way (Barr.) G78   59   L18
Laurence Dr. (Bears.) G61   7   Q5
Laurie Ct. (Udd.) G71   57   HH16
  Hillcrest Rd.
Laurieston La. G51   34   T13
  Paisley Rd. W.
Laurieston Rd. G5   51   V14
Laurieston Way (Ruther.)   65   Y18
  G73
Lauriston Rd. G5   51   V14
Laverock Ter. (Chry.) G69   15   GG7
Laverockhall St. G21   22   X10
Law St. G40   37   Y13
Lawers Dr. (Bears.) G61   7   Q5
Lawers Rd. G43   62   S17
Lawers Rd., Renf. PA4   31   M11
Lawhill Av. G44   64   W18
Lawmoor Av. G5   52   W14
Lawmoor La. G5   36   W13
  Ballater St.
Lawmoor Pl. G5   52   W15
  Lawmoor Av.
Lawmoor Rd. G5   52   W14
Lawmoor St. G5   52   W14
Lawn St., Pais. PA1   30   K13
Lawrence Av. (Giff.) G46   62   T19
Lawrence St. G11   34   T11
Lawrie St. G11   34   S11
Lawside Dr. G53   49   Q16
Laxford Av. G44   63   V18
Laxton Dr. (Lenzie) G66   13   DD6
Leabank Av., Pais. PA2   46   K16
Leadburn Rd. G21   23   Z10
  Rye Rd.
Leadburn St. G32   38   AA12
Leader St. G33   37   Z11
Leander Cres., Renf. PA4   32   N11

Leckethill St. G21   22   X10
  Springburn Rd.
Leckie St. G43   50   T16
Ledaig Pl. G31   37   Z12
Ledaig St. G31   37   Z12
Ledard Rd. G42   51   U16
Ledcameroch Cres. (Bears.)   7   Q6
  G61
Ledcameroch Pk. (Bears.) G61   7   Q6
  Ledcameroch Rd.
Ledcameroch Rd. (Bears.)   7   Q6
  G61
Ledgowan Pl. G20   20   T8
Ledi Dr. (Bears.) G61   7   Q5
Ledi Rd. G43   62   T17
Ledmore Dr. G15   6   N6
Lednock Rd. (Stepps) G33   25   CC9
Lednock Rd. G52   32   P13
Lee Av. G33   38   AA11
Lee Cres. (Bishop.) G64   22   X8
Leebank Dr. G44   63   U19
Leefield Dr. G44   63   U19
Leehill Rd. G21   22   X8
Leeside Rd. G21   22   X8
Leesland (Udd.) G71   57   HH16
Leewood Dr. G44   63   U19
Leggatston Rd. G53   61   Q19
Leglen Wd. Cres. G21   23   Z9
Leglen Wd. Dr. G21   23   Z9
Leglen Wd. Pl. G21   24   AA9
Leglen Wd. Rd. G21   23   Z9
Leicester Av. G12   20   S9
Leighton St. G20   21   U9
Leitchland Rd. (Elder.), John.   44   F16
  PA5
Leitchland Rd., Pais. PA2   44   F16
Leitchs Ct. G1   36   W13
  Trongate
Leith St. G33   37   Z12
Leithland Av. G53   48   P16
Leithland Rd. G53   48   P15
Lendale La. (Bishop.) G64   11   Y6
Lendel Pl. G51   35   U13
  Paisley Rd. W.
Lenihall Dr. G45   64   X19
Lenihall Ter. G45   64   X19
Lennox Av. G14   19   Q10
Lennox Cres. (Bishop.)   22   X8
  G64
Lennox Dr. (Bears.) G61   7   R5
Lennox Gdns. G14   19   Q10
Lennox La. W. G14   19   Q10
  Lennox Av.
Lennox Pl. G14   19   Q10
  Scotstoun St.
Lennox Pl., Clyde. G81   4   K6
  Swindon St.
Lennox Rd. (Cumb.) G67   70   NN3
Lennox St. G20   20   T8
  Maryhill Rd.
Lennox Ter., Pais. PA3   31   L12
Lennox Vw., Clyde. G81   5   L6
  Granville St.
Lentran St. G34   40   FF12
Leny St. G20   21   V10
Lenzie Pl. G21   22   X9
Lenzie Rd. (Stepps) G33   25   CC9
Lenzie St. G21   22   X9
Lenzie Ter. G21   22   X9
Lenzie Way G21   22   X9
Lenziemill Rd. (Cumb.) G67   71   PP4
Lerwick St. G4   35   V11
  Dobbies Ln.
Leslie Rd. G41   51   U15
Leslie St. G41   51   U14
Lesmuir Dr. G14   18   P9
Lesmuir Pl. G14   18   N9
Letham Ct. G43   63   U17
Letham Dr. G43   63   U17
Letham Dr. (Bishop.) G64   23   Z8
Letham Gra. (Cumb.) G68   70   NN2
Lethamhill Cres. G33   38   AA11
Lethamhill Pl. G33   38   AA11
Lethamhill Rd. G33   38   AA11
Letherby Dr. G42   51   V16
Letherby Dr. G44   51   V16
Lethington Av. G41   51   U16
Lethington Pl. G41   51   U16
Letterfearn Dr. G23   9   U7
Letterickhills Cres. (Camb.)   67   DD18
  G72
Lettoch St. G51   34   S13

Street	Page	Grid
Leven Av. (Bishop.) G64	11	Y7
Leven Ct. (Barr.) G78	59	L17
Leven Dr. (Bears.) G61	7	R6
Leven Sq., Renf. PA4	17	L10
Leven St. G41	51	U14
Leven Vw., Clyde. G81	5	L6
Radnor St.		
Leven Way, Pais. PA2	45	G15
Levern Cres. (Barr.) G78	59	L19
Levern Gdns. (Barr.) G78	59	L18
Leverndale Rd. G53	48	N15
Levernside Av. (Barr.) G78	59	L19
Levernside Cres. G53	48	P15
Levernside Rd. G53	48	P15
Lewis Av., Renf. PA4	31	M11
Lewis Cres. (Old Kil.) G60	4	J5
Lewis Cres. (Mill.Pk.), John. PA10	42	B15
Lewis Gdns. (Old Kil.) G60	4	J5
Lewis Cres.		
Lewis Gdns. (Bears.) G61	6	P5
Lewis Gro. (Old Kil.) G60	4	J5
Lewiston Dr. G23	8	T7
Lewiston Rd.		
Lewiston Pl. G23	8	T7
Lewiston Rd.		
Lewiston Rd. G23	8	T7
Lexwell Av. (Elder.), John. PA5	44	F14
Leyden Ct. G20	21	U9
Leyden St.		
Leyden Gdns. G20	21	U9
Leyden St.		
Leyden St. G20	21	U9
Leys, The (Bishop.) G64	11	Y7
Liberton St. G33	37	Z12
Liberty Av. (Bail.) G69	41	HH13
Libo Av. G53	49	Q15
Library Gdns. (Camb.) G72	66	AA17
Liddel Rd. (Cumb.) G67	70	NN3
Liddell St. G32	55	CC15
Liddesdale Av., Pais. PA2	44	F16
Liddesdale Pl. G22	22	W8
Liddesdale Sq.		
Liddesdale Rd. G22	22	W8
Liddesdale Sq. G22	22	W8
Liddesdale Ter. G22	22	X8
Liddoch Way (Ruther.) G73	52	X16
Liff Gdns. (Bishop.) G64	23	Z8
Liff Pl. G34	40	FF11
Lightburn Pl. G32	38	BB12
Lightburn Rd. G31	37	Z13
Duke St.		
Lightburn Rd. (Camb.) G72	67	CC18
Lilac Av., Clyde. G81	4	J6
Lilac Cres. (Udd.) G71	57	HH16
Lilac Gdns. (Bishop.) G64	23	Y8
Lilac Wynd (Camb.) G72	67	DD18
Lillyburn Pl. G15	6	N5
Lily St. G40	53	Y14
Lilybank Av. (Muir.) G69	26	FF8
Lilybank Av. (Camb.) G72	67	CC16
Lilybank Gdns. G12	34	T11
Lilybank Gdns. La. G12	20	T10
Great George St.		
Lilybank La. G12	34	T11
Lilybank Gdns.		
Lilybank Ter. G12	20	T10
Great George St.		
Lilybank Ter. La. G12	20	T10
Great George St.		
Lime Gro. (Lenzie) G66	13	CC5
Lime Gro. (Blan.) G72	68	FF19
Lime La. G14	19	Q10
Lime St.		
Lime St. G14	19	Q10
Limecraigs Cres., Pais. PA2	46	J16
Limecraigs Rd., Pais. PA2	45	H16
Limeside Av. (Ruther.) G73	53	Y16
Limeside Gdns. (Ruther.) G73	53	Z16
Calderwood Rd.		
Limetree Av. (Udd.) G71	57	HH16
Limetree Dr., Clyde. G81	5	L6
Limeview Av., Pais. PA2	45	H16
Limeview Cres., Pais. PA2	45	H16
Limeview Rd., Pais. PA2	45	H16
Limeview Av.		
Limeview Way, Pais. PA2	45	H16
Limeview Av.		
Linacre Dr. G32	39	CC13
Linacre Gdns. G32	39	CC13
Linburn Pl. G52	32	P13
Linburn Rd. G52	32	N12
Linclive Link Rd. (Linw.), Pais. PA3	28	F13
Linclive Ter. (Linw.), Pais. PA3	28	F13
Lincluden Path G41	51	U14
McCulloch St.		
Lincoln Av. G13	18	P9
Lincoln Av. (Udd.) G71	57	GG15
Lindams (Udd.) G71	69	GG17
Linden Dr., Clyde. G81	5	L5
Linden Pl. G13	19	R8
Linden St. G13	19	R8
Lindores Av. (Ruther.) G73	53	Y16
Lindores St. G42	51	V16
Somerville Dr.		
Lindrick Dr. G23	9	U7
Lindsay Dr. G12	20	S9
Lindsay Pl. G12	20	S9
Lindsay Pl. (Lenzie) G66	13	CC6
Lindsay Pl., John. PA5	44	E14
Thorn Brae		
Lindsaybeg Rd. (Lenzie) G66	13	DD6
Lindsaybeg Rd. (Chry.) G69	14	EE7
Linfern Rd. G12	20	T10
Links Rd. G32	55	CC14
Links Rd. G44	64	W18
Linkwood Av. G15	6	N6
Kinfauns Dr.		
Linkwood Cres. G15	6	N6
Linkwood Dr. G15	6	N6
Linkwood Gdns. G15	6	P6
Linkwood Pl. G15	6	N6
Kinfauns Dr.		
Linlithgow Gdns. G32	39	CC13
Linn Brae, John. PA5	43	D15
Linn Cres., Pais. PA2	46	J16
Linn Dr. G44	63	U18
Linn Pk. G44	63	V18
Linn Pk. Gdns., John. PA5	44	E15
Linn Valley Vw. G45	64	W18
Linnet Av., John. PA5	43	C16
Linnet Pl. G13	18	N8
Linnhe Av. G44	63	V18
Linnhe Av. (Bishop.) G64	11	Y7
Linnhe Dr. (Barr.) G78	59	L17
Linnhe Pl. (Blan.) G72	68	FF19
Linnhead Dr. G53	60	P17
Linnhead Pl. G14	18	P10
Linnpark Av. G44	63	U19
Linnpark Ct. G44	63	U19
Linnwell Cres., Pais. PA2	46	J16
Linnwood Ct. G44	63	V17
Bowling Grn. Rd.		
Linside Av., Pais. PA1	47	L14
Lintfield Ln. (Udd.) G71	69	HH17
Myers Cres.		
Linthaugh Rd. G53	48	P15
Linthaugh Ter. G53	49	Q15
Linthaugh Rd.		
Linthouse Bldgs. G51	33	R12
Holmfauld Rd.		
Linthouse Rd. G51	33	R11
Lintlaw (Blan.) G72	68	FF19
Lintlaw Dr. G52	33	Q13
Linton St. G33	38	AA12
Linwood Moss Rd. (Linw.), Pais. PA3	28	F13
Linwood Rd., Pais. PA1	28	F13
Linwood Rd. (Linw.), Pais. PA3	28	F13
Linwood Ter. G12	21	U10
Glasgow St.		
Lismore Av., Renf. PA4	31	M11
Lismore Dr., Pais. PA2	46	J16
Lismore Gdns. (Mill.Pk.), John. PA10	43	C15
Tandlehill Rd.		
Lismore Pl. (Chry.) G69	15	HH6
Altnacreag Gdns.		
Lismore Rd. G12	20	S10
Lister Rd. G52	32	P12
Lister St. G4	36	W11
Lithgow Cres., Pais. PA2	47	L15
Little Dovehill G1	36	W13
Little Mill Gdns. G53	48	P16
Dalmellington Rd.		
Little St. G3	35	U12
Littlehill St. G21	22	X10
Edgefauld Rd.		
Littleholm, Clyde. G81	4	K6
Littlemill Cres. G53	48	P16
Littlemill Dr. G53	48	P16
Littleton Dr. G23	8	T7
Rothes Dr.		
Littleton St. G23	8	T7
Rothes Dr.		
Livingstone Av. G52	32	P12
Livingstone Cres. (Blan.) G72	68	FF19
Livingstone St. G21	22	W10
Keppochhill Rd.		
Livingstone St., Clyde. G81	5	M7
Lloyd Av. G32	54	BB15
Lloyd St. G31	37	Y12
Lloyd St. (Ruther.) G73	53	Y15
Loanbank Quad. G51	34	S12
Loancroft Av. (Bail.) G69	56	FF14
Loancroft Gdns. (Udd.) G71	69	GG17
Loancroft Gate (Udd.) G71	69	GG17
Loancroft Pl. (Bail.) G69	56	EE14
Loanend Cotts. (Camb.) G72	67	DD19
Loanfoot Av. G13	18	P8
Loanhead Av. (Linw.), Pais. PA3	28	E13
Loanhead Av., Renf. PA4	17	M10
Loanhead La. (Linw.), Pais. PA3	28	E13
Loanhead Rd.		
Loanhead Rd. (Linw.), Pais. PA3	28	E13
Loanhead St. G32	38	AA12
Lobnitz Av., Renf. PA4	17	M10
Loch Achray St. G32	55	CC14
Loch Katrine St. G32	55	CC14
Loch Laidon St. G32	55	CC14
Loch Rd. (Stepps) G33	25	CC9
Loch Voil St. G32	55	CC14
Lochaber Dr. (Ruther.) G73	65	Z18
Lochaber Rd. (Bears.) G61	8	S7
Lochaline Av., Pais. PA2	45	H15
Lochaline Dr. G44	63	V18
Lochalsh Dr., Pais. PA2	45	G15
Lochalsh Pl. (Blan.) G72	68	EE19
Lochar Cres. G53	49	Q15
Lochard Dr., Pais. PA2	45	H15
Lochay St. G32	55	CC14
Lochbrae Dr. (Ruther.) G73	65	Z18
Lochbridge Rd. G34	40	EE12
Lochbroom Dr., Pais. PA2	45	H15
Lochburn Cres. G20	21	U8
Lochburn Gro. G20	21	U8
Cadder Rd.		
Lochburn Pas. G20	21	U8
Lochburn Rd. G20	20	T9
Lochdochart Path G34	40	FF12
Lochdochart Rd.		
Lochdochart Rd. G34	40	FF12
Lochearn Cres., Pais. PA2	45	H15
Lochearnhead Rd. G33	25	CC9
Lochend Av. (Gart.) G69	27	GG8
Lochend Cres. (Bears.) G61	7	Q6
Lochend Dr. (Bears.) G61	7	Q6
Lochend Rd. G34	40	EE11
Lochend Rd. (Bears.) G61	7	R6
Lochend Rd. (Gart.) G69	27	GG8
Locher Rd. (Kilb.), John. PA10	42	A14
Lochfauld Rd. G23	9	V7
Lochfield Cres., Pais. PA2	46	K15
Lochfield Dr., Pais. PA2	47	L15
Lochfield Gdns. G34	40	FF11
Lochfield Rd., Pais. PA2	46	K15
Lochgilp St. G20	20	T8
Lochgoin Av. G15	6	N6
Lochgreen St. G33	23	Z10
Lochhead Av. (Linw.), Pais. PA3	28	E13
Lochiel La. (Ruther.) G73	65	Z18
Lochiel Rd. (Thorn.) G46	61	R18
Lochinver Cres., Pais. PA2	45	H15
Lochinver Dr. G44	63	V18
Lochinver Gro. (Camb.) G72	67	CC17
Andrew Sillars Av.		
Lochlea Av., Clyde. G81	5	M6
Lochlea Rd. G43	62	T17
Lochlea Rd. (Cumb.) G67	71	QQ2
Lochlea Rd. (Ruther.) G73	64	X17
Lochleven La. G42	51	V16
Battlefield Rd.		
Lochleven Rd. G42	51	V16
Lochlibo Av. G13	18	N9
Lochlibo Cres. (Barr.) G78	59	L19

Lochlibo Rd. (Barr.) G78	59	L19
Lochlibo Ter. (Barr.) G78	59	L19
Lochmaben Rd. G52	48	N14
Lochmaddy Av. G44	63	V18
Lochore Av., Pais. PA3	31	L12
Lochside (Bears.) G61	7	R6
Drymen Rd.		
Lochside (Gart.) G69	27	GG9
Lochside St. G41	51	U15
Minard Rd.		
Lochview Cotts. (Gart.)	27	GG10
G69		
Lochview Cres. G33	24	AA10
Lochview Dr. G33	24	AA10
Lochview Gdns. G33	24	AA10
Lochview Pl. G33	24	AA10
Lochview Rd. (Bears.) G61	7	R6
Lochview Ter. (Gart.) G69	27	GG10
Lochwood Ln. (Mood.) G69	15	HH6
Lochwood St. G33	38	AA11
Lochy Av., Renf. PA4	32	N11
Lochy Gdns. (Bishop.) G64	11	Y7
Lockerbie Av. G43	63	U17
Lockhart Av. (Camb.) G72	67	CC17
Lockhart Dr. (Camb.) G72	67	CC17
Lockhart St. G21	37	Y11
Locksley Av. G13	19	Q8
Locksley Rd., Pais. PA2	45	G15
Logan Dr. (Cumb.) G68	70	MM2
Logan Dr., Pais. PA3	30	J13
Logan St. G5	52	W15
Logan Twr. (Camb.) G72	67	DD18
Claude Av.		
Loganswell Dr. (Thorn.) G46	61	Q19
Loganswell Gdns. (Thorn.)	61	R19
G46		
Loganswell Pl. (Thorn.) G46	61	R19
Loganswell Rd. (Thorn.) G46	61	R19
Lomax St. G33	37	Z12
Lomond Av., Renf. PA4	31	L11
Lomond Ct. (Barr.) G78	59	M19
Lomond Cres., Pais. PA2	46	J16
Lomond Dr. (Both.) G71	69	HH18
Lomond Dr. (Barr.) G78	59	L18
Lomond Gdns. (Elder.), John.	44	F15
PA5		
Lomond Pl. (Stepps) G33	25	CC10
Lomond Rd. (Bears.) G61	7	R7
Lomond Rd. (Bishop.) G64	10	X6
Lomond Rd. (Lenzie) G66	13	CC5
Lomond Rd. (Udd.) G71	57	GG15
Lomond St. G22	21	V9
Lomond Vw., Clyde. G81	5	L6
Granville St.		
London Arc. G1	36	W13
London Rd.		
London La. G1	36	W13
London Rd.		
London Rd. G1	36	W13
London Rd. G31	53	Z14
London Rd. G32	54	BB15
London Rd. G40	52	X14
London St., Renf. PA4	17	M9
Lonend, Pais. PA1	46	K14
Long Row (Bail.) G69	40	FF13
Longay Pl. G22	22	W8
Longay St. G22	22	W8
Longcroft Dr., Renf. PA4	17	M10
Longden St., Clyde. G81	17	M8
Longford St. G33	37	Z12
Longlee (Bail.) G69	56	EE14
Longmeadow, John. PA5	43	C15
Longstone Rd. G33	38	BB12
Longwill Ter. (Cumb.) G67	71	PP2
Lonmay Rd. G33	39	CC12
Lonsdale Av. (Giff.) G46	62	T18
Loom St. G40	36	X13
Stevenson St.		
Loom Wk. (Kilb.), John.	42	B14
PA10		
Shuttle St.		
Lora Dr. G52	49	R14
Lord Way (Bail.) G69	41	GG13
Dukes Rd.		
Loretto Pl. G33	38	AA12
Loretto St. G33	38	AA12
Lorn Av. (Chry.) G69	26	FF8
Lorne Cres. (Bishop.) G64	11	Z7
Lorne Dr. (Linw.), Pais. PA3	28	E13
Lorne Rd. G52	32	N12
Lorne St. G51	34	T13
Lorne Ter. (Camb.) G72	66	AA18

Lorraine Gdns. G12	20	T10
Kensington Rd.		
Lorraine Rd. G12	20	T10
Loskin Dr. G22	21	V8
Lossie Cres., Renf. PA4	32	N11
Lossie St. G33	37	Z11
Lothian Cres., Pais. PA2	46	J15
Lothian Gdns. G20	21	U10
Lothian St. G52	32	N12
Louden Hill Dr. G21	24	AA9
Louden Hill Gdns. G21	24	AA9
Louden Hill Pl. G21	24	AA9
Louden Hill Rd. G21	24	AA9
Louden Hill Way G21	24	AA9
Loudon Gdns., John. PA5	44	E14
Loudon Rd. G33	24	BB9
Loudon Ter. G12	20	T10
Observatory Rd.		
Lounsdale Av., Pais. PA2	45	H14
Lounsdale Cres., Pais. PA2	45	H15
Lounsdale Dr., Pais. PA2	45	H15
Lounsdale Gro., Pais. PA2	45	H15
Lounsdale Ho., Pais. PA2	45	H15
Gallacher Av.		
Lounsdale Pl. G14	18	P10
Lounsdale Rd., Pais. PA2	45	H15
Lounsdale Way, Pais. PA2	45	H14
Lourdes Av. G52	49	Q14
Lourdes Ct. G52	49	Q14
Lourdes Av.		
Lovat Pl. (Ruther.) G73	65	Z18
Lovat St. G4	36	W11
Love St., Pais. PA3	30	K13
Low Barholm (Kilb.), John.	42	B15
PA10		
Low Cres., Clyde. G81	18	N8
Low Parksail, Ersk. PA8	16	J8
Low Rd. (Castlehead), Pais.	46	J14
PA2		
Lower Bourtree Dr. (Ruther.)	65	Z18
G73		
Lower English Bldgs. G42	51	V14
Lower Millgate (Udd.) G71	57	GG16
Lowndes La., Pais. PA3	30	K13
New Sneddon St.		
Lowndes St. (Barr.) G78	59	M19
Lowther Ter. G12	20	T10
Loyne Dr., Renf. PA4	32	N11
Morriston Cres.		
Luath St. G51	34	S12
Lubas Av. G42	52	W16
Lubas Pl. G42	52	W16
Lubnaig Rd. G43	63	U17
Luckingsford Av. (Inch.),	16	J8
Renf. PA4		
Luckingsford Dr. (Inch.),	16	J8
Renf. PA4		
Luckingsford Rd. (Inch.),	16	J8
Renf. PA4		
Lucy Brae (Udd.) G71	57	GG16
Ludovic Sq., John. PA5	43	D14
Luffness Gdns. G32	54	BB15
Lugar Dr. G52	49	R14
Lugar Pl. G44	64	X17
Luggiebank Pl. (Bail.) G69	57	HH14
Luing Rd. G52	33	R13
Luma Gdns. G51	33	Q12
Lumloch St. G21	23	Y10
Lumsden La. G3	34	T12
Lumsden St.		
Lumsden St. G3	34	T12
Lunan Dr. (Bishop.) G64	23	Z8
Lunan Pl. G51	33	R12
Luncarty Pl. G32	54	BB14
Luncarty St. G32	54	BB14
Lunderston Dr. G53	48	P16
Lundie Gdns. (Bishop.) G64	23	Z8
Lundie St. G32	54	AA14
Luss Rd. G51	33	R12
Lusset Vw., Clyde. G81	5	L6
Radnor St.		
Lusshill Ter. (Udd.) G71	56	EE15
Lyall Pl. G21	22	W10
Keppochhill Rd.		
Lyall St. G21	22	W10
Lybster Cres. (Ruther.) G73	65	Z18
Lye Brae (Cumb.) G67	71	PP3
Lyle Pl., Pais. PA2	46	K15
Lylesland Ct., Pais. PA2	46	K15
Lymburn St. G3	34	T12
Lyndale Pl. G20	20	T8
Lyndale Rd. G20	20	T8

Lyndhurst Gdns. G20	21	U10
Lyndhurst Gdns. La. G20	21	U10
Melrose Gdns.		
Lyne Cft. (Bishop.) G64	11	Y6
Lyne Dr. G23	9	U7
Lynedoch Cres. G3	35	U11
Lynedoch Cres. La. G3	35	U11
Woodlands Rd.		
Lynedoch Pl. G3	35	U11
Lynedoch St. G3	35	U11
Lynedoch Ter. G3	35	U11
Lynn Gdns. G12	20	T10
Great George St.		
Lynn Wk. (Udd.) G71	69	HH17
Flax Rd.		
Lynnhurst (Udd.) G71	57	GG16
Lynton Av. (Giff.) G46	62	S19
Lyon Rd., Pais. PA2	45	G15
Lyon Rd. (Linw.), Pais. PA3	44	E14
Lyoncross Av. (Barr.) G78	59	M19
Lyoncross Cres. (Barr.) G78	59	M18
Lyoncross Rd. G53	48	P15
Lytham Dr. G23	9	U7
Lytham Meadows (Both.)	69	GG19
G71		

M

Macarthur Wynd (Camb.)	67	CC17
G72		
Macbeth Pl. G31	53	Z14
Macbeth St.		
Macbeth St. G31	53	Z14
Maccallum Dr. (Camb.) G72	67	CC17
Macdonald St. (Ruther.) G73	53	Y16
Greenhill Rd.		
Macdougall Dr. (Camb.) G72	67	CC17
Macdougall St. G43	50	T16
Macdowall St., John. PA5	43	D14
Macdowall St., Pais. PA3	30	J13
Macduff Pl. G31	53	Z14
Macduff St. G31	53	Z14
Mace Rd. G13	7	Q7
Macfarlane Cres. (Camb.)	67	CC17
G72		
Macfarlane Rd. (Bears.) G61	7	R6
Macgregor Ct. (Camb.) G72	67	CC17
Machrie Dr. G45	64	X18
Machrie Rd. G45	64	X18
Machrie St. G45	64	X18
Mackean St., Pais. PA3	30	J13
Mackechnie St. G51	34	S12
Mackeith St. G40	52	X14
Mackenzie Dr. (Mill.Pk.),	42	B15
John. PA10		
Mackie St. G4	22	W10
Borron St.		
Mackiesmill Rd. (Elder.),	44	F16
John. PA5		
Mackinlay St. G5	51	V14
Maclay Av. (Kilb.), John.	42	B15
PA10		
Maclean St. G51	34	T13
Maclean St., Clyde. G81	18	N8
Wood Quad.		
Maclehose Rd. (Cumb.) G67	71	QQ2
Maclellan St. G41	34	T13
Macleod Way (Camb.) G72	67	CC17
Macarthur Wynd		
Macmillan Gdns. (Udd.) G71	57	HH16
Madison Av. G44	63	V17
Madison La. G44	63	V17
Carmunnock Rd.		
Madras Pl. G40	52	X14
Madras St.		
Madras St. G40	52	X14
Mafeking St. G51	34	S13
Magdalen Way, Pais. PA2	44	F16
Magnolia Dr. (Camb.) G72	67	DD18
Magnus Cres. G44	63	V18
Mahon Ct. (Mood.) G69	15	GG7
Maidland Rd. G53	49	Q16
Mailerbeg Gdns. (Chry.) G69	15	GG6
Mailing Av. (Bishop.) G64	11	Y7
Main Rd. (Elder.), John. PA5	44	F14
Main Rd. (Millarston), Pais.	44	F14
PA1		
Main Rd. (Castlehead), Pais.	46	J14
PA2		
Main St. G40	52	X14
Main St. (Thorn.) G46	61	R18
Main St. (Cumb.) G67	71	PP1

123

Name		
Main St. (Bail.) G69	56	EE14
Main St. (Chry.) G69	26	FF8
Main St. (Both.) G71	69	HH19
Main St. (Udd.) G71	69	GG17
Main St. (Camb.) G72	66	BB17
Main St. (Ruther.) G73	53	Y16
Main St. (Barr.) G78	59	L19
Mainhead Ter. (Cumb.) G67	71	PP1
Roadside		
Mainhill Av. (Bail.) G69	40	FF13
Mainhill Dr. (Bail.) G69	40	FF13
Mainhill Pl. (Bail.) G69	40	FF13
Mainhill Rd. (Bail.) G69	41	GG13
Mains Av. (Giff.) G46	62	S19
Mains Dr., Ersk. PA8	4	J7
Mains Hill, Ersk. PA8	4	J7
Mains River, Ersk. PA8	4	J7
Mains Wd., Ersk. PA8	4	J7
Mainscroft, Ersk. PA8	4	J7
Mair St. G51	35	U13
Maitland Pl., Renf. PA4	31	L11
Maitland St. G4	35	V11
Malcolm St. G31	37	Z13
Malin Pl. G33	38	AA12
Mallaig Path G51	33	Q12
Mallaig Pl. G51	33	Q12
Mallaig Rd. G51	33	Q12
Mallard Rd., Clyde. G81	5	L5
Malloch Cres. (Elder.), John. PA5	44	E15
Malloch St. G20	21	U9
Maltbarns St. G20	21	V10
Malvern Ct. G31	37	Y13
Malvern Way, Pais. PA3	30	J12
Mambeg Dr. G51	33	R12
Mamore Pl. G43	62	T17
Mamore St. G43	62	T17
Manchester Dr. G12	20	S9
Manitoba Pl. G31	37	Y13
Janefield St.		
Mannering Ct. G41	50	T16
Pollokshaws Rd.		
Mannering Rd. G41	50	T16
Mannering Rd., Pais. PA2	45	G16
Mannofield (Bears.) G61	7	Q6
Chesters Rd.		
Manor Rd. G14	19	R10
Manor Rd. G15	6	N7
Manor Rd. (Gart.) G69	27	GG9
Manor Rd., Pais. PA2	45	G15
Manor Way (Ruther.) G73	65	Y18
Manresa Pl. G4	35	V11
Braid Sq.		
Manse Av. (Bears.) G61	7	R5
Manse Av. (Both.) G71	69	HH19
Manse Brae G44	63	V17
Manse Ct. (Barr.) G78	59	M18
Manse Gdns. G32	55	CC14
Manse Rd. G32	55	CC14
Manse Rd. (Bears.) G61	7	R5
Manse Rd. (Bail.) G69	41	GG13
Manse St., Renf. PA4	17	M10
Mansefield Av. (Camb.) G72	66	BB18
Mansefield Dr. (Udd.) G71	69	GG17
Mansel St. G21	22	X9
Mansewood Rd. G43	62	S17
Mansfield Rd. G52	32	N12
Mansfield St. G11	34	T11
Mansion Ct. (Camb.) G72	66	BB17
Mansion St. G22	22	W9
Mansion St. (Camb.) G72	66	BB17
Mansionhouse Av. G32	55	CC16
Mansionhouse Dr. G32	39	CC13
Mansionhouse Gdns. G41	51	U16
Mansionhouse Rd.		
Mansionhouse Gro. G32	55	DD14
Mansionhouse Rd. G32	55	DD14
Mansionhouse Rd. G41	51	U16
Mansionhouse Rd. G42	51	U16
Mansionhouse Rd., Pais. PA1	31	L13
Manus Duddy Ct. (Blan.) G72	68	FF19
Maple Cres. (Camb.) G72	67	DD18
Maple Dr. (Kirk.) G66	12	BB5
Maple Dr. (Barr.) G78	59	M19
Maple Dr., Clyde. G81	4	K5
Maple Dr., John. PA5	44	E16
Maple Rd. G41	50	S14
Mar Gdns. (Ruther.) G73	65	Z18
March La. G41	51	U15
Nithsdale Dr.		
March St. G41	51	U15
Marchbank Gdns., Pais. PA1	47	M14
Marchfield (Bishop.) G64	10	X6
Marchfield Av., Pais. PA3	30	J12
Marchglen Pl. G51	33	Q12
Mallaig Rd.		
Marchmont Gdns. (Bishop.) G64	10	X6
Marchmont Ter. G12	20	T10
Observatory Rd.		
Maree Dr. G52	49	R14
Maree Gdns. (Bishop.) G64	11	Y7
Maree Rd., Pais. PA2	45	H15
Marfield St. G32	38	AA13
Margaret St. G1	36	W12
Martha St.		
Margaretta Bldgs. G44	63	V17
Clarkston Rd.		
Marguerite Av. (Lenzie) G66	13	CC5
Marguerite Dr. (Kirk.) G66	13	CC5
Marguerite Gdns. (Kirk.) G66	13	CC5
Marguerite Gdns. (Both.) G71	69	HH18
Marguerite Gro. (Kirk.) G66	13	CC5
Marine Cres. G51	35	U13
Marine Gdns. G51	35	U13
Mavisbank Gdns.		
Mariscat Rd. G41	51	U15
Marjory Dr., Pais. PA3	31	L12
Marjory Rd., Renf. PA4	31	L11
Markdown Av. G53	48	P15
Market St. G40	36	X13
Markinch St. G5	35	V13
West St.		
Marlach Pl. G53	48	P16
Marlborough Av. G11	19	R10
Marlborough La. N. G11	19	R10
Marlborough Av.		
Marlborough La. S. G11	19	R10
Marlborough Av.		
Marldon La. G11	19	R10
Marlborough Av.		
Marlow St. G41	51	U14
Marlow Ter. G41	35	U13
Seaward St.		
Marmion Pl. (Cumb.) G67	70	NN4
Marmion Rd. (Cumb.) G67	70	NN4
Marmion Rd., Pais. PA2	45	G16
Marmion St. G20	21	U10
Marne St. G31	37	Y12
Marnock Ter., Pais. PA2	47	L15
Marnock Way (Chry.) G69	15	GG7
Braeside Av.		
Marquis Gate (Udd.) G71	69	GG17
Marshall's La., Pais. PA1	46	K14
Mart St. G1	36	W13
Martha St. G1	36	W12
Martin Cres. (Bail.) G69	40	FF13
Martin St. G40	52	X14
Martlet Dr., John. PA5	43	C16
Martyrs Pl. (Bishop.) G64	23	Y8
Marwick St. G31	37	Y12
Mary Sq. (Bail.) G69	41	GG13
Mary St. G4	35	V11
Mary St., John. PA5	44	E14
Mary St., Pais. PA2	46	K15
Maryhill Rd. G20	20	S8
Maryhill Rd. (Bears.) G61	8	S7
Maryland Dr. G52	33	R13
Maryland Gdns. G52	33	R13
Marys La., Renf. PA4	17	M10
Maryston Pl. G33	37	Z11
Maryston St. G33	37	Z11
Maryview Gdns. (Udd.) G71	56	FF15
Old Edinburgh Rd.		
Maryville Av. (Giff.) G46	62	T19
Maryville Gdns. (Giff.) G46	62	S19
Maryville Vw. (Udd.) G71	56	FF15
Marywood Sq. G41	51	U15
Masonfield Av. (Cumb.) G68	70	MM3
Masterton St. G21	22	W10
Mathieson La. G5	52	W14
Mathieson St.		
Mathieson Rd. (Ruther.) G73	53	Z15
Mathieson St. G5	52	W14
Mathieson St., Pais. PA1	31	L13
Matilda Rd. G41	51	U14
Mauchline St. G5	51	V14
Maukinfauld Ct. G32	54	AA14
Maukinfauld Rd. G32	54	AA14
Mauldslie St. G40	53	Y14
Maule Dr. G11	34	S11
Mavis Bk. (Bishop.) G64	22	X8
Mavisbank Gdns. G51	35	U13
Mavisbank Rd. G51	34	S12
Govan Rd.		
Mavisbank Ter., Pais. PA1	46	K14
Maxton Av. (Barr.) G78	59	L18
Maxton Gro. (Barr.) G78	59	L18
Maxton Ter. (Camb.) G72	66	AA18
Maxwell Av. G41	51	U14
Maxwell Av. (Bears.) G61	7	R7
Maxwell Av. (Bail.) G69	56	EE14
Maxwell Dr. G41	50	T14
Maxwell Dr. (Bail.) G69	40	EE13
Maxwell Gdns. G41	50	T14
Maxwell Gro. G41	50	T14
Maxwell La. G41	51	U14
Maxwell Oval G41	51	U14
Maxwell Pl. G41	51	V14
Maxwell Pl. (Udd.) G71	69	HH17
North British Road		
Maxwell Rd. G41	51	U14
Maxwell Sq. G41	51	U14
Maxwell St. G1	36	W13
Maxwell St. (Bail.) G69	56	EE14
Maxwell St., Clyde. G81	4	K6
Maxwell St., Pais. PA3	30	K13
Old Sneddon St.		
Maxwellton Rd., Pais. PA1	45	H14
Maxwellton St., Pais. PA1	46	J14
Maxwellton Trd. Est., Pais. PA1	45	H14
Maxwelton Rd. G33	37	Z11
May Rd., Pais. PA2	46	K16
May Ter. G42	51	V16
Prospecthill Rd.		
May Ter. (Giff.) G46	62	T18
Maybank La. G42	51	V15
Victoria Rd.		
Maybank St. G42	51	V15
Mayberry Cres. G32	39	CC13
Mayberry Gdns. G32	39	CC13
Mayberry Gro. G32	39	CC13
Maybole St. G53	60	N17
Mayfield St. G20	21	U9
McAlpine St. G2	35	V13
McArthur St. G43	50	T16
Pleasance St.		
McAslin Ct. G4	36	W12
McAslin St. G4	36	X12
McCallum Av. (Ruther.) G73	53	Y16
McClue Av., Renf. PA4	17	L10
McClue Rd., Renf. PA4	17	L10
McCracken Av., Renf. PA4	31	L11
McCreery St., Clyde. G81	17	M8
McCulloch St. G41	51	U14
McDonald Av., John. PA5	43	D15
McDonald Cres., Clyde. G81	17	M8
McFarlane St. G4	36	X13
McFarlane St., Pais. PA3	30	J12
McGhee St., Clyde. G81	5	L6
McGown St., Pais. PA3	30	J13
McGregor Av., Renf. PA4	31	L11
Porterfield Rd.		
McGregor Rd. (Cumb.) G67	70	NN3
McGregor St. G51	33	R13
McGregor St., Clyde. G81	17	M8
McIntosh Ct. G31	36	X12
McIntosh St.		
McIntosh St. G31	36	X12
McIntyre Pl., Pais. PA2	46	K15
McIntyre St. G3	35	U12
McIntyre Ter. (Camb.) G72	66	BB17
McIver St. (Camb.) G72	67	CC17
McKay Cres., John. PA5	44	E15
McKenzie Av., Clyde. G81	5	L6
McKenzie St., Pais. PA3	29	H13
McKerrell St., Pais. PA1	31	L13
McLaren Av., Renf. PA4	31	M11
Newmains Rd.		
McLaren Ct. (Giff.) G46	62	S19
Fenwick Pl.		
McLaren Cres. G20	21	U8
McLaren Gdns. G20	21	U8
McLaurin Cres., John. PA5	43	C15
McLean Pl., Pais. PA3	30	J12
McLean Sq. G51	34	T13
McLennan St. G42	51	V16
McLeod St. G4	36	X12
McNair St. G32	38	BB13
McNeil St. G5	52	W14
McNeill Av., Clyde. G81	6	N7
McPhail St. G40	52	X14

McPhater St. G4   35   V11
Dunblane St.
McPherson Dr. (Both.) G71   69   HH18
Wordsworth Way
McPherson St. G1   36   W13
High St.
McTaggart Rd. (Cumb.) G67   70   NN4
Meadow La., Renf. PA4   17   M9
Meadow Rd. G11   34   S11
Meadow Vw. (Cumb.) G67   71   QQ2
Meadowbank La. (Udd.) G71   68   FF17
Meadowburn (Bishop.) G64   11   Y6
Meadowburn Av. (Lenzie)   13   DD5
G66
Meadowhead Av. (Chry.)   15   GG7
G69
Meadowpark St. G31   37   Y12
Meadowside Av. (Elder.),   44   F15
John. PA5
Meadowside Quay St. G11   33   R11
Meadowside St. G11   34   S11
Meadowside St., Renf. PA4   17   M9
Meadowwell St. G32   38   BB13
Meadside Av. (Kilb.), John.   42   B14
PA10
Meadside Rd. (Kilb.), John.   42   B14
PA10
Mearns Way (Bishop.) G64   11   Z7
Medlar Ct. (Camb.) G72   67   DD18
Maple Cres.
Medlar Rd. (Cumb.) G67   71   QQ3
Medwin St. (Camb.) G72   67   DD17
Mill Rd.
Medwyn St. G14   19   Q10
Meek Pl. (Camb.) G72   66   BB17
Meetinghouse La., Pais. PA1   30   K13
Moss St.
Megan Gate G40   52   X14
Megan St.
Megan St. G40   52   X14
Meikle Av., Renf. PA4   31   M11
Meikle Rd. G53   49   Q16
Meiklerig Cres. G53   49   Q15
Meikleriggs Dr., Pais. PA2   45   H15
Meiklewood Rd. G51   33   Q13
Melbourne Av., Clyde. G81   4   J5
Melbourne Ct. (Giff.) G46   62   T18
Melbourne St. G31   36   X13
Meldon Pl. G51   33   R12
Meldrum Gdns. G41   50   T15
Meldrum St., Clyde. G81   18   N8
Melford Av. (Giff.) G46   62   T19
Melford Way, Pais. PA3   31   L12
Knock Way
Melfort Av. G41   50   S14
Melfort Av., Clyde. G81   5   L6
Melfort Gdns. (Mill.Pk.),   43   C15
John. PA10
Milliken Pk. Rd.
Mellerstain Dr. G14   18   N9
Melness Pl. G51   33   Q12
Mallaig Rd.
Melrose Av. (Bail.) G69   41   GG13
Melrose Av. (Ruther.) G73   53   Y16
Melrose Av., Pais. PA2   45   H15
Melrose Av. (Linw.), Pais.   28   E13
PA3
Melrose Ct. (Ruther.) G73   53   Y16
Dunard Rd.
Melrose Gdns. G20   21   U10
Melrose Gdns. (Udd.) G71   57   GG15
Lincoln Av.
Melrose Pl. (Blan.) G72   68   FF19
Melrose St. G4   35   V11
Queens Cres.
Melvaig Pl. G20   20   T9
Melvick Pl. G51   33   Q12
Mallaig Rd.
Melville Ct. G1   36   W12
Brunswick St.
Melville Gdns. (Bishop.) G64   11   Y7
Melville St. G41   51   U14
Memel St. G21   22   X9
Memus Av. G52   49   Q14
Mennock Dr. (Bishop.) G64   11   Y6
Menock Rd. G44   63   V17
Menteith Av. (Bishop.)   11   Y7
G64
Menteith Dr. (Ruther.) G73   65   Z19
Menteith Pl. (Ruther.) G73   65   Z19
Menzies Dr. G21   23   Y9
Menzies Pl. G21   23   Y9

Menzies Rd. G21   23   Y9
Merchant La. G1   36   W13
Clyde St.
Merchants Clo. (Kilb.), John.   42   B14
PA10
Church St.
Merchiston St. G32   38   AA12
Merkland Ct. G11   34   S11
Vine St.
Merkland St. G11   34   S11
Merksworth Way, Pais. PA3   30   J12
Mosslands Rd.
Merlewood Av. (Both.) G71   69   HH18
Merlin Way, Pais. PA3   31   L12
Merlinford Av., Renf. PA4   18   N10
Merlinford Cres., Renf. PA4   18   N10
Merlinford Dr., Renf. PA4   18   N10
Merlinford Way, Renf. PA4   18   N10
Merrick Gdns. G51   34   S13
Merrick Ter. (Udd.) G71   57   HH16
Merrick Way (Ruther.) G73   65   Y18
Merryburn Av. (Giff.) G46   62   T17
Merrycrest Av. (Giff.) G46   62   T18
Merrycroft Av. (Giff.) G46   62   T18
Merryland Pl. G51   34   T12
Merryland St. G51   34   S12
Merrylee Cres. (Giff.) G46   62   T17
Merrylee Pk. Av. (Giff.) G46   62   T17
Merrylee Pk. La. (Giff.) G46   62   T18
Merrylee Pk. Ms. (Giff.) G46   62   T18
Merrylee Rd. G43   62   T17
Merrylee Rd. G44   62   T17
Merryton Av. G15   6   P6
Merryton Av. (Giff.) G46   62   T18
Merryton Pl. G15   6   P6
Merryvale Av. (Giff.) G46   62   T18
Merryvale Pl. (Giff.) G46   62   T17
Merton Dr. G52   32   P13
Meryon Gdns. G32   55   CC15
Meryon Rd. G32   55   CC15
Methil St. G14   19   Q10
Methuen Rd., Pais. PA3   31   L11
Methven Av. (Bears.) G61   8   S5
Methven St. G31   53   Z14
Methven St., Clyde. G81   4   K6
Metropole La. G1   35   V13
Howard St.
Mews La., Pais. PA3   30   K12
Renfrew Rd.
Mickelhouse Oval (Bail.) G69   40   EE13
Micklehouse Rd.
Micklehouse Pl. (Bail.) G69   40   EE13
Micklehouse Rd.
Micklehouse Rd. (Bail.) G69   40   EE13
Micklehouse Wynd (Bail.)   40   EE13
G69
Micklehouse Rd.
Mid Cotts. (Gart.) G69   26   FF10
Midcroft (Bishop.) G64   10   X6
Midcroft Av. G44   64   W17
Middle Pk., Pais. PA2   46   J15
Middlemuir Av. (Kirk.) G66   13   CC5
Middlemuir Rd. (Lenzie) G66   13   CC5
Middlerigg Rd. (Cumb.) G68   70   MM3
Middlesex Gdns. G41   35   U13
Middlesex St. G41   35   U13
Middleton Cres., Pais. PA3   30   J13
Middleton Rd., Pais. PA3   28   F13
Middleton St. G51   34   T13
Midfaulds Av., Renf. PA4   32   N11
King George Pk. Av.
Midland St. G1   35   V13
Midlem Dr. G52   33   Q13
Midlem Oval G52   33   Q13
Midlock St. G51   34   T13
Midlothian Dr. G41   50   T15
Midton Cotts. (Mood.) G69   15   HH7
Midton St. G21   22   X10
Midwharf St. G4   36   W11
Migvie Pl. G20   20   T9
Wyndford Rd.
Milan St. G41   51   V14
Milford St. G33   38   BB12
Mill Ct. (Ruther.) G73   53   Y16
Mill Cres. G40   52   X14
Mill Pl. (Linw.), Pais. PA3   28   E13
Mill Ri. (Lenzie) G66   13   CC6
Mill Rd. (Both.) G71   69   HH19
Mill Rd. (Camb.) G72   67   CC18
Mill Rd., Clyde. G81   17   M8
Mill St. G40   52   X14
Mill St. (Ruther.) G73   53   Y16

Mill St., Pais. PA1   46   K14
Mill Vennel, Renf. PA4   18   N10
High St.
Millands Av. (Blan.) G72   68   FF19
Millar St., Pais. PA1   30   K13
Millar Ter. (Ruther.) G73   53   Y15
Millarbank St. G21   22   X10
Millarston Av., Pais. PA1   45   H14
Millarston Dr., Pais. PA1   45   H14
Millbeg Cres. G33   39   DD13
Millbeg Pl. G33   39   DD13
Millbrae Ct. G42   51   U16
Millbrae Rd.
Millbrae Cres. G42   51   U16
Millbrae Cres., Clyde. G81   17   M8
Millbrae Gdns. G42   51   U16
Millbrae Rd.
Millbrae Rd. G42   51   U16
Millbrix Av. G14   18   P9
Millburn Av. (Ruther.) G73   65   Y17
Millburn Av., Clyde. G81   18   N8
Millburn Av., Renf. PA4   17   M10
Millburn Dr., Renf. PA4   18   N10
Millburn Rd., Renf. PA4   17   M10
Millburn St. G21   37   Y11
Millburn Way, Renf. PA4   18   N10
Millcroft Rd. (Cumb.) G67   71   PP3
Millcroft Rd. (Ruther.) G73   52   X15
Millennium Gdns. G34   40   FF12
Miller St. G1   36   W12
Miller St. (Bail.) G69   56   EE14
Miller St., Clyde. G81   5   L7
Miller St., John. PA5   44   E14
Millerfield Pl. G40   53   Y14
Millerfield Rd. G40   53   Y14
Millers Pl. (Lenzie) G66   13   CC6
Millersneuk Av. (Lenzie) G66   13   CC6
Millersneuk Cres. G33   24   BB9
Millersneuk Dr. (Lenzie) G66   13   CC6
Millerston St. G31   37   Y13
Millford Dr. (Linw.), Pais. PA3   28   E13
Millgate (Udd.) G71   57   GG16
Millgate Av. (Udd.) G71   57   GG16
Millgate Ct. (Udd.) G71   57   GG16
Millholm Rd. G44   63   V18
Millhouse Cres. G20   20   T8
Millhouse Dr. G20   20   T8
Millichen Rd. G23   8   T5
Milliken Dr. (Mill.Pk.), John.   43   C15
PA10
Milliken Pk. Rd. (Mill.Pk.),   43   C15
John. PA10
Milliken Rd. (Mill.Pk.), John.   43   C15
PA10
Millpond Dr. G40   36   X13
Millport Av. G44   52   W16
Millroad Dr. G40   36   X13
Millroad Gdns. G40   36   X13
Millroad St. G40   36   X13
Millview (Barr.) G78   59   M18
Millview Pl. G53   60   P18
Millwood St. G41   51   U16
Milnbank St. G31   37   Y12
Milncroft Rd. G33   38   BB11
Milner La. G13   19   R9
Southbrae Dr.
Milner Rd. G13   19   R9
Milngavie Rd. (Bears.) G61   7   R6
Milnpark Gdns. G41   35   U13
Milnpark St. G41   35   U13
Milovaig Av. G23   8   T7
Milovaig St. G23   8   T7
Milrig Rd. (Ruther.) G73   52   X16
Milton Av. (Camb.) G72   66   AA17
Milton Douglas Rd., Clyde.   5   L5
G81
Milton Dr. (Bishop.) G64   22   X8
Milton Gdns. (Udd.) G71   57   GG16
Milton Mains Rd., Clyde.   5   L5
G81
Milton St. G4   35   V11
Milverton Av. (Bears.) G61   7   Q5
Milverton Rd. (Giff.) G46   62   S19
Minard Rd. G41   51   U15
Minard Way (Udd.) G71   57   HH16
Newton Dr.
Minerva St. G3   35   U12
Minerva Way G3   35   U12
Mingarry La. G20   20   T10
Clouston St.
Mingarry St. G20   21   U10
Mingulay Cres. G22   22   W8

Name	Page	Grid
Mingulay Pl. G22	22	X8
Mingulay St. G22	22	W8
Minister Wk. (Bail.) G69	41	GG13
Dukes Rd.		
Minmoir Rd. G53	48	N16
Minstrel Rd. G13	7	Q7
Minto Av. (Ruther.) G73	65	Z18
Minto Cres. G52	33	R13
Minto St. G52	33	R13
Mireton St. G22	21	V9
Mirrlees Dr. G12	20	T10
Mirrlees La. G12	20	T10
Redlands Rd.		
Mitchell Av. (Camb.) G72	67	DD17
Mitchell Av., Renf. PA4	31	L11
Mitchell Dr. (Ruther.) G73	65	Y17
Mitchell La. G1	35	V12
Buchanan St.		
Mitchell Rd. (Cumb.) G67	71	PP3
Mitchell St. G1	35	V12
Mitchell St., Coat. ML5	57	HH14
Mitchellhill Rd. G45	64	X19
Mitchison Rd. (Cumb.) G67	71	PP2
Mitre Ct. G11	19	R10
Mitre Rd.		
Mitre La. G14	19	R10
Mitre La. W. G14	19	R10
Mitre La.		
Mitre Rd. G11	19	R10
Mitre Rd. G14	19	R10
Moat Av. G13	19	Q8
Mochrum Rd. G43	63	U17
Moffat Pl. (Blan.) G72	68	FF19
Moffat St. G5	52	W14
Mogarth Av., Pais. PA2	45	H16
Amochrie Rd.		
Moidart Av., Renf. PA4	17	L10
Moidart Ct. (Barr.) G78	59	L18
Moidart Cres. G52	33	R13
Moidart Rd.		
Moidart Pl. G52	33	R13
Moidart Rd.		
Moidart Rd. G52	33	R13
Moir La. G1	36	W13
Moir St.		
Moir St. G1	36	W13
Molendinar St. G1	36	W13
Mollinsburn St. G21	22	X10
Monach Rd. G33	39	CC12
Monachie Gdns. (Bishop.) G64	11	Z7
Muirhead Way		
Monar Dr. G22	21	V10
Monar Pl. G22	21	V10
Monar St. G22	21	V10
Monart Pl. G20	21	U10
Caithness St.		
Moncrieff Av. (Lenzie) G66	13	CC5
Moncrieff Gdns. (Kirk.) G66	13	CC5
Moncrieff Av.		
Moncrieff Pl. G20	35	V11
North Woodside Rd.		
Moncrieff St. G4	35	V11
Braid Sq.		
Moncur St. G40	36	X13
Moness Dr. G52	49	R14
Monifieth Av. G52	49	Q14
Monikie Gdns. (Bishop.) G64	11	Z7
Muirhead Way		
Monkcastle Dr. (Camb.) G72	66	BB17
Monkland Av. (Kirk.) G66	13	CC5
Monkland Vw. (Udd.) G71	57	HH15
Lincoln Av.		
Monkland Vw. Cres. (Bail.) G69	41	HH13
Monksbridge Av. G13	7	Q7
Monkscroft Av. G11	20	S10
Monkscroft Ct. G11	34	S11
Monkscroft Gdns. G11	20	S10
Monkscroft Av.		
Monkton Dr. G15	6	P7
Monmouth Av. G12	20	S9
Monreith Av. (Bears.) G61	7	Q7
Monreith Rd. G43	62	T17
Monreith Rd. E. G44	63	V17
Monroe Dr. (Udd.) G71	57	GG15
Monroe Pl. (Udd.) G71	57	GG15
Montague La. G12	20	S10
Montague St. G4	35	U11
Montague Ter. G12	20	S10
Hyndland Rd.		
Montclair Pl. (Linw.), Pais. PA3	28	E13
Monteith Dr. (Clark.) G76	63	V19
Monteith Pl. G40	36	X13
Monteith Row G40	36	X13
Monteith Row La. G40	36	X13
Monteith Pl.		
Montford Av. G44	52	W16
Montford Av. (Ruther.) G73	52	W16
Montgomerie Gdns. G14	19	Q10
Lennox Av.		
Montgomery Av., Pais. PA3	31	L12
Montgomery Dr. (Giff.) G46	62	T19
Montgomery Dr. (Kilb.), John. PA10	42	B14
Meadside Av.		
Montgomery La. G42	51	V16
Somerville Dr.		
Montgomery Pl. (Camb.) G72	68	EE17
Newton Fm. Rd.		
Montgomery Rd., Pais. PA3	31	L12
Montgomery St. G40	52	X14
London Rd.		
Montgomery St. (Camb.) G72	67	DD17
Mill Rd.		
Montrave St. G52	49	Q14
Montrave St. (Ruther.) G73	53	Z15
Montreal Ho., Clyde. G81	4	J5
Perth Cres.		
Montrose Av. G32	54	BB15
Montrose Av. G52	32	N12
Montrose Gdns. (Blan.) G72	68	FF19
Montrose Pl. (Linw.), Pais. PA3	28	E13
Montrose Rd., Pais. PA2	45	G16
Montrose St. G1	36	W12
Montrose St. G4	36	W12
Montrose St., Clyde. G81	5	L7
Montrose Ter. (Bishop.) G64	23	Z8
Monument Dr. G33	24	AA9
Monymusk Gdns. (Bishop.) G64	11	Z7
Monymusk Pl. G15	6	N5
Moodies Ct. G1	36	W13
Osborne St.		
Moodiesburn St. G33	37	Z11
Moorburn Av. (Giff.) G46	62	S18
Moore Dr. (Bears.) G61	7	R6
Moore St. G31	37	Y13
Gallowgate		
Moorfoot (Bishop.) G64	11	Z7
Moorfoot Av. (Thorn.) G46	62	S18
Moorfoot Av., Pais. PA2	46	J15
Moorfoot St. G32	38	AA13
Moorhouse Av. G13	18	N9
Moorhouse Av., Pais. PA2	45	H15
Moorhouse St. (Barr.) G78	59	M19
Moorings, The, Pais. PA2	45	H14
Moorpark Av. G52	32	N13
Moorpark Av. (Muir.) G69	26	FF8
Cumbernauld Rd.		
Moorpark Dr. G52	32	P13
Moorpark Pl. G52	32	N13
Moorpark Sq., Renf. PA4	31	L11
Morag Av. (Blan.) G72	68	FF19
Moraine Av. G15	6	P7
Moraine Circ. G15	6	P7
Moraine Dr. G15	6	P7
Moraine Pl. G15	6	P7
Moraine Dr.		
Morar Av., Clyde. G81	5	L6
Morar Ct. (Cumb.) G67	70	LL4
Morar Ct., Clyde. G81	5	L6
Morar Cres. (Bishop.) G64	10	X7
Morar Cres., Clyde. G81	5	L6
Morar Dr. (Bears.) G61	8	S6
Morar Dr. (Cumb.) G67	70	LL4
Morar Dr. (Ruther.) G73	65	Y18
Morar Dr., Clyde. G81	5	L6
Morar Dr., Pais. PA2	45	G15
Morar Dr. (Linw.), Pais. PA3	28	E13
Morar Pl., Clyde. G81	5	L6
Morar Pl., Renf. PA4	17	L10
Morar Rd. G52	33	R13
Morar Rd., Clyde. G81	5	L6
Morar Ter. (Udd.) G71	57	HH16
Morar Ter. (Ruther.) G73	65	Z18
Moravia Av. (Both.) G71	69	HH18
Moray Ct. (Ruther.) G73	53	Y16
Moray Gdns. (Cumb.) G68	71	PP1
Moray Gdns. (Udd.) G71	57	GG16
Moray Gate (Both.) G71	69	GG18
Moray Pl. G41	51	U15
Moray Pl. (Bishop.) G64	11	Z7
Moray Pl. (Linw.), Pais. PA3	28	E13
Mordaunt St. G40	53	Y14
Moredun Cres. G32	39	CC12
Moredun Dr., Pais. PA2	45	H15
Moredun Rd., Pais. PA2	45	H15
Moredun St. G32	39	CC12
Morefield Rd. G51	33	Q12
Morgan Ms. G42	51	V14
Morina Gdns. G53	61	Q19
Morion Rd. G13	19	Q8
Morley St. G42	51	V16
Morna Pl. G14	33	R11
Victoria Pk. Dr. S.		
Morningside St. G33	37	Z12
Morrin Path G21	22	X10
Crichton St.		
Morrin Sq. G4	36	X12
Collins St.		
Morrin St. G21	22	X10
Morris Pl. G40	36	X13
Morrison Quad., Clyde. G81	6	N7
Morrison St. G5	35	V13
Morrison St., Clyde. G81	4	K5
Morrisons Ct. G2	35	V12
Argyle St.		
Morriston Cres., Renf. PA4	32	N11
Morriston Pk. Dr. (Camb.) G72	54	BB16
Morriston St. (Camb.) G72	66	BB17
Mortimer St. G20	21	U10
Hotspur St.		
Morton Gdns. G41	50	T15
Morven Av. (Bishop.) G64	11	Z7
Morven Av. (Blan.) G72	68	FF19
Morven Av., Pais. PA2	46	J16
Morven Dr. (Linw.), Pais. PA3	28	E13
Morven Gdns. (Udd.) G71	57	GG16
Morven Rd. (Bears.) G61	7	R5
Morven Rd. (Camb.) G72	66	AA18
Morven St. G52	33	R13
Mosesfield St. G21	22	X9
Mosesfield Ter. G21	22	X9
Balgrayhill Rd.		
Moss Av. (Linw.), Pais. PA3	28	E13
Moss Dr. (Barr.) G78	59	L17
Moss Hts. Av. G52	33	Q13
Moss Knowe (Cumb.) G67	71	QQ3
Moss Path (Bail.) G69	55	DD14
Castle St.		
Moss Rd. G51	33	Q12
Moss Rd. (Kirk.) G66	13	CC5
Moss Rd. (Cumb.) G67	71	RR2
Moss Rd. (Muir.) G69	26	FF8
Moss St., Pais. PA1	30	K13
Moss-side Rd. G41	50	T15
Mossbank Av. G33	24	AA10
Mossbank Dr. G33	24	AA10
Mosscastle Rd. G33	39	CC11
Mossend La. G33	39	CC12
Mossend Rd., Pais. PA3	30	J12
Mosslands Rd.		
Mossend St. G33	39	CC12
Mossgiel Av. (Ruther.) G73	65	Y17
Mossgiel Dr., Clyde. G81	5	M6
Mossgiel Gdns. (Udd.) G71	57	GG16
Mossgiel Pl. (Ruther.) G73	65	Y17
Mossgiel Rd. G43	62	T17
Mossgiel Rd. (Cumb.) G67	71	PP3
Mossgiel Ter. (Blan.) G72	68	FF19
Mossland Rd. G52	32	N12
Mosslands Rd., Pais. PA3	30	J12
Mossneuk Dr., Pais. PA2	46	J16
Mosspark Av. G52	49	R14
Mosspark Boul. G52	49	R14
Mosspark Dr. G52	49	Q14
Mosspark La. G52	49	R15
Mosspark Dr.		
Mosspark Oval G52	49	R14
Mosspark Sq. G52	49	R14
Mossvale Cres. G33	39	CC11
Mossvale La., Pais. PA3	30	J13
Mossvale Path G33	25	CC10
Mossvale Rd. G33	24	BB10
Mossvale Sq. G33	39	CC11
Mossvale Sq., Pais. PA3	30	J13
Mossvale St., Pais. PA3	30	J12
Mossvale Ter. (Chry.) G69	15	HH6

Name	Page	Grid
Ochil St. G32	54	BB14
Ochil Vw. (Udd.) G71	57	HH16
Ochiltree Av. G13	19	R8
Ogilvie Pl. G31	54	AA14
Ogilvie St. G31	53	Z14
Old Bothwell Rd. (Both.) G71	69	HH19
Old Castle Rd. G44	63	V17
Old Cotts., Pais. PA2	47	M16
Grahamston Rd.		
Old Dalmarnock Rd. G40	52	X14
Old Dalnottar Rd. (Old Kil.) G60	4	J5
Old Dumbarton Rd. G3	34	T11
Old Edinburgh Rd. (Udd.) G71	57	GG15
Old Gartloch Rd. (Gart.) G69	27	GG9
Old Glasgow Rd. (Udd.)	56	FF16
Old Govan Rd., Renf. PA4	18	N10
Old Greenock Rd. (Inch.), Renf. PA4	16	J8
Old Manse Rd. G32	39	CC13
Old Mill Rd. (Both.) G71	69	HH19
Old Mill Rd. (Udd.) G71	69	GG17
Old Mill Rd. (Camb.) G72	67	CC17
Old Mill Rd., Clyde. G81	5	L5
Old Mill Rd., Pais. PA2	45	H14
Old Rd. (Elder.), John. PA5	44	E14
Old Rutherglen Rd. G5	52	W14
Old Shettleston Rd. G32	38	AA13
Old Sneddon St., Pais. PA3	30	K13
Old St., Clyde. G81	4	K5
Old Wd. Rd. (Bail.) G69	56	EE14
Old Wynd G1	36	W13
Oldhall Rd., Pais. PA1	47	M14
Olifard Av. (Both.) G71	69	HH18
Oliphant Cres., Pais. PA2	45	G16
Olive St. G33	23	Z10
Olrig Ter. G41	51	U14
Shields Rd.		
Olympia St. G40	36	X13
O'Neil Av. (Bishop.) G64	23	Y8
Onslow Dr. G31	37	Y12
Onslow Rd., Clyde. G81	5	M7
Onslow Sq. G31	37	Y12
Onslow Dr.		
Oran Gdns. G20	21	U9
Oran Gate G20	21	U10
Oran Pl. G20	21	U9
Oran St. G20	21	U9
Oransay Ct. (Old Kil.) G60	4	J5
Oransay Cres. (Old Kil.) G60	4	J5
Oransay Gdns. (Old Kil.) G60	4	J5
Orbiston Gdns. G32	38	BB13
Balintore St.		
Orcades Dr. G44	63	V18
Orchard Av. (Both.) G71	69	HH19
Orchard Brae (Lenzie) G66	13	DD6
Lindsaybeg Rd.		
Orchard Ct. G32	54	BB16
Orchard Ct. (Thorn.) G46	62	S18
Orchard Dr. (Giff.) G46	62	S18
Orchard Dr. (Ruther.) G73	52	X16
Orchard Gro. (Giff.) G46	62	S18
Orchard Pk. (Giff.) G46	62	T18
Orchard Pk. Av. (Giff.) G46	62	S18
Orchard St., Pais. PA1	46	K14
Orchard St., Renf. PA4	17	M10
Orchardfield (Lenzie) G66	13	DD6
Orchy Ct., Clyde. G81	5	M5
Orchy Cres. (Bears.) G61	7	Q7
Orchy Cres., Pais. PA2	45	G15
Orchy Dr. (Clark.) G76	63	U19
Orchy Gdns. (Clark.) G76	63	U19
Orchy St. G44	63	V17
Oregon Pl. G5	52	W14
Orion Way (Camb.) G72	66	BB17
Orkney Pl. G51	34	S12
Orkney St.		
Orkney St. G51	34	S12
Orleans Av. G14	19	R10
Orleans La. G14	19	R10
Ormiston Av. G14	19	Q10
Ormiston La. G14	19	Q10
Ormiston Av.		
Ormiston La. N. G14	19	Q10
Ormiston Av.		
Ormiston La. S. G14	19	Q10
Ormiston Av.		
Ormonde Av. G44	63	U18
Ormonde Ct. G44	63	U18
Ormonde Cres. G44	63	U18
Ormonde Dr. G44	63	U18
Ornsay St. G22	22	W8
Oronsay Cres. (Bears.) G61	8	S6
Orr Pl. G40	36	X13
Orr Sq., Pais. PA1	30	K13
Orr St. G40	36	X13
Orr St., Pais. PA1	30	J13
Orr St., Pais. PA2	30	K13
Orton Pl. G51	34	S13
Orton St. G51	34	S13
Orwell St. G21	22	X10
Osborn Ter. G51	34	S13
Copland Rd.		
Osborne St. G1	36	W13
Osborne St., Clyde. G81	5	L6
Osborne Vill. G44	63	V17
Holmhead Rd.		
Osprey Dr. (Udd.) G71	57	HH16
Ossian Av., Pais. PA1	32	N13
Auchmannoch Av.		
Ossian Rd. G43	63	U17
Oswald La. G1	35	V13
Oswald St.		
Oswald St. G1	35	V13
Otago La. G12	35	U11
Otago St.		
Otago La. N. G12	35	U11
Otago St.		
Otago St. G12	35	U11
Ottawa Cres., Clyde. G81	4	J6
Otter La. G11	34	S11
Castlebank St.		
Otterburn Dr. (Giff.) G46	62	T19
Otterswick Pl. G33	39	CC11
Oval, The (Clark.) G76	63	U19
Overbrae Pl. G15	6	N5
Overdale Av. G42	51	U16
Overdale Gdns. G42	51	U16
Overdale St. G42	51	U16
Overdale Vills. G42	51	U16
Overdale St.		
Overlea Av. (Ruther.) G73	65	Z17
Overnewton Pl. G3	34	T12
Kelvinhaugh St.		
Overnewton Sq. G3	34	T12
Overnewton St. G3	34	T11
Overton Cres., John. PA5	44	E14
Overton Rd. (Camb.) G72	67	CC18
Overton Rd., John. PA5	44	E15
Overton St. (Camb.) G72	67	CC18
Overtoun Ct., Clyde. G81	4	K6
Dunswin Av.		
Overtoun Dr. (Ruther.) G73	53	Y16
Overtoun Dr., Clyde. G81	4	K6
Overtoun Rd., Clyde. G81	4	K6
Overtown Av. G53	60	P17
Overtown St. G31	37	Y13
Overwood Dr. G44	64	W17
Oxford Dr. (Linw.), Pais. PA3	28	E13
Oxford La. G5	35	V13
Oxford La., Renf. PA4	17	M10
Oxford Rd., Renf. PA4	17	M10
Oxford St. G5	35	V13
Oxton Dr. G52	32	P13

P

Name	Page	Grid
Pacific Dr. G51	34	T13
Pacific Quay G51	34	T12
Paisley Ct. (Barr.) G78	59	L18
Paisley Rd.		
Paisley Rd. G5	35	U13
Paisley Rd. (Barr.) G78	59	L18
Paisley Rd., Renf. PA4	31	L11
Paisley Rd. W. G51	34	S13
Paisley Rd. W. G52	48	P14
Palace St. G31	53	Z14
Paladin Av. G13	19	Q8
Palermo St. G21	22	X10
Atlas Rd.		
Palladium Pl. G14	19	Q10
Palmer Av. G13	7	Q7
Palmerston Pl. G3	34	T12
Kelvinhaugh St.		
Palmerston Pl., John. PA5	43	C16
Pandora Way (Udd.) G71	57	HH16
Hillcrest Rd.		
Panmure St. G20	21	V10
Park Av. G3	35	U11
Park Av. (Bishop.) G64	11	Y6
Park Av. (Barr.) G78	59	L19
Park Av. (Elder.), John. PA5	44	F15
Park Av., Pais. PA2	46	J15
Park Brae, Ersk. PA8	16	J8
Park Dr.		
Park Circ. G3	35	U11
Park Circ. La. G3	35	U11
Lynedoch Pl.		
Park Circ. Pl. G3	35	U11
Park Ct. (Giff.) G46	62	S19
Park Ct. (Bishop.) G64	11	Y6
Park Ct., Clyde. G81	4	K6
Littleholm		
Park Cres. (Bears.) G61	6	P5
Park Cres. (Bishop.) G64	11	Y6
Park Cres. (Inch.), Renf. PA4	16	J8
Park Dr. G3	35	U11
Park Dr. (Ruther.) G73	53	Y16
Park Dr., Ersk. PA8	16	J8
Park Gdns. G3	35	U11
Park Gdns. (Kilb.), John. PA10	42	B14
Park Gdns. La. G3	35	U11
Clifton St.		
Park Gate G3	35	U11
Park Gro., Ersk. PA8	16	J8
Park Holdings, Ersk. PA8	16	J8
Park La. G40	36	X13
Park La., Pais. PA3	30	K13
Netherhill Rd.		
Park Pl. G20	20	T8
Fingal St.		
Park Quad. G3	35	U11
Park Ridge, Ersk. PA8	16	J8
Park Dr.		
Park Rd. G4	35	U11
Park Rd. G32	55	CC16
Park Rd. (Giff.) G46	62	T19
Park Rd. (Bishop.) G64	11	Y7
Park Rd. (Bail.) G69	41	GG13
Park Rd. (Chry.) G69	26	FF8
Park Rd., Clyde. G81	4	K6
Park Rd., John. PA5	43	D15
Park Rd., Pais. PA2	46	J15
Park Rd. (Inch.), Renf. PA4	16	J8
Park St. S. G3	35	U11
Park Ter. G3	35	U11
Park Ter. G42	51	U15
Queens Dr.		
Park Ter. (Giff.) G46	62	T19
Park Top, Ersk. PA8	16	J8
Park Vw. (Kilb.), John. PA10	42	B14
Park Vw., Pais. PA2	46	J15
Park Way G32	55	CC16
Park Rd.		
Park Way (Cumb.) G67	71	PP2
Park Winding, Ersk. PA8	16	J8
Parkbrae Gdns. G20	21	V9
Parkbrae Pl. G20	21	V9
Parkburn Av. (Kirk.) G66	13	CC5
Parker St. G14	33	R11
Parkgrove Av. (Giff.) G46	62	T18
Parkgrove Ct. (Giff.) G46	62	T18
Parkgrove Ter. G3	35	U11
Parkgrove Ter. La. G3	35	U12
Derby St.		
Parkhall Rd., Clyde. G81	4	K6
Parkhall Ter., Clyde. G81	4	K5
Parkhead Cross G31	37	Z13
Parkhill Dr. (Ruther.) G73	53	Y16
Parkhill Rd. G43	50	T16
Parkholm La. G5	35	U13
Paisley Rd.		
Parkhouse Path G53	60	P18
Parkhouse Rd. G53	60	N18
Parkhouse Rd. (Barr.) G78	60	N18
Parkinch, Ersk. PA8	16	J8
Parklands Rd. G44	63	U18
Parklea (Bishop.) G64	10	X6
Midcroft		
Parkneuk Rd. G43	62	T18
Parksail, Ersk. PA8	16	J8
Parksail Dr., Ersk. PA8	16	J8
Parkside Gdns. G20	21	V9
Parkside Pl. G20	21	V9
Parkvale Av., Ersk. PA8	16	J8
Parkvale Cres., Ersk. PA8	16	J8
Parkvale Av.		
Parkvale Dr., Ersk. PA8	16	J8
Parkvale Av.		
Parkvale Gdns., Ersk. PA8	16	J8
Parkvale Av.		

Street		
Parkvale Pl., Ersk. PA8	16	J8
Parkvale Av.		
Parkvale Way, Ersk. PA8	16	J8
Parkvale Av.		
Parkview Av. (Kirk.) G66	13	CC5
Parkview Ct. (Kirk.) G66	13	CC5
Parkview Dr. (Stepps) G33	25	DD9
Parnie St. G1	36	W13
Parson St. G4	36	X12
Parsonage Row G1	36	W12
Parsonage Sq. G4	36	W12
Partick Bri. St. G11	34	T11
Partickhill Av. G11	20	S10
Partickhill Ct. G11	20	S10
Partickhill Av.		
Partickhill Rd. G11	20	S10
Paterson St. G5	35	V13
Pathead Gdns. G33	24	AA9
Patna St. G40	53	Y14
Paton St. G31	37	Y12
Patrick St., Pais. PA2	46	K14
Patterton Dr. (Barr.) G78	59	M19
Pattison St., Clyde. G81	4	K6
Payne St. G4	36	W11
Peacock Av., Pais. PA2	45	G15
Peacock Dr.		
Peacock Dr., Pais. PA2	45	G14
Pearce La. G51	34	S12
Pearce St.		
Pearce St. G51	34	S12
Pearson Dr., Renf. PA4	31	M11
Pearson Pl. (Linw.), Pais. PA3	28	E13
Peat Pl. G53	60	P17
Peat Rd. G53	60	P17
Peathill Av. (Chry.) G69	26	EE8
Peathill St. G21	22	W10
Peebles Dr. (Ruther.) G73	53	Z16
Peel Glen Gdns. G15	6	P5
Peel Glen Rd. G15	6	P6
Peel Glen Rd. (Bears.) G61	6	N5
Peel La. G11	34	S11
Burgh Hall St.		
Peel Pl. (Both.) G71	69	HH18
Peel St. G11	34	S11
Peel Vw., Clyde. G81	5	M6
Kirkoswald Dr.		
Pembroke St. G3	35	U12
Pencaitland Dr. G32	54	BB14
Falside Rd.		
Pencaitland Gro. G32	54	BB14
Falside Rd.		
Pencaitland Pl. G23	9	U7
Pendale Ri. G45	64	W18
Pendeen Cres. G33	39	DD13
Pendeen Pl. G33	39	DD13
Pendeen Rd. G33	39	DD13
Pendicle Cres. (Bears.) G61	7	Q6
Pendicle Rd. (Bears.) G61	7	Q6
Penicuik St. G32	37	Z13
Penilee Rd. G52	32	N12
Penilee Rd., Pais. PA1	32	N13
Penilee Ter. G52	32	N12
Peninver Dr. G51	33	R12
Penman Av. (Ruther.) G73	52	X16
Pennan Pl. G14	18	P9
Penneld Rd. G52	32	N13
Penrith Av. (Giff.) G46	62	T19
Penrith Dr. G12	20	S9
Penryn Gdns. G32	55	CC14
Penston Rd. G33	39	CC12
Pentland Av. (Linw.), Pais. PA3	28	E13
Pentland Ct. (Barr.) G78	59	L19
Pentland Cres., Pais. PA2	46	J16
Pentland Dr. (Bishop.) G64	11	Z7
Pentland Dr. (Barr.) G78	59	M19
Pentland Dr., Renf. PA4	31	L12
Pentland Rd. G40	52	X14
Pentland Rd. G43	62	T17
Pentland Rd. (Chry.) G69	26	FF8
Penzance Way (Chry.) G69	15	GG6
Peockland Gdns., John. PA5	44	E14
Peockland Pl., John. PA5	44	E14
Percy Dr. (Giff.) G46	62	T19
Percy Rd., Renf. PA4	31	L12
Percy St. G51	34	T13
Perran Gdns. (Chry.) G69	15	GG7
Perth Cres., Clyde. G81	4	J5
Perth St. G3	35	U12
Argyle St.		
Peters Ct. G20	20	T8
Maryhill Rd.		
Petershill Ct. G21	23	Y10
Petershill Dr. G21	23	Y10
Petershill Pl. G21	23	Y10
Petershill Rd. G21	22	X10
Peterson Dr. G13	18	N8
Peterson Gdns. G13	18	N8
Petition Pl. (Udd.) G71	69	HH17
Pettigrew St. G32	38	BB13
Peveril Av. G41	50	T15
Peveril Av. (Ruther.) G73	65	Z17
Pharonhill St. G31	38	AA13
Phoenix Business Pk., Pais. PA1	29	G13
Phoenix Pk. Ter. G4	35	V11
Corn St.		
Phoenix Pl. (Elder.), John. PA5	44	F14
Phoenix Rd. G4	35	V11
Great Western Rd.		
Piccadilly St. G3	35	U12
Piershill St. G32	38	AA12
Pikeman Rd. G13	19	Q9
Pilmuir Av. G44	63	U18
Pilrig St. G32	38	AA12
Pilton Rd. G15	6	P6
Pine Av. (Camb.) G72	67	DD18
Pine Cres., John. PA5	44	E15
Pine Gro. (Udd.) G71	57	HH16
Pine Pl. G5	52	W14
Pine Pl. (Cumb.) G67	71	RR2
Pine Rd. (Cumb.) G67	71	RR2
Pine Rd., Clyde. G81	4	J6
Pine St., Pais. PA2	47	L15
Pinelands (Bishop.) G64	11	Y6
Pinewood Av. (Kirk.) G66	12	BB5
Pinewood Ct. (Kirk.) G66	12	BB5
Pinewood Pl. (Kirk.) G66	12	BB5
Pinewood Sq. G15	6	N6
Pinkerton Av. (Ruther.) G73	52	X16
Pinkerton La., Renf. PA4	31	M11
Pinkston Dr. G21	36	W11
Pinkston Rd. G4	36	W11
Pinkston Rd. G21	22	W10
Pinmore Path G53	60	N17
Pinmore Pl. G53	60	N17
Pinmore St. G53	60	N17
Pinwherry Dr. G33	24	AA9
Pinwherry Pl. (Both.) G71	69	HH18
Hume Dr.		
Pirn St. G40	52	X14
Pitcairn St. G31	54	AA14
Pitcaple Dr. G43	62	S17
Pitlochry Dr. G52	48	P14
Pitmedden Rd. (Bishop.) G64	11	Z7
Pitmilly Rd. G15	7	Q6
Pitreavie Pl. G33	39	CC11
Pitt St. G2	35	V12
Pladda Rd., Renf. PA4	31	M11
Plaintrees Ct., Pais. PA2	46	K15
Carriagehill Dr.		
Planetree Pl., John. PA5	44	E15
Planetree Rd., Clyde. G81	5	L5
Planetrees Av., Pais. PA2	46	K15
Carriagehill Dr.		
Plant St. G31	37	Z13
Plantation Pk. Gdns. G51	34	T13
Plantation Pl. G51	35	U13
Govan Rd.		
Plantation Sq. G51	35	U13
Playfair St. G40	53	Y14
Pleaknowe Cres. (Chry.) G69	15	GG7
Pleamuir Pl. (Cumb.) G68	70	MM3
Plean St. G14	18	P9
Pleasance La. G43	50	T16
Pleasance St. G43	50	T16
Plover Pl., John. PA5	43	C16
Pointhouse Rd. G3	35	U12
Finnieston St.		
Pollock Dr. (Bishop.) G64	10	X7
Pollock Rd. (Bears.) G61	8	S6
Pollok Av. G43	50	T16
Pollokshaws Rd.		
Pollokshaws Rd. G41	51	U15
Pollokshaws Rd. G43	50	S16
Pollokshields Sq. G41	51	U15
Polmadie Av. G5	52	W15
Polmadie Rd. G5	52	W15
Polmadie Rd. G42	52	W15
Polmadie St. G42	52	W15
Polnoon Av. G13	18	P9
Polquhap Ct. G53	48	P16
Polquhap Gdns. G53	48	P16
Polquhap Pl. G53	48	P16
Polquhap Rd. G53	48	P16
Polson Cres., Pais. PA2	46	J15
Polson Dr., John. PA5	43	D15
Polsons Cres., Pais. PA2	46	J15
Polwarth Gdns. G12	20	S10
Novar Dr.		
Polwarth La. G12	20	S10
Novar Dr.		
Polwarth St. G12	20	S10
Poplar Av. G11	19	R10
Poplar Av., John. PA5	43	D15
Poplar Cotts. G14	18	N9
Dumbarton Rd.		
Poplar Dr. (Kirk.) G66	12	BB5
Poplar Dr., Clyde. G81	4	K5
Poplar Pl. (Blan.) G72	68	FF19
Poplar Rd. G41	34	S13
Urrdale Rd.		
Poplar Way (Camb.) G72	67	DD18
Poplin St. G40	52	X14
Porchester St. G33	39	CC11
Port Dundas Pl. G2	36	W12
Port Dundas Rd. G4	36	W11
Port St. G3	35	U12
Portal Rd. G13	19	Q8
Porterfield Rd., Renf. PA4	31	L11
Portland Rd. (Cumb.) G68	70	NN1
Portland St., Pais. PA2	47	L14
Portman Pl. G12	35	U11
Cowan St.		
Portman St. G41	35	U13
Portmarnock Dr. G23	20	T8
Portreath Rd. (Chry.) G69	15	GG6
Portsoy Av. G13	18	N8
Portsoy Pl. G13	18	N8
Portugal La. G5	35	V13
Bedford St.		
Portugal St. G5	35	V13
Bedford St.		
Possil Cross G22	21	V10
Possil Rd. G4	21	V10
Post La., Renf. PA4	17	M10
Potassels Rd. (Muir.) G69	26	FF8
Potter Clo. G32	54	AA14
Potter Pl.		
Potter Gro. G32	54	AA14
Potter Pl.		
Potter Pl. G32	54	AA14
Potter St. G32	54	AA14
Potterhill Av., Pais. PA2	46	K16
Potterhill Rd. G53	48	P15
Powburn Cres. (Udd.) G71	56	FF16
Powfoot St. G31	37	Z13
Powrie St. G33	25	CC10
Prentice La. (Udd.) G71	57	HH16
Preston Pl. G42	51	V15
Preston St. G42	51	V15
Cathcart Rd.		
Prestwick Ct. (Cumb.) G68	70	NN2
Prestwick St. G53	60	P17
Priesthill Av. G53	61	Q17
Priesthill Cres. G53	61	Q17
Priesthill Rd. G53	60	P17
Primrose Ct. G14	19	Q10
Primrose St. G14	19	Q10
Prince Albert Rd. G12	20	S10
Prince Edward St. G42	51	V15
Prince of Wales Gdns. G20	20	T8
Prince of Wales Ter. G12	20	T10
Byres Rd.		
Prince's Dock G51	34	T12
Princes Gdns. G12	20	S10
Princes Gate (Udd.) G71	69	GG18
Princes Gate (Ruther.) G73	53	Y16
Greenbank St.		
Princes Pl. G12	20	T10
Princes Sq. G1	36	W12
Princes Sq. (Barr.) G78	59	M18
Princes St. (Ruther.) G73	53	Y16
Princes Ter. G12	20	T10
Princess Cres., Pais. PA1	31	L13
Princess Dr. (Bail.) G69	41	GG13
Priory Av., Pais. PA3	31	L12
Priory Cotts. (Blan.) G72	68	FF19
Priory Dr. (Udd.) G71	56	FF16
Priory Pl. G13	19	Q8
Priory Rd. G13	19	Q8

Prosen St. G32   54 AA14
Prospect Av. (Udd.) G71   57 GG16
Prospect Av. (Camb.) G72   66 AA17
Prospect Rd. G43   50 T16
Prospecthill Circ. G42   52 W15
Prospecthill Cres. G42   52 X16
Prospecthill Dr. G42   52 W16
Prospecthill Pl. G42   52 X16
Prospecthill Rd. G42   51 V16
Prospecthill Sq. G42   52 W16
Provan Rd. G33   37 Z11
Provand Hall Cres. (Bail.) G69   56 EE14
Provanhill St. G21   36 X11
Provanmill Pl. G33   23 Z10
Provanmill Rd.
Provanmill Rd. G33   23 Z10
Provost Driver Ct., Renf. PA4   31 M11
King George Pk. Av.
Purdon St. G11   34 S11

Q

Quadrant Rd. G43   63 U17
Quarrelton Rd., John. PA5   43 D15
Quarry Av. (Camb.) G72   67 DD18
Quarry Pl. (Camb.) G72   66 AA17
Quarry Rd. (Barr.) G78   59 L18
Quarry Rd., Pais. PA2   46 K15
Quarry St., John. PA5   43 D14
Quarrybank (Mill.Pk.), John. PA10   43 C15
Quarrybrae St. G31   38 AA13
Quarryknowe (Ruther.) G73   52 X16
Quarryknowe St. G31   38 AA13
Quarrywood Av. G21   23 Z10
Quarrywood Rd. G21   23 Z10
Quay Rd. (Ruther.) G73   53 Y15
Quay Rd. N. (Ruther.) G73   53 Y15
Quebec Ho., Clyde. G81   4 J5
Perth Cres.
Queen Arc. G2   35 V12
Renfrew St.
Queen Elizabeth Av. G52   32 N12
Queen Elizabeth Sq. G5   52 W14
Queen Margaret Ct. G20   21 U10
Queen Margaret Cres. G12   21 U10
Hamilton Dr.
Queen Margaret Dr. G12   20 T10
Queen Margaret Dr. G20   21 U10
Queen Margaret Rd. G20   21 U10
Queen Mary Av. G42   51 V15
Queen Mary Av., Clyde. G81   5 M7
Queen Mary St. G40   52 X14
Queen Sq. G41   51 U15
Queen St. G1   36 W12
Queen St. (Ruther.) G73   53 Y16
Queen St., Pais. PA1   46 J14
Queen St., Renf. PA4   17 M10
Queen Victoria Dr. G13   19 Q10
Queen Victoria Dr. G14   19 Q10
Queen Victoria Gate G13   19 Q9
Queens Av. (Camb.) G72   66 BB17
Queens Cres. G4   35 V11
Queens Cres. (Bail.) G69   41 GG13
Queens Cross G20   21 U10
Queens Dr. G42   51 U15
Queens Dr. (Cumb.) G68   70 NN1
Queens Dr. La. G42   51 V15
Queens Gdns. G12   20 T10
Victoria Cres. Rd.
Queens Gate La. G12   20 T10
Victoria Cres. Rd.
Queens Pk. Av. G42   51 V15
Queens Pl. G12   20 T10
Queens Rd. (Elder.), John. PA5   44 F15
Queensbank Av. (Gart.) G69   27 GG8
Queensborough Gdns. G12   20 S10
Queensby Av. (Bail.) G69   40 EE13
Queensby Rd.
Queensby Dr. (Bail.) G69   40 EE13
Queensby Rd.
Queensby Pl. (Bail.) G69   40 EE13
Queensby Rd.
Queensby Rd. (Bail.) G69   40 EE13
Queensferry St. G5   52 X15
Rosebery St.

Queenshill St. G21   22 X10
Queensland Ct. G52   33 Q13
Queensland Dr. G52   33 Q13
Queensland Gdns. G52   33 Q13
Queensland La. E. G52   32 P13
Kingsland Dr.
Queensland La. W. G52   33 Q13
Queensland Dr.
Queenslie Ind. Est. G33   39 CC12
Queenslie St. G33   37 Z11
Quendale Dr. G32   54 AA14
Quentin St. G41   51 U15
Quinton Gdns. (Bail.) G69   40 EE13

R

Raasay Dr., Pais. PA2   46 J16
Raasay Pl. G22   22 W8
Raasay St. G22   22 W8
Rachan St. G34   40 FF11
Radnor St. G3   34 T11
Argyle St.
Radnor St., Clyde. G81   5 L6
Raeberry St. G20   21 U10
Raeswood Dr. G53   48 N16
Raeswood Gdns. G53   48 N16
Raeswood Pl. G53   48 N16
Raeswood Rd. G53   48 N16
Rafford St. G51   34 S12
Raglan St. G4   35 V11
Raith Av. G44   64 W18
Raithburn Av. G45   64 W18
Raithburn Rd. G45   64 W18
Ralston Av. G52   48 N14
Ralston Av., Pais. PA1   48 N14
Ralston Ct. G52   48 N14
Ralston Dr. G52   48 N14
Ralston Path G52   48 N14
Ralston Dr.
Ralston Pl. G52   48 N14
Ralston Rd. (Bears.) G61   7 R5
Ralston Rd. (Barr.) G78   59 M19
Ralston St., Pais. PA1   47 L14
Seedhill Rd.
Ram St. G32   38 AA13
Rampart Av. G13   18 P8
Ramsay Av., John. PA5   43 D15
Ramsay Cres. (Mill.Pk.), John. PA10   42 B15
Ramsay Pl., John. PA5   43 D15
Ramsay St., Clyde. G81   4 K6
Ranald Gdns. (Ruther.) G73   65 Z18
Randolph Av. (Clark.) G76   63 U19
Randolph Dr. (Clark.) G76   63 U19
Randolph Gdns. (Clark.) G76   63 U19
Randolph Rd. G11   19 R10
Randolph Ter. (Camb.) G72   66 BB17
Hamilton Rd.
Ranfurly Dr. (Cumb.) G68   70 NN2
Ranfurly Rd. G52   32 N13
Rankine Pl., John. PA5   43 D14
Rankine St., John. PA5   43 D14
Rankines La., Renf. PA4   17 M10
Manse St.
Rannoch Av. (Bishop.) G64   11 Y7
Rannoch Dr. (Bears.) G61   8 S7
Rannoch Dr., Renf. PA4   17 M10
Rannoch Gdns. (Bishop.) G64   11 Y7
Rannoch Pl., Pais. PA2   47 L14
Rannoch Rd. (Udd.) G71   57 GG15
Rannoch Rd., John. PA5   43 D15
Rannoch St. G44   63 V17
Raploch Av. G14   18 P10
Raploch La. G14   18 P10
Raploch Av.
Rathlin St. G51   34 S12
Ratho Dr. G21   22 X9
Rattray St. G32   54 AA14
Ravel Row G31   37 Z13
Ravel Wynd (Udd.) G71   57 HH16
Ravelston Rd. (Bears.) G61   7 R7
Ravelston St. G32   37 Z13
Ravens Ct. (Bishop.) G64   22 X8
Lennox Cres.
Ravenscliffe Dr. (Giff.) G46   62 S18
Ravenscraig Av., Pais. PA2   46 J15
Ravenscraig Dr. G53   60 P17
Ravenscraig Ter. G53   61 Q17
Ravenshall Rd. G41   50 T16
Ravenstone Dr. (Giff.) G46   62 T18
Ravenswood Av., Pais. PA2   45 G16

Ravenswood Dr. G41   50 T15
Ravenswood Rd. (Bail.) G69   40 FF13
Rayne Pl. G15   6 P6
Red Rd. G21   23 Y10
Red Rd. Ct. G21   23 Y10
Redan St. G40   36 X13
Redcastle Sq. G33   39 CC11
Redford St. G33   37 Z12
Redgate Pl. G14   18 P10
Redhill Rd. (Cumb.) G68   70 MM2
Redhurst Cres., Pais. PA2   45 H16
Redhurst La., Pais. PA2   45 H16
Redhurst Way, Pais. PA2   45 H16
Redlands La. G12   20 T10
Kirklee Rd.
Redlands Rd. G12   20 T10
Redlands Ter. G12   20 T10
Redlands Ter. La. G12   20 T10
Julian Av.
Redlawood Pl. (Camb.) G72   68 EE17
Redlawood Rd.
Redlawood Rd. (Camb.) G72   68 EE17
Redmoss St. G22   21 V9
Rednock St. G22   22 W10
Redpath Dr. G52   32 P13
Redwood Ct. (Camb.) G72   67 DD18
Redwood Cres.
Redwood Cres. (Camb.) G72   67 DD18
Redwood Dr. G21   23 Y10
Foresthall Dr.
Redwood Pl. (Kirk.) G66   12 BB5
Redwood Rd. (Cumb.) G67   71 QQ3
Redwood Way (Camb.) G72   67 DD18
Reelick Av. G13   18 N8
Reelick Quad. G13   18 N8
Reen Pl. (Both.) G71   69 HH18
Regent Dr. (Ruther.) G73   53 Y16
King St.
Regent Moray St. G3   34 T11
Regent Pk. Sq. G41   51 U15
Regent Pk. Ter. G41   51 U15
Pollokshaws Rd.
Regent Pl., Clyde. G81   4 K6
Regent Sq. (Lenzie) G66   13 CC6
Regent St., Clyde. G81   4 K6
Regent St., Pais. PA1   31 L13
Regents Gate (Both.) G71   69 GG18
Regwood St. G41   50 T16
Reid Av. (Bears.) G61   8 S5
Reid Av. (Linw.), Pais. PA3   28 E13
Reid Pl. G40   52 X14
Reid St. G40   52 X14
Reid St. (Ruther.) G73   53 Y16
Reidhouse St. G21   22 X10
Muir St.
Reidvale St. G31   36 X13
Renfield St. G2   35 V12
Renfield St., Renf. PA4   17 M10
Renfrew Ct. G2   35 V12
Renfrew St.
Renfrew La. G2   35 V12
Renfield St.
Renfrew Rd. G51   32 P11
Renfrew Rd., Pais. PA3   30 K13
Renfrew Rd., Renf. PA4   32 P11
Renfrew St. G2   35 V11
Renfrew St. G3   35 V11
Rennies Rd. (Inch.), Renf. PA4   16 J8
Renshaw Dr. G52   32 P13
Renshaw Rd. (Elder.), John. PA5   44 F15
Renton St. G4   36 W11
Renwick St. G41   35 U13
Scotland St.
Resipol Rd. (Stepps) G33   25 DD9
Reston Dr. G52   32 P13
Reuther Av. (Ruther.) G73   53 Y16
Revoch Dr. G13   18 P8
Rhannan Rd. G44   63 V17
Rhannan Ter. G44   63 V17
Rhindhouse Dr. (Bail.) G69   40 EE13
Rhindhouse Pl. (Bail.) G69   40 FF13
Rhindhouse Rd. (Bail.) G69   40 FF13
Swinton Av.
Rhindmuir Av. (Bail.) G69   40 FF13
Rhindmuir Ct. (Bail.) G69   40 FF13
Rhindmuir Cres. (Bail.) G69   40 FF13
Rhindmuir Dr. (Bail.) G69   40 FF13
Rhindmuir Gdns. (Bail.) G69   40 FF13
Rhindmuir Gro. (Bail.) G69   40 FF13
Rhindmuir Path (Bail.) G69   40 FF13

Rhindmuir Pl. (Bail.) G69 40 FF13
Rhindmuir Rd. (Bail.) G69 40 FF13
Rhindmuir Vw. (Bail.) G69 40 FF13
Rhindmuir Wynd (Bail.) G69 40 FF13
Rhindmuir Cres.
Rhinds St., Coat. ML5 57 HH14
Rhinsdale Cres. (Bail.) G69 40 FF13
Rhumhor Gdns., John. 42 B15
PA10
Rhymer St. G21 36 X11
Rhymie Rd. G32 55 CC14
Rhynie Dr. G51 34 S13
Riccarton St. G42 52 W15
Riccartsbar Av., Pais. PA2 46 J14
Richard St. G2 35 V12
Cadogan St.
Richard St., Renf. PA4 17 M10
Richmond Ct. (Ruther.) G73 53 Z16
Richmond Dr. (Bishop.) G64 11 Y6
Richmond Dr. (Camb.) G72 66 AA17
Richmond Dr. (Ruther.) G73 53 Z16
Richmond Dr. (Linw.), Pais. 28 E12
PA3
Richmond Gdns. (Chry.) G69 14 EE7
Richmond Gro. (Ruther.) G73 53 Z16
Richmond Pl. (Ruther.) G73 53 Z16
Richmond St. G1 36 W12
Richmond St., Clyde. G81 5 M7
Riddell St., Clyde. G81 5 M6
Riddon Av. G13 18 N8
Riddon Av., Clyde. G81 18 N8
Riddon Pl. G13 18 N8
Riddrie Cres. G33 38 AA12
Riddrie Knowes G33 38 AA12
Riddrie Ter. G33 23 Z10
Provanmill Rd.
Riddrievale Ct. G33 38 AA11
Riddrievale St. G33 38 AA11
Rigby St. G32 37 Z13
Rigg Pl. G33 39 DD12
Rigghead Av. (Cumb.) G67 71 PP1
Riggside Rd. G33 39 CC11
Riglands Way, Renf. PA4 17 M10
Riglaw Pl. G13 18 P8
Rigmuir Rd. G51 33 Q13
Rimsdale St. G40 37 Y13
Ringford St. G21 22 X10
Ripon Dr. G12 20 S9
Risk St. G40 36 X13
Risk St., Clyde. G81 4 K6
Ristol Rd. G13 19 Q9
Anniesland Rd.
Ritchie Cres. (Elder.), John. 44 F14
PA5
Ritchie Pk., John. PA5 44 E14
Ritchie St. G5 51 V14
River Dr. (Inch.), Renf. PA4 16 J10
River Rd. G32 54 BB16
River Rd. G41 51 U16
Mansionhouse Rd.
Riverbank St. G43 50 T16
Riverford Rd. G43 50 T16
Riverford Rd. (Ruther.) G73 53 Z15
Riversdale Cotts. G14 18 N9
Dumbarton Rd.
Riversdale La. G14 18 P10
Ardsloy Pl.
Riverside Ct. G44 63 V19
Riverside Pk. G44 63 V19
Linnpark Av.
Riverside Pl. (Camb.) G72 67 DD17
Riverside Rd. G43 51 U16
West St.
Riverview Av. G5 35 V13
Riverview Dr. G5 35 V13
Riverview Gdns. G5 35 V13
Riverview Pl. G5 35 V13
Roaden Av., Pais. PA2 45 G16
Roaden Rd., Pais. PA2 45 G16
Roadside (Cumb.) G67 71 PP1
Robb St. G21 22 X10
Rober Dr. G51 34 S12
Robert Burns Av., Clyde. 5 M6
G81
Robert St. G51 34 S12
Robert Templeton Dr. 67 CC17
(Camb.) G72
Roberton Av. G41 50 T15
Roberts St., Clyde. G81 4 K6
Robertson La. G2 35 V12
Robertson St.
Robertson St. G2 35 V12

Robertson St. (Barr.) G78 59 L18
Robertson Ter. (Bail.) G69 40 FF13
Edinburgh Rd.
Robin Way G32 55 CC16
Robroyston Av. G33 24 AA10
Robroyston Dr. G33 24 AA9
Robroyston Rd. G33 24 AA9
Robroyston Rd. (Bishop.) 12 AA7
G64
Robslee Cres. (Giff.) G46 62 S18
Robslee Dr. (Giff.) G46 62 S18
Robslee Rd. (Thorn.) G46 62 S19
Robson Gro. G42 51 V15
Rock Dr. (Kilb.), John. PA10 42 B15
Rock St. G4 21 V10
Rockall Dr. G44 64 W18
Rockbank Pl. G40 37 Y13
Broad St.
Rockbank Pl., Clyde. G81 5 L5
Glasgow Rd.
Rockbank St. G40 37 Y13
Rockcliffe St. G40 52 X14
Rockfield Pl. G21 23 Z9
Rockfield Rd. G21 23 Z9
Rockmount Av. (Thorn.) 62 S18
G46
Rockmount Av. (Barr.) G78 59 M19
Rockwell Av., Pais. PA2 46 J16
Rodger Dr. (Ruther.) G73 65 Y17
Rodger Pl. (Ruther.) G73 65 Y17
Rodil Av. G44 64 W18
Rodney St. G4 35 V11
Roebank Dr. (Barr.) G78 59 M19
Roebank St. G31 37 Y12
Roffey Pk. Rd., Pais. PA1 31 M13
Rogart St. G40 36 X13
Orr St.
Rogerfield Rd. (Bail.) G69 40 FF12
Rokeby Ter. G12 20 T10
Great Western Rd.
Roman Av. G15 6 P7
Roman Ct. (Bears.) G61 7 R5
Roman Dr. (Bears.) G61 7 R5
Roman Gdns. (Bears.) G61 7 R5
Roman Rd. (Bears.) G61 7 R5
Roman Rd., Clyde. G81 5 L5
Romney Av. G44 64 W17
Rona St. G21 37 Y11
Rona Ter. (Camb.) G72 66 AA18
Ronaldsay Dr. (Bishop.) G64 11 Z7
Ronaldsay Pl. (Cumb.) G67 70 MM4
Ronaldsay St. G22 22 W8
Ronay St. G22 22 W8
Rooksdell Av., Pais. PA2 46 J15
Ropework La. G1 36 W13
Clyde St.
Rose Cotts. G13 19 R9
Crow Rd.
Rose Dale (Bishop.) G64 23 Y8
Rose Knowe Rd. G42 52 X15
Rose St. G3 35 V12
Rosebank Av. (Blan.) G72 69 GG19
Rosebank Dr. (Camb.) G72 67 CC18
Rosebank Gdns. (Udd.) G71 56 EE15
Rosebank Pl. (Udd.) G71 56 EE15
Rosebank St. (Udd.) G71 57 GG14
Rosebery Pl., Clyde. G81 5 L7
Miller St.
Rosebery St. G5 52 X15
Rosedale Av., Pais. PA2 44 F16
Rosedale Dr. (Bail.) G69 56 EE14
Rosedale Gdns. G20 20 T8
Rosefield Gdns. (Udd.) G71 57 GG16
Roselea Gdns. G13 19 R8
Roselea Pl. (Blan.) G72 68 FF19
Rosemount (Cumb.) G68 70 NN1
Rosemount Cres. G21 37 Y11
Rosemount St. G21 36 X11
Rosemount Ter. G51 35 U13
Paisley Rd. W.
Rosemout Meadows (Both.) 69 GG19
G71
Roseness Pl. G33 38 BB12
Rosevale Rd. (Bears.) G61 7 R6
Rosevale St. G11 34 S11
Rosewood Av., Pais. PA2 45 H15
Rosewood St. G13 19 R8
Roslea Dr. G31 37 Y12
Roslyn Dr. (Bail.) G69 41 GG13
Rosneath St. G51 34 S12
Ross Av., Renf. PA4 31 L11

Ross Hall Pl., Renf. PA4 17 M10
Ross St. G40 36 W13
Ross St., Pais. PA1 47 L14
Rossendale Rd. G41 50 T16
Rossendale Rd. G43 50 T16
Rosshall Av., Pais. PA1 47 M14
Rosshill Av. G52 32 N13
Rosshill Rd. G52 32 N13
Rossie Cres. (Bishop.) G64 23 Z8
Rosslea Dr. (Giff.) G46 62 T19
Rosslyn Av. (Ruther.) G73 53 Y16
Rosslyn Rd. (Bears.) G61 6 P5
Rosslyn Ter. G12 20 T10
Rostan Rd. G43 62 T17
Rosyth Rd. G5 52 X15
Rosyth St. G5 52 X15
Rotherwick Dr., Pais. PA1 48 N14
Rotherwood Av. G13 7 Q7
Rotherwood Av., Pais. PA2 45 G16
Rotherwood La. G13 7 Q7
Rotherwood Av.
Rotherwood Pl. G13 19 Q8
Rothes Dr. G23 8 T7
Rothes Pl. G23 8 T7
Rottenrow G4 36 W12
Rottenrow E. G4 36 W12
Roual Ter., Pais. PA1 31 L13
Greenlaw Av.
Rouken Glen Pk. (Thorn.) 61 R19
G46
Rouken Glen Rd. (Thorn.) 61 R19
G46
Roukenburn St. (Thorn.) 61 R18
Roundhill Dr. (Elder.), John. 45 G14
PA5
Roundknowe Rd. (Udd.) G71 56 FF15
Rowallan Gdns. G11 20 S10
Rowallan La. G11 20 S10
Churchill Dr.
Rowallan La. E. G11 20 S10
Churchill Dr.
Rowallan Rd. (Thorn.) G46 61 R19
Rowallan Ter. G33 24 BB10
Rowan Av., Renf. PA4 17 M10
Rowan Cres. (Lenzie) G66 13 CC5
Rowan Dr., Clyde. G81 4 K6
Rowan Gdns. G41 50 S14
Rowan Gdns. (Both.) G71 69 HH18
Rowan Gate, Pais. PA2 46 K15
Rowan Pl. (Camb.) G72 67 CC17
Elm Dr.
Rowan Rd. G41 50 S14
Rowan Rd. (Cumb.) G67 71 QQ2
Rowan St., Pais. PA2 46 K15
Rowand Av. (Giff.) G46 62 T19
Rowandale Av. (Bail.) G69 56 EE14
Rowanlea Av., Pais. PA2 44 F16
Rowanlea Dr. (Giff.) G46 62 T18
Rowanpark Dr. (Barr.) G78 59 L17
Rowans, The (Bishop.) G64 10 X7
Rowans Gdns. (Both.) G71 69 HH18
Rowantree Av. (Ruther.) G73 65 Y17
Rowantree Gdns. (Ruther.) 65 Y17
G73
Rowantree Pl., John. PA5 43 D15
Rowantree Rd.
Rowantree Rd., John. PA5 43 D15
Rowchester St. G40 37 Y13
Rowena Av. G13 7 Q7
Roxburgh La. G12 20 T10
Saltoun St.
Roxburgh Rd., Pais. PA2 44 F16
Roxburgh St. G12 20 T10
Roy St. G21 22 W10
Royal Bk. Pl. G1 36 W12
Buchanan St.
Royal Cres. G3 35 U11
Royal Cres. G42 51 V15
Royal Ex. Bldgs. G1 36 W12
Royal Ex. Sq.
Royal Ex. Ct. G1 36 W12
Queen St.
Royal Ex. Sq. G1 36 W12
Royal Inch Cres., Renf. PA4 17 M9
Royal Ter. G3 35 U11
Royal Ter. G42 51 V15
Queens Dr.
Royal Ter. La. G3 35 U11
North Claremont St.
Royston Rd. G21 36 X11
Royston Rd. G33 24 AA10

Royston Sq. G21	36	X11
Roystonhill G21	36	X11
Rozelle Av. G15	6	P6
Rubislaw Dr. (Bears.) G61	7	R6
Ruby St. G40	53	Y14
Ruchazie Pl. G33	38	AA12
Ruchazie Rd. G32	38	AA13
Ruchazie Rd. G33	38	AA13
Ruchill Pl. G20	21	U9
Ruchill St. G20	21	U9
Ruel St. G44	51	V16
Rufflees Av. (Barr.) G78	59	M18
Rugby Av. G13	18	P8
Rullion Pl. G33	38	AA12
Rumford St. G40	52	X14
Rupert St. G4	35	U11
Rushyhill St. G21	23	Y10
Cockmuir St.		
Ruskin Pl. G12	20	T10
Great Western Rd.		
Ruskin Sq. (Bishop.) G64	11	Y7
Ruskin Ter. G12	21	U10
Ruskin Ter. (Ruther.) G73	53	Y15
Russell Cres. (Bail.) G69	56	FF14
Russell Dr. (Bears.) G61	7	R5
Russell Gdns. (Udd.) G71	57	HH16
Kingston Av.		
Russell St. G11	34	S11
Vine St.		
Russell St., John. PA5	44	E14
Russell St., Pais. PA3	30	J12
Rutherford Av. (Kirk.) G66	14	EE5
Chryston Rd.		
Rutherford Gra. (Kirk.) G66	13	CC5
Rutherford La. G2	35	V12
Hope St.		
Rutherglen Bri. G40	52	X14
Rutherglen Bri. G42	52	X14
Rutherglen Rd. G5	52	W14
Rutherglen Rd. (Ruther.) G73	52	W14
Ruthven Av. (Giff.) G46	62	T19
Ruthven La. G12	20	T10
Byres Rd.		
Ruthven Pl. (Bishop.) G64	23	Z8
Ruthven St. G12	20	T10
Rutland Ct. G51	35	U13
Govan Rd.		
Rutland Cres. G51	35	U13
Rutland La. G51	35	U13
Govan Rd.		
Rutland Pl. G51	35	U13
Ryan Rd. (Bishop.) G64	11	Y7
Ryan Way (Ruther.) G73	65	Z18
Rye Cres. G21	23	Z9
Rye Rd. G21	23	Z9
Rye Way, Pais. PA2	45	G15
Ryebank Rd. G21	23	Z9
Ryecroft Dr. (Bail.) G69	40	EE13
Ryedale Pl. G15	6	P6
Ryefield Av., John. PA5	43	C15
Ryefield Pl., John. PA5	43	C15
Ryefield Rd. G21	23	Y9
Ryehill Pl. G21	23	Z9
Ryehill Rd. G21	23	Z9
Ryemount Rd. G21	23	Z9
Ryeside Rd. G21	23	Y9
Ryewraes Rd. (Linw.), Pais. PA3	28	E13
Rylands Dr. G32	55	DD14
Rylands Gdns. G32	55	DD14
Rylees Cres. G52	32	N12
Rylees Pl. G52	32	N13
Rylees Rd. G52	32	N13
Ryvra Rd. G13	19	Q9

S

Sackville Av. G13	19	R9
Sackville La. G13	19	R9
Sackville Av.		
Saddell Rd. G15	6	P6
St. Abbs Dr., Pais. PA2	45	H15
St. Andrews Av. (Bishop.) G64	10	X7
St. Andrew's Av. (Both.) G71	69	HH19
St. Andrews Cres. G41	51	U14
St. Andrews Cres., Pais. PA3	30	J11
St. Andrews Cross G41	51	V14
St. Andrews Dr. G41	50	T15
St. Andrews Dr. (Abbots.), Pais. PA3	30	J12
St. Andrews Dr. W. (Abbots.), Pais. PA3	30	J11
St. Andrews La. G1	36	W13
Gallowgate		
St. Andrews Rd. G41	51	U14
St. Andrews Rd., Renf. PA4	31	M11
St. Andrews Sq. G1	36	W13
St. Andrews St. G1	36	W13
St. Annes Av., Ersk. PA8	16	J8
St. Annes Wynd, Ersk. PA8	16	J8
St. Anns Dr. (Giff.) G46	62	T19
St. Blanes Dr. (Ruther.) G73	64	X17
St. Boswell's Cres., Pais. PA2	45	H15
St. Brides Rd. G43	50	T16
St. Brides Way (Both.) G71	69	HH18
St. Catherines Rd. (Giff.) G46	62	T19
St. Clair Av. (Giff.) G46	62	T18
St. Clair St. G20	35	U11
Woodside Rd.		
St. Conval Pl. G43	50	S16
Shawbridge St.		
St. Cyrus Gdns. (Bishop.) G64	11	Z7
St. Cyrus Rd. (Bishop.) G64	11	Y7
St. Enoch Pl. G1	35	V13
Howard St.		
St. Enoch Sq. G1	35	V13
St. Enoch Wynd G2	35	V12
Argyle St.		
St. Fillans Rd. G33	25	CC9
St. Georges Cross G3	35	V11
St. Georges Pl. G20	35	V11
St. Georges Rd.		
St. Georges Rd. G3	35	V11
St. Germains (Bears.) G61	7	R6
St. Helena Cres., Clyde. G81	5	M5
St. Ives Rd. (Mood.) G69	15	GG6
St. James Av., Pais. PA3	29	H12
St. James Pl., Pais. PA3	30	K13
Love St.		
St. James Rd. G4	36	W12
St. James St., Pais. PA3	30	J13
St. Johns Ct. G41	51	U14
St. Johns Quad. G41	51	U14
St. Johns Rd. G41	51	U14
St. Johns Ter. G12	35	U11
Southpark Av.		
St. Joseph's Ct. G21	36	X11
St. Joseph's Pl. G21	36	X11
St. Josephs Pl. G40	36	X13
Abercromby St.		
St. Joseph's Vw. G21	36	X11
St. Kenneth Dr. G51	33	R12
St. Kilda Dr. G14	19	R10
St. Leonards Dr. (Giff.) G46	62	T18
St. Margarets Pl. G1	36	W13
Bridgegate		
St. Mark Gdns. G32	38	AA13
St. Mark St.		
St. Mark St. G32	38	AA13
St. Marnock St. G40	37	Y13
St. Mary's Cres. (Barr.) G78	59	M19
St. Mary's Gdns. (Barr.) G78	59	M19
Heys St.		
St. Marys La. G2	35	V12
West Nile St.		
St. Marys Rd. (Bishop.) G64	10	X7
St. Michael's Ct. G31	37	Z13
St. Michael's La. G31	37	Z13
St. Mirren St., Pais. PA1	46	K14
St. Monance St. G21	22	X9
St. Mungo Av. G4	36	W12
St. Mungo Pl. G4	36	W12
St. Mungo St. (Bishop.) G64	22	X8
St. Mungo's Rd. (Cumb.) G67	70	NN3
St. Ninian St. G5	36	W13
St. Ninian Ter. G5	36	W13
Old Rutherglen Rd.		
St. Ninians Cres., Pais. PA2	46	K15
Rowan St.		
St. Ninians Rd., Pais. PA2	46	K15
St. Peters La. G2	35	V12
Blythswood St.		
St. Peters Path G4	35	V11
Gladstone St.		
St. Peter's Path G4	35	V11
Braid St.		
St. Peters St. G4	35	V11
St. Rollox Brae G21	36	X11
St. Ronans Dr. G41	50	T15
St. Ronans Dr. (Ruther.) G73	65	Z17
St. Stephens Av. (Ruther.) G73	65	Z18
St. Stephens Cres. (Ruther.) G73	66	AA18
St. Valleyfield St. G21	22	X10
Ayr St.		
St. Vincent Cres. G3	34	T12
St. Vincent Cres. La. G3	35	U12
Corunna St.		
St. Vincent La. G2	35	V12
Hope St.		
St. Vincent Pl. G1	36	W12
St. Vincent St. G2	35	U12
St. Vincent St. G3	35	U12
St. Vincent Ter. G3	35	U12
Salamanca St. G31	37	Z13
Salasaig Ct. G33	38	BB12
Sutherness Dr.		
Salen St. G52	33	R13
Salisbury Pl. G12	20	T10
Great Western Rd.		
Salisbury Pl., Clyde. G81	4	J5
Salisbury St. G5	51	V14
Salkeld St. G5	51	V14
Salmona St. G22	21	V10
Saltaire Av. (Udd.) G71	69	HH17
Salterland Rd. G53	60	N17
Salterland Rd. (Barr.) G78	60	N17
Saltmarket G1	36	W13
Saltmarket Pl. G1	36	W13
King St.		
Saltoun Gdns. G12	20	T10
Roxburgh St.		
Saltoun La. G12	20	T10
Ruthven St.		
Saltoun St. G12	20	T10
Salvia St. (Camb.) G72	66	AA17
Sanda St. G20	21	U10
Sandaig Rd. G33	39	DD13
Sandbank Av. G20	20	T9
Sandbank Dr. G20	20	T8
Sandbank St. G20	20	T9
Sandbank Ter. G20	20	T8
Sandend Rd. G53	48	P16
Sanderling Pl., John. PA5	43	C16
Sanderling Rd., Pais. PA3	30	J12
Sandfield St. G20	21	U9
Maryhill Rd.		
Sandford Gdns. (Bail.) G69	56	EE14
Scott St.		
Sandgate Av. G32	55	CC14
Sandhaven Rd. G53	48	P16
Sandholes, Pais. PA1	46	J14
Sandholm Pl. G14	18	N9
Sandholm Ter. G14	18	N9
Sandielands Av., Ersk. PA8	16	J8
Sandilands St. G32	38	BB13
Sandmill St. G21	37	Y11
Sandra Rd. (Bishop.) G64	11	Z7
Sandringham Dr. (Elder.), John. PA5	44	E15
Glamis Av.		
Sandringham La. G12	20	T10
Kersland St.		
Sandwood Cres. G52	32	P13
Sandwood Rd.		
Sandwood Rd. G52	32	P13
Sandy La. G11	34	S11
Crawford St.		
Sandy Rd. G11	34	S11
Sandy Rd., Renf. PA4	31	M11
Sandyfaulds Sq. G5	52	W14
Sandyford Pl. G3	35	U12
Sandyford Pl. La. G3	35	U11
Elderslie St.		
Sandyford Rd., Pais. PA3	31	L12
Sandyford St. G3	34	T12
Sandyhills Cres. G32	54	BB14
Sandyhills Dr. G32	54	BB14
Sandyhills Gro. G32	55	CC15
Hamilton Rd.		
Sandyhills Pl. G32	54	BB14
Sandyhills Rd. G32	54	BB14
Sandyknowes Rd. (Cumb.) G67	71	PP4
Sannox Gdns. G31	37	Y12
Sanquhar Dr. G53	48	P16
Sanquhar Gdns. G53	48	P16
Sanquhar Gdns. (Blan.) G72	68	EE19
Sanquhar Pl. G53	48	P16

Street		
Sanquhar Rd. G53	48	P16
Saracen Gdns. G22	22	W9
Saracen Head La. G1	36	W13
Gallowgate		
Saracen St. G22	22	W10
Sardinia La. G12	20	T10
Great George St.		
Sardinia Ter. G12	20	T10
Cecil St.		
Saucel, Pais. PA1	46	K14
Saucel St., Pais. PA1	46	K14
Saucelhill Ter., Pais. PA2	46	K14
Sauchenhall Rd. (Kirk.) G66	15	GG5
Sauchiehall La. G2	35	V12
Sauchiehall St.		
Sauchiehall St. G2	35	U12
Sauchiehall St. G3	35	U12
Saughs Av. G33	24	AA9
Saughs Dr. G33	24	AA9
Saughs Gate G33	24	AA9
Saughs Pl. G33	24	AA9
Saughs Av.		
Saughs Rd. G33	24	AA9
Saughton St. G32	38	AA12
Saunders Ct. (Barr.) G78	59	L18
John St.		
Savoy Arc. G40	52	X14
Main St.		
Savoy St. G40	52	X14
Sawfield Pl. G4	35	V11
Garscube Rd.		
Sawmill Rd. G11	33	R11
South St.		
Sawmillfield St. G4	35	V11
Saxon Rd. G13	19	Q8
Scadlock Rd., Pais. PA3	29	H13
Scalpay Pl. G22	22	W8
Scalpay St. G22	22	W8
Scapa St. G23	21	U8
Scapa St. G40	53	Y14
Springfield Rd.		
Scaraway Dr. G22	22	W8
Scaraway Pl. G22	22	W8
Scaraway St. G22	22	W8
Scaraway Ter. G22	22	W8
Scarba Dr. G43	62	S17
Scarrel Dr. G45	65	Y18
Scarrel Gdns. G45	65	Y18
Scarrel Rd. G45	65	Y18
Scarrel Ter. G45	65	Y18
Schaw Ct. (Bears.) G61	7	Q5
Schaw Dr. (Bears.) G61	7	R5
Schaw Rd., Pais. PA3	31	L13
Schipka Pas. G1	36	W13
Gallowgate		
School Av. (Camb.) G72	66	BB17
School Rd. (Stepps) G33	25	DD9
School Rd., Pais. PA1	32	N13
School Wynd, Pais. PA1	30	K13
Scioncroft Av. (Ruther.) G73	53	Z16
Scone St. G21	22	W10
Sconser St. G23	9	U7
Scorton Gdns. (Bail.) G69	55	DD14
Scotland St. G5	35	U13
Scotland St. W. G41	34	T13
Scotsblair Av. (Kirk.) G66	13	CC5
Scotsburn Rd. G21	23	Z10
Scotstoun Mill Rd. G11	34	T11
Partick Bri. St.		
Scotstoun Pl. G14	19	Q10
Scotstoun St.		
Scotstoun St. G14	19	Q10
Scott Av., John. PA5	43	D16
Scott Dr. (Bears.) G61	7	Q5
Scott Rd. G52	32	N12
Scott St. G3	35	V11
Scott St. (Bail.) G69	56	EE14
Scott St., Clyde. G81	4	K6
Scotts Rd., Pais. PA2	47	M14
Seafar Rd. (Cumb.) G67	70	NN4
Seafield Dr. (Ruther.) G73	65	Z18
Seaforth Cres. (Barr.) G78	59	L18
Seaforth La. (Chry.) G69	15	HH7
Burnbrae Av.		
Seaforth Rd. G52	32	P12
Seaforth Rd., Clyde. G81	5	L7
Seaforth Rd. N. G52	32	P12
Seaforth Rd. S. G52	32	P12
Seagrove St. G32	37	Z13
Seamill Path G53	60	N17
Seamill Pl. G53	60	N17
Seamill St. G53	60	N17
Seamore St. G20	35	U11
Seath Rd. (Ruther.) G73	53	Y15
Seath St. G42	52	W15
Seaward La. G41	35	U13
Seaward St.		
Seaward Pl. G41	35	U13
Seaward St. G41	35	U13
Second Av. (Stepps) G33	24	BB9
Second Av. G44	63	V17
Second Av. (Bears.) G61	8	S6
Second Av. (Kirk.) G66	13	CC7
Second Av. (Udd.) G71	57	GG15
Second Av., Clyde. G81	5	L6
Second Av., Renf. PA4	31	M11
Second Gdns. G41	50	S14
Second St. (Udd.) G71	57	GG16
Seedhill, Pais. PA1	46	K14
Seedhill Rd., Pais. PA1	46	K14
Seggielea La. G13	19	Q9
Helensburgh Dr.		
Seggielea Rd. G13	19	Q9
Seil Dr. G44	64	W18
Selborne Pl. G13	19	R9
Selborne Rd.		
Selborne Pl. La. G13	19	R9
Selborne Rd.		
Selborne Rd. G13	19	R9
Selby Gdns. G32	39	DD13
Selkirk Av. G52	49	Q14
Selkirk Av., Pais. PA2	45	H15
Selkirk Dr. (Ruther.) G73	53	Z16
Sella Rd. (Bishop.) G64	11	Z6
Selvieland Rd. G52	32	N13
Semple Pl. (Linw.), Pais. PA3	28	E12
Seton Ter. G31	36	X12
Settle Gdns. (Bail.) G69	55	DD14
Seven Sisters (Kirk.) G66	13	DD5
Seventh Av. (Udd.) G71	57	GG16
Seyton Av. (Giff.) G46	62	T19
Shaftesbury St. G3	35	U12
Shaftesbury St., Clyde. G81	4	K7
Shafton Pl. G13	19	R8
Shafton Rd. G13	19	R8
Shakespeare Av., Clyde. G81	4	K6
Shakespeare St. G20	21	U9
Shamrock Cotts. G13	19	R9
Crow Rd.		
Shamrock St. G4	35	V11
Shandon St. G51	34	T12
Govan Rd.		
Shandwick St. G34	40	EE12
Shanks Av. (Barr.) G78	59	M19
Hunter Rd.		
Shanks Cres., John. PA5	43	C15
Shanks St. G20	21	U9
Shannon St. G20	21	U9
Shapinsay St. G22	22	W8
Sharrocks St. G51	34	T13
Clifford St.		
Shaw Pl. (Linw.), Pais. PA3	28	E13
Shaw St. G51	34	S12
Shawbridge St. G43	50	S16
Shawfield Dr. G5	52	X15
Shawfield Rd. G5	52	X15
Shawhill Rd. G41	50	T16
Shawhill Rd. G43	50	T16
Shawholm Cres. G43	50	S16
Shawlands Arc. G41	51	U16
Shawlands Sq. G41	51	U16
Shawmoss Rd. G41	50	T15
Shawpark St. G20	21	U9
Shearer La. G5	35	U13
Shearer Pl. G51	35	U13
Sheddens Pl. G32	38	AA13
Sheepburn Rd. (Udd.) G71	57	GG16
Sheila St. G33	24	AA10
Sheldrake Pl., John. PA5	43	C16
Shelley Ct. G12	20	S9
Shelley Rd.		
Shelley Dr. (Both.) G71	69	HH18
Shelley Dr., Clyde. G81	5	L6
Shelley Rd. G12	19	R9
Sheppard St. G21	22	X10
Cowlairs Rd.		
Sherbrooke Av. G41	50	T14
Sherbrooke Dr. G41	50	T14
Sherbrooke Gdns. G41	50	T14
Sherburn Gdns. (Bail.) G69	55	DD14
Sheriff Pk. Av. (Ruther.) G73	53	Y16
Sherwood Av. (Udd.) G71	69	HH17
Sherwood Av., Pais. PA1	31	L13
Sherwood Dr. (Thorn.) G46	62	S18
Sherwood Pl. G15	6	P6
Shetland Dr. G44	64	W18
Shettleston Rd. G31	37	Z13
Shettleston Rd. G32	38	AA13
Shettleston Sheddings G31	38	AA13
Shettleston Rd.		
Shiel Ct. (Barr.) G78	59	L17
Shiel Rd. (Bishop.) G64	11	Y7
Shieldaig Dr. (Ruther.) G73	65	Y18
Shieldaig Rd. G22	21	V8
Shieldbridge Gdns. G23	9	U7
Shieldburn Rd. G51	33	Q12
Shieldhall Gdns. G51	33	Q12
Shieldhall Rd. G51	32	P12
Shields Rd. G41	35	U13
Shilford Av. G13	18	P8
Shillay St. G22	22	X8
Shilton Dr. G53	60	P17
Shinwell Av., Clyde. G81	5	M7
Shipbank La. G1	36	W13
Clyde St.		
Shiskine Dr. G20	20	T8
Shiskine Pl. G20	20	T8
Shiskine St.		
Shiskine St. G20	20	T8
Shore St. G40	52	X15
Shortridge St. G20	21	U9
Shanks St.		
Shortroods Av., Pais. PA3	30	J12
Shortroods Cres., Pais. PA3	30	J12
Shortroods Rd., Pais. PA3	30	J12
Shotts St. G33	39	CC12
Shuna Pl. G20	21	U9
Shuna St. G20	21	U9
Shuttle La. G1	36	W12
George St.		
Shuttle St. G1	36	W12
Shuttle St. (Kilb.), John. PA10	42	A14
Shuttle St., Pais. PA1	46	K14
Sidland Rd. G21	23	Z9
Sidlaw Av. (Barr.) G78	59	M19
Ochil Dr.		
Sidlaw Rd. (Bears.) G61	6	P5
Sielga Pl. G34	40	EE12
Siemens Pl. G21	37	Y11
Siemens St. G21	37	Y11
Sievewright St. (Ruther.) G73	53	Z15
Hunter Rd.		
Silk St., Pais. PA1	30	K13
Silkin Av., Clyde. G81	5	M7
Silverburn St. G33	38	AA12
Silverdale St. G31	53	Z14
Silverfir Pl. G5	52	W14
Silverfir St. G5	52	W14
Silvergrove St. G40	36	X13
Silverwells (Both.) G71	69	HH19
Silverwells Cres. (Both.) G71	69	HH19
Simons Cres., Renf. PA4	17	M9
Simpson Ct. (Udd.) G71	69	GG17
Simpson Ct., Clyde. G81	5	L7
Simpson Gdns. (Barr.) G78	59	L19
Simpson St. G20	21	U10
Simshill Rd. G44	63	V18
Sinclair Av. (Bears.) G61	7	R5
Sinclair Dr. G42	51	U16
Sinclair Gdns. (Bishop.) G64	23	Y8
Sinclair St., Clyde. G81	17	M8
Singer Rd., Clyde. G81	4	K6
Singer St., Clyde. G81	5	L6
Sir Michael Pl., Pais. PA1	46	J14
Sixth Av., Renf. PA4	31	M11
Sixth St. (Udd.) G71	57	GG15
Skaethorn Rd. G20	20	S8
Skaterig La. G13	19	R9
Skaterigg Dr. G13	19	R9
Skaterigg Gdns. G13	19	R9
Skaterigg Rd. G13	19	R9
Crow Rd.		
Skelbo Path G34	40	FF11
Auchingill Rd.		
Skelbo Pl. G34	40	FF11
Skene Rd. G51	34	S13
Skerray Quad. G22	22	W8
Skerray St. G22	22	W8
Skerryvore Pl. G33	38	BB12

Street	Page	Grid
Skerryvore Rd. G33	38	BB12
Skibo Dr. (Thorn.) G46	61	R18
Skibo La. (Thorn.) G46	61	R18
Skipness Dr. G51	33	R12
Skirsa Ct. G23	21	V8
Skirsa Pl. G23	21	U8
Skirsa Sq. G23	21	U8
Skirsa St. G23	21	U8
Skirving St. G41	51	U16
Skye Av., Renf. PA4	31	M11
Skye Ct. (Cumb.) G60	70	MM4
Skye Cres. (Old Kil.) G60	4	J5
Skye Cres., Pais. PA2	46	J16
Skye Dr. (Old Kil.) G60	4	J5
Skye Dr. (Cumb.) G67	70	MM4
Skye Gdns. (Bears.) G61	6	P5
Skye Pl. (Cumb.) G67	70	MM4
Skye Rd. (Cumb.) G67	70	MM4
Skye Rd. (Ruther.) G73	65	Z18
Skye St. G20	20	T8
Bantaskin St.		
Slakiewood Av. (Gart.) G69	27	GG8
Slatefield St. G31	37	Y13
Sleads St. G41	35	U13
Sloy St. G22	22	W10
Smeaton Dr. (Bishop.) G64	11	Y6
Smeaton St. G20	21	U9
Smith Cres., Clyde. G81	5	L5
Smith St. G14	33	R11
Smith Ter. (Ruther.) G73	53	Y15
Smithhills St., Pais. PA1	30	K13
Smiths La., Pais. PA3	30	K13
Smithycroft Rd. G33	38	AA11
Smithyends (Cumb.) G67	71	PP1
Snaefell Av. (Ruther.) G73	65	Z18
Snaefell Cres. (Ruther.) G73	65	Z17
Snuff Mill Rd. G44	63	V17
Society St. G31	37	Y13
Soho St. G40	37	Y13
Sollas Pl. G13	18	N8
Solway Pl. (Chry.) G69	26	FF8
Solway Rd. (Bishop.) G64	11	Z7
Solway St. G40	52	X15
Somerford Rd. (Bears.) G61	7	R7
Somerled Av., Pais. PA3	30	K11
Somerset Pl. G3	35	U11
Somerset Pl. Ms. G3	35	U11
Elderslie St.		
Somervell St. (Camb.) G72	66	AA17
Somerville Dr. G42	51	V16
Somerville St., Clyde. G81	5	L7
Sorby St. G31	37	Z13
Sorn St. G40	53	Y14
South Annandale St. G42	51	V15
South Av., Clyde. G81	5	L7
South Av., Pais. PA2	46	K16
South Av., Renf. PA4	17	M10
South Bk. St., Clyde. G81	17	M8
South Brook St., Clyde. G81	4	K6
South Campbell St., Pais. PA2	46	K14
South Carbrain Rd. (Cumb.) G67	71	PP4
South Chester St. G32	38	BB13
South Cotts. G14	33	R11
Curle St.		
South Cft. St., Pais. PA1	30	K13
Lawn St.		
South Crosshill Rd. (Bishop.) G64	11	Y7
South Dean Pk. Av. (Both.) G71	69	HH19
South Douglas St., Clyde. G81	17	M8
South Dr. (Linw.), Pais. PA3	28	E13
South Elgin Pl., Clyde. G81	17	M8
South Elgin St.		
South Elgin St., Clyde. G81	17	M8
South Erskine Pk. (Bears.) G61	7	Q5
South Ex. Ct. G1	36	W12
Queen St.		
South Frederick St. G1	36	W12
South Moraine La. G15	7	Q7
Moraine Av.		
South Muirhead Rd. (Cumb.) G67	71	PP3
South Pk. Av. (Barr.) G78	59	M19
South Pk. Dr., Pais. PA2	46	K15
South Portland St. G5	35	V13
South Scott St. (Bail.) G69	56	EE14
South Spiers Wf. G4	35	V11
South St. G11	33	Q11
South St. G14	18	P10
South Vesalius St. G32	38	BB13
South Vw. (Kirk.) G66	13	CC7
Gadloch Av.		
South Vw. (Blan.) G72	68	FF19
South Vw., Clyde. G81	4	K6
South Wardpark Ct. (Cumb.) G67	71	QQ1
South Wardpark Pl. (Cumb.) G67	71	QQ1
South William St., John. PA5	43	D15
South Woodside Rd. G4	35	U11
South Woodside Rd. G20	21	U10
Southampton Dr. G12	20	S9
Southbank St. G31	37	Z13
Sorby St.		
Southbar Av. G13	18	P8
Southbrae Dr. G13	19	Q9
Southbrae La. G13	19	R9
Milner Rd.		
Southcroft Rd. (Ruther.) G73	52	X15
Southcroft St. G51	34	S12
Southdeen Av. G15	6	P6
Southdeen Rd. G15	6	P6
Southend Rd., Clyde. G81	5	L5
Southern Av. (Ruther.) G73	65	Y17
Southerness Dr. (Cumb.) G68	71	PP1
Dornoch Way		
Southesk Av. (Bishop.) G64	10	X7
Southesk Gdns. (Bishop.) G64	10	X6
Southfield Av., Pais. PA2	46	K16
Southfield Cres. G53	49	Q16
Southfield Rd. (Cumb.) G68	70	MM3
Southhill Av. (Ruther.) G73	65	Z17
Southinch Av. G14	18	N9
Southinch La. G14	18	N9
Tweedvale Av.		
Southlea Av. (Thorn.) G46	62	S18
Southloch St. G21	22	X10
Southmuir Pl. G20	20	T9
Southpark Av. G12	34	T11
Southpark La. G12	21	U10
Glasgow St.		
Southpark Ter. G12	35	U11
Southpark Av.		
Southview Ct. (Bishop.) G64	22	X8
Southview Dr. (Bears.) G61	7	Q5
Southview Pl. (Gart.) G69	27	GG9
Southview Ter. (Bishop.) G64	22	X8
Southwold Rd., Pais. PA1	32	N13
Southwood Dr. G44	64	W17
Spateston Rd., John. PA5	43	C16
Spean St. G44	51	V16
Speirs Rd., John. PA5	44	E14
Speirshall Clo. G14	18	N9
Speirshall Ter. G14	18	N9
Spence St. G20	20	T8
Spencer Dr., Pais. PA2	44	F16
Spencer St. G13	19	R8
Spencer St., Clyde. G81	5	L6
Spey Av., Pais. PA2	45	G15
Spey Dr., Renf. PA4	32	N11
Almond Av.		
Spey Pl., John. PA5	43	C16
Spey Rd. (Bears.) G61	7	Q7
Spey St. G33	38	AA12
Spiers Gro. (Thorn.) G46	61	R18
Spiers Pl. (Linw.), Pais. PA3	28	E12
Spiers Rd. (Bears.) G61	8	S6
Spiersbridge Av. (Thorn.) G46	61	R18
Spiersbridge La. (Thorn.) G46	61	R18
Spiersbridge Rd. (Thorn.) G46	61	R19
Spiersbridge Ter. (Thorn.) G46	61	R18
Spiersfield Gdns., Pais. PA2	46	J14
Spindlehowe Rd. (Udd.) G71	69	GG17
Spinners Gdns., Pais. PA2	45	H14
Spinners Row, John. PA5	43	C15
Spittal Rd. (Ruther.) G73	64	X18
Spittal Ter. (Camb.) G72	68	EE19
Spoolers Rd., Pais. PA1	46	J14
Spoutmouth G1	36	W13
Spring La. G5	52	W14
Lawmoor St.		
Springbank Rd., Pais. PA3	30	J12
Springbank St. G20	21	U10
Springbank Ter., Pais. PA3	30	J12
Springboig Av. G32	39	CC13
Springboig Rd. G32	39	CC12
Springburn Rd. G21	22	X9
Springburn Rd. (Bishop.) G64	22	X9
Springburn Way G21	22	X10
Springcroft Av. (Bail.) G69	40	EE13
Springcroft Cres. (Bail.) G69	40	EE13
Springcroft Gdns. (Bail.) G69	40	FF13
Springcroft Gro. (Bail.) G69	40	EE13
Springcroft Rd. (Bail.) G69	40	FF13
Springcroft Wynd (Bail.) G69	40	EE13
Springdale Dr., Pais. PA2	45	G15
Springfield Av. (Bishop.) G64	23	Y8
Springfield Av. (Udd.) G71	69	GG17
Springfield Av., Pais. PA1	47	M14
Springfield Ct. G1	36	W12
Buchanan St.		
Springfield Cres. (Bishop.) G64	23	Y8
Springfield Cres. (Udd.) G71	69	GG17
Springfield Dr. (Barr.) G78	60	N19
Springfield Gro. (Barr.) G78	59	M19
Springfield Pk., John. PA5	44	E15
Springfield Pk. Rd. (Ruther.) G73	65	Z17
Springfield Quay G5	35	U13
Springfield Rd. G31	53	Z14
Springfield Rd. G40	53	Y14
Springfield Rd. (Bishop.) G64	11	Y7
Springfield Rd. (Cumb.) G67	71	PP2
Springfield Sq. (Bishop.) G64	23	Y8
Springhill Dr. N. (Bail.) G69	40	EE12
Springhill Dr. S. (Bail.) G69	40	EE12
Springhill Fm. Gro. (Bail.) G69	40	EE13
Springhill Fm. Pl. (Bail.) G69	40	EE13
Springhill Fm. Rd. (Bail.) G69	40	EE13
Springhill Fm. Way (Bail.) G69	40	EE13
Springhill Gdns. G41	51	U15
Springhill Parkway (Bail.) G69	40	EE13
Springhill Rd. (Bail.) G69	39	DD13
Springhill Rd. (Barr.) G78	59	L19
Springkell Av. G41	50	T14
Springkell Dr. G41	50	S14
Springkell Gdns. G41	50	T15
Springkell Gate G41	50	T15
Springside Pl. G15	6	P6
Springvale Ter. G21	22	X10
Hillkirk Pl.		
Spruce Av., John. PA5	44	E15
Spruce Dr. (Kirk.) G66	12	BB5
Spruce Dr. (Camb.) G72	67	DD18
Spruce Rd. (Cumb.) G67	71	QQ2
Spruce St. G22	22	W9
Spruce Way (Camb.) G72	67	DD18
Spynie Pl. (Bishop.) G64	11	Z7
Squire St. G14	33	R11
Stable Gro., Pais. PA1	45	H14
Staffa Av., Renf. PA4	31	M11
Staffa Dr., Pais. PA2	46	K16
Staffa Rd. (Camb.) G72	66	AA18
Staffa St. G31	37	Y12
Staffa Ter. (Camb.) G72	66	AA18
Staffin Dr. G23	8	T7
Staffin St. G23	9	U7
Stafford St. G4	36	W11
Stag St. G51	34	T12
Stair St. G20	21	U10
Stamford St. G31	37	Y13
Stamford St. G40	37	Y13
Stamperland Gdns. (Clark.) G76	63	U19
Stanalane St. (Thorn.) G46	61	R18
Standburn Rd. G21	23	Z8
Stanely Av., Pais. PA2	45	H15
Stanely Ct., Pais. PA2	45	H16
Stanely Cres., Pais. PA2	45	H16
Stanely Dr., Pais. PA2	46	J15
Stanely Rd., Pais. PA2	46	J15
Stanford St., Clyde. G81	5	M7
Stanhope Dr. (Ruther.) G73	65	Z17
Stanley Dr. (Bishop.) G64	11	Y6
Stanley Pl. (Blan.) G72	68	FF19
Stanley St. G41	35	U13

Street	Map	Grid
Stanley St. La. G41	35	U13
Milnpark St.		
Stanmore Rd. G42	51	V16
Stark Av., Clyde. G81	4	K5
Startpoint St. G33	38	BB12
Station Cres., Renf. PA4	17	M10
Station Rd. G20	20	T8
Station Rd. (Millerston) G33	24	BB9
Station Rd. (Stepps) G33	25	CC9
Station Rd. (Giff.) G46	62	T18
Fenwick Rd.		
Station Rd. (Bears.) G61	7	Q6
Station Rd. (Bail.) G69	56	FF14
Station Rd. (Muir.) G69	26	FF9
Station Rd. (Both.) G71	69	HH19
Station Rd. (Udd.) G71	69	GG17
Station Rd. (Blan.) G72	69	GG19
Station Rd. (Kilb.), John. PA10	42	B15
Station Rd., Pais. PA1	45	H14
Station Rd., Renf. PA4	17	M10
Station Way (Udd.) G71	69	HH17
Mansefield Dr.		
Station Wynd (Kilb.), John. PA10	42	B15
Steel St. G1	36	W13
Steeple St. (Kilb.), John. PA10	42	B14
Stenhouse Av. (Muir.) G69	26	FF8
Station Rd.		
Stenton St. G32	38	AA12
Stepford Path G33	40	EE12
Stepford Rd.		
Stepford Pl. G33	39	DD12
Stepford Rd. G33	39	DD12
Stephen Cres. (Bail.) G69	39	DD13
Stephenson St. G52	32	N12
Stepps Rd. G33	39	CC11
Stepps Rd. (Kirk.) G66	13	DD7
Steppshill Ter. G33	25	CC9
Stevenson St. G40	36	X13
Stevenson St., Clyde. G81	4	K6
Stevenson St., Pais. PA2	46	K14
Stewart Av., Renf. PA4	31	L11
Stewart Ct. (Barr.) G78	59	M18
Stewart St.		
Stewart Cres. (Barr.) G78	59	M18
Stewart Dr. (Bail.) G69	41	HH13
Coatbridge Rd.		
Stewart Dr., Clyde. G81	5	L5
Stewart Pl. (Barr.) G78	59	L18
Stewart Rd., Pais. PA2	46	K16
Stewart St. G4	35	V11
Stewart St. (Barr.) G78	59	M18
Stewart St., Clyde. G81	4	K6
Stewarton Dr. (Camb.) G72	66	AA17
Stewarton Dr. (Thorn.) G46	61	R19
Stewartville St. G11	34	S11
Stirling Av. (Bears.) G61	7	R7
Stirling Dr. (Bears.) G61	7	Q5
Stirling Dr. (Bishop.) G64	10	X6
Stirling Dr. (Ruther.) G73	65	Y17
Stirling Dr., John. PA5	43	C15
Stirling Gdns. (Bishop.) G64	10	X6
Stirling Rd. G4	36	W12
Stirling St. (Cumb.) G67	71	PP2
Stirling Way, Renf. PA4	31	M11
York Way		
Stirlingfauld Pl. G5	35	V13
Stirrat St. G20	20	T9
Stirrat St., Pais. PA3	29	H12
Stobcross Rd. G3	35	U12
Stobcross St. G3	35	U12
Stobcross Wynd G3	34	T12
Stobhill Rd. G21	22	X8
Stobs Dr. (Barr.) G78	59	L17
Stobs Pl. G34	40	FF11
Stock Av., Pais. PA2	46	K14
Stock St., Pais. PA2	46	K15
Stockholm Cres., Pais. PA2	46	K14
Stockwell Pl. G1	36	W13
Stockwell St. G1	36	W13
Stoddard Sq. (Elder.), John. PA5	44	F14
Glenpatrick Rd.		
Stonebank Gro. G45	64	W18
Stonedyke Gro. G15	6	P7
Stonefield Av. G12	20	T9
Stonefield Av., Pais. PA2	46	K15
Stonefield Cres., Pais. PA2	46	K15
Stonefield Dr., Pais. PA2	46	K15

Street	Map	Grid
Stonefield Gdns., Pais. PA2	46	K15
Stonefield Grn., Pais. PA2	46	K15
Stonefield Gro., Pais. PA2	46	K15
Stonefield Pk., Pais. PA2	46	K16
Stonelaw Dr. (Ruther.) G73	53	Y16
Stonelaw Rd. (Ruther.) G73	53	Y16
Stoneside Dr. G43	62	S17
Stoneside Sq. G43	62	S17
Stoney Brae, Pais. PA1	30	K13
Stoney Brae, Pais. PA2	46	K16
Stoneyetts Cotts. (Chry.) G69	15	GG6
Stoneyetts Rd. (Chry.) G69	15	GG7
Stonyhurst St. G22	21	V10
Stonylee Rd. (Cumb.) G67	71	PP3
Storie St., Pais. PA1	46	K14
Stormyland Way (Barr.) G78	59	M19
Stornoway St. G22	22	W8
Stow Brae, Pais. PA1	46	K14
Stow St., Pais. PA1	46	K14
Strachur St. G22	21	V8
Straiton Pl. (Blan.) G72	68	FF19
Straiton St. G32	38	AA12
Stranka Av., Pais. PA2	46	J14
Stranraer Dr. G15	7	Q7
Moraine Av.		
Stratford St. G20	21	U9
Strathallan La. G12	34	T11
Highburgh Rd.		
Strathallan Ter. G12	34	T11
Caledon St.		
Strathallon Pl. (Ruther.) G73	65	Z18
Ranald Gdns.		
Strathbran St. G31	53	Z14
Strathcarron Cres., Pais. PA2	47	L16
Strathcarron Dr., Pais. PA2	47	L15
Strathcarron Pl. G20	20	T9
Glenfinnan Rd.		
Strathcarron Pl., Pais. PA2	47	L15
Strathcarron Rd., Pais. PA2	47	L16
Strathcarron Way, Pais. PA2	47	L15
Strathclyde Dr. (Ruther.) G73	53	Y16
Strathclyde Path (Udd.) G71	69	GG17
Strathclyde St. G40	53	Y15
Strathclyde Vw. (Both.) G71	69	HH19
Strathcona Dr. G13	19	R8
Strathcona Gdns. G13	20	S8
Strathcona Pl. (Ruther.) G73	65	Z18
Strathcona St. G13	19	R9
Strathdee Av., Clyde. G81	5	L5
Strathdee Rd. G44	63	U19
Strathdon Av. G44	63	U19
Strathdon Av., Pais. PA2	46	J15
Strathdon Dr. G44	63	U19
Strathendrick Dr. G44	63	U18
Strathkelvin Retail Pk. (Bishop.) G64	11	Z6
Strathmore Av. (Blan.) G72	68	FF19
Strathmore Av., Pais. PA1	47	M14
Strathmore Gdns. G12	35	U11
Gibson St.		
Strathmore Gdns. (Ruther.) G73	65	Z18
Strathmore Rd. G22	21	V8
Strathord Pl. (Chry.) G69	15	HH6
Strathord St. G32	54	BB14
Strathtay Av. G44	63	U19
Strathview Gdns. (Bears.) G61	7	Q6
Strathview Gro. G44	63	U19
Strathview Pk. G44	63	U19
Strathy Pl. G20	20	T9
Glenfinnan Rd.		
Strathyre Gdns. (Bears.) G61	8	S5
Strathyre Gdns. (Chry.) G69	15	HH7
Heathfield Av.		
Strathyre St. G41	51	U16
Stratton Dr. (Giff.) G46	62	S19
Strauss Av., Clyde. G81	6	N7
Stravaig Path, Pais. PA2	45	H16
Stravaig Wk., Pais. PA2	45	H16
Stravanan Av. G45	64	W19
Stravanan Ct. G45	64	X19
Stravanan Rd. G45	64	W19
Stravanan St. G45	64	W19
Stravanan Ter. G45	64	W19
Streamfield Gdns. G33	23	Z8
Streamfield Gate G33	23	Z8
Brookfield Dr.		
Streamfield Lea G33	23	Z8
Brookfield Dr.		
Streamfield Pl. G33	24	AA8

Street	Map	Grid
Strenabey Av. (Ruther.) G73	65	Z18
Striven Gdns. G20	21	U10
Stroma St. G21	37	Y11
Stromness St. G5	51	V14
Strone Rd. G33	38	BB12
Stronend St. G22	21	V9
Stronsay Pl. (Bishop.) G64	11	Z7
Stronsay St. G21	37	Y11
Stronvar Dr. G14	18	P10
Stronvar La. G14	18	P10
Larchfield Av.		
Strowan Cres. G32	54	BB14
Strowan St. G32	54	BB14
Struan Av. (Giff.) G46	62	S18
Struan Gdns. G44	63	V17
Struan Rd. G44	63	V17
Struie St. G34	40	EE12
Stuart Av. (Ruther.) G73	65	Y17
Stuart Dr. (Bishop.) G64	22	X8
Succoth St. G13	19	R8
Suffolk St. G40	36	X13
Kent St.		
Sugworth Av. (Bail.) G69	40	EE13
Sumburgh St. G33	38	AA12
Summer St. G40	36	X13
Summerfield Cotts. G14	33	R11
Smith St.		
Summerfield Pl. G40	53	Y14
Ardenlea St.		
Summerfield St. G40	53	Y15
Summerhill Dr. G15	6	P6
Summerhill Gdns. G15	6	P6
Summerhill Pl. G15	6	P6
Summerhill Rd. G15	6	P6
Summerlea Rd. (Thorn.) G46	61	R18
Summerlee St. G33	39	CC12
Summertown Rd. G51	34	S12
Sunart Av., Renf. PA4	17	L10
Sunart Gdns. (Bishop.) G64	11	Y7
Sunart Rd. G52	33	R13
Sunart Rd. (Bishop.) G64	11	Y7
Sunningdale Rd. G23	20	T8
Sunningdale Wynd (Both.) G71	69	GG18
Sunnybank St. G40	53	Y14
Sunnylaw Dr., Pais. PA2	45	H15
Sunnylaw St. G22	21	V10
Sunnyside Av. (Udd.) G71	69	GG17
Sunnyside Dr. G15	6	P7
Sunnyside Dr. (Bail.) G69	41	GG13
Sunnyside Oval, Pais. PA2	46	K15
Sunnyside Pl. G15	6	P7
Sunnyside Pl. (Barr.) G78	59	L19
Sunnyside Rd., Pais. PA2	46	J15
Surrey St. G5	51	V14
Pollokshaws Rd.		
Sussex St. G41	35	U13
Sutcliffe Ct. G13	19	R8
Sutcliffe Rd. G13	19	R8
Sutherland Av. G41	50	T14
Sutherland Dr. (Giff.) G46	62	T19
Sutherland La. G12	34	T11
University Av.		
Sutherland Rd., Clyde. G81	5	L7
Sutherland St., Pais. PA1	30	J13
Sutherness Dr. G33	38	BB12
Swallow Gdns. G13	18	N8
Swan La. G4	36	W11
Swan Pl., John. PA5	43	C16
Swan St. G4	36	W11
Swan St., Clyde. G81	4	K6
Swanston St. G40	53	Y15
Sween Av. G44	63	V18
Sweethope Gdns. (Both.) G71	69	HH19
Sweethope Pl. (Both.) G71	69	HH18
Swift Cres. G13	18	N8
Swift Pl., John. PA5	43	C16
Swindon St., Clyde. G81	4	K6
Swinton Av. (Bail.) G69	40	FF13
Swinton Cres. (Bail.) G69	40	FF13
Swinton Cres., Coat. ML5	57	HH14
Swinton Dr. G52	32	P13
Swinton Gdns. (Bail.) G69	40	FF13
Swinton Av.		
Swinton Path (Bail.) G69	40	FF13
Swinton Av.		
Swinton Pl. G52	32	P13
Swinton Rd. (Bail.) G69	40	EE13

Name	No.	Ref.
Swinton Vw. (Bail.) G69	40	FF13
Swinton Av.		
Switchback Rd. (Bears.) G61	7	R7
Sword St. G31	36	X13
Swordale Path G34	40	EE12
Swordale Pl.		
Swordale Pl. G34	40	EE12
Sycamore Av. (Lenzie) G66	13	CC5
Sycamore Av., John. PA5	44	E15
Sycamore Dr., Clyde. G81	5	L6
Sycamore Way (Camb.) G72	67	DD18
Sydenham La. G12	20	S10
Crown Rd. S.		
Sydenham Rd. G12	20	T10
Sydney Ct. G2	35	V12
Argyle St.		
Sydney St. G31	36	X13
Sydney St., Clyde. G81	4	J6
Sylvania Way, Clyde. G81	5	L7
Sylvania Way S., Clyde. G81	5	L7
Symington Dr., Clyde. G81	5	L7
Syriam Pl. G21	22	X10
Syriam St.		
Syriam St. G21	22	X10

T

Name	No.	Ref.
Tabard Pl. G13	19	Q8
Tabard Pl. N. G13	19	Q8
Tabard Rd.		
Tabard Pl. S. G13	19	Q8
Tabard Rd.		
Tabard Rd. G13	19	Q8
Tabernacle La. (Camb.) G72	66	BB17
Tabernacle St. (Camb.) G72	66	BB17
Tain Pl. G34	40	FF12
Tait Av. (Barr.) G78	59	M18
Talbot Ct. G13	18	P9
Talbot Dr. G13	18	P9
Talbot Pl. G13	18	P9
Talbot Ter. G13	18	P9
Talbot Ter. (Udd.) G71	57	GG16
Talisman Rd. G13	19	Q9
Talisman Rd., Pais. PA2	45	G16
Talla Rd. G52	32	P13
Tallant Rd. G15	6	P6
Tallant Ter. G15	7	Q6
Tallisman, Clyde. G81	5	M7
Onslow Rd.		
Tambowie St. G13	19	R8
Tamshill St. G20	21	U9
Tamworth St. G40	37	Y13
Rimsdale St.		
Tanar Av., Renf. PA4	32	N11
Tanar Way, Renf. PA4	32	N11
Tandlehill Rd. (Mill.Pk.), John. PA10	42	B15
Tanera Av. G44	64	W18
Tanfield Pl. G32	39	CC12
Tanfield St.		
Tanfield St. G32	39	CC12
Tankerland Rd. G44	63	V17
Tanna Dr. G52	49	R14
Tannadice Av. G52	49	Q14
Tannahill Cres., John. PA5	43	D15
Tannahill Rd. G43	63	U17
Tannahill Rd., Pais. PA3	29	H13
Tannahill Ter., Pais. PA3	29	H13
Tannoch Dr. (Cumb.) G67	71	PP4
Tannoch Pl. (Cumb.) G67	71	PP4
Tannochside Dr. (Udd.) G71	57	HH15
Tannock St. G22	21	V10
Tantallon Dr., Pais. PA2	45	H15
Tantallon Rd. G41	51	U16
Tantallon Rd. (Bail.) G69	56	EE14
Tanzieknowe Av. (Camb.) G72	66	BB18
Tanzieknowe Dr. (Camb.) G72	66	BB18
Tanzieknowe Pl. (Camb.) G72	66	BB18
Tanzieknowe Rd. (Camb.) G72	66	BB18
Taransay St. G51	34	S12
Tarbert Av. (Blan.) G72	68	FF19
Tarbolton Dr., Clyde. G81	5	M6
Tarbolton Rd. G43	62	T17
Tarbolton Rd. (Cumb.) G67	71	PP3
Tarbolton Sq., Clyde. G81	5	M6
Tarbolton Dr.		
Tarfside Av. G52	49	Q14
Tarfside Gdns. G52	49	Q14
Tarfside Oval G52	49	Q14
Tarland St. G51	33	R13
Tarn Gro. G33	24	AA8
Tarras Dr., Renf. PA4	32	N11
Tarras Pl. (Camb.) G72	67	CC17
Tassie St. G41	50	T16
Tattershall Rd. G33	39	CC11
Tavistock Dr. G43	62	T17
Tay Av., Renf. PA4	18	N10
Tay Cres. G33	38	AA11
Tay Cres. (Bishop.) G64	11	Y7
Tay Pl., John. PA5	43	C16
Tay Rd. (Bears.) G61	7	Q7
Tay Rd. (Bishop.) G64	11	Y7
Taylor Av. (Kilb.), John. PA10	42	A14
Taylor Pl. G4	36	W12
Taylor St. G4	36	W12
Taylor St., Clyde. G81	17	M8
Taymouth St. G32	54	BB14
Taynish Dr. G44	64	W18
Teal Dr. G13	18	N8
Tealing Av. G52	49	Q14
Tealing Cres. G52	49	Q14
Teasel Av. G53	60	P18
Teith Av., Renf. PA4	32	N11
Teith Dr. (Bears.) G61	7	Q6
Teith Pl. (Camb.) G72	67	CC17
Teith St. G33	38	AA11
Telephone La. G12	34	T11
Highburgh Rd.		
Telford Ct., Clyde. G81	5	L7
Telford Pl. (Cumb.) G67	71	PP4
Telford Rd. (Cumb.) G67	71	PP4
Templar Av. G13	7	Q7
Temple Gdns. G13	19	R8
Temple Locks Ct. G13	19	R8
Temple Locks Pl. G13	19	R8
Temple Pl. G13	19	R8
Temple Rd. G13	20	S8
Templeland Av. G53	49	Q15
Templeland Rd. G53	49	Q15
Templeton St. G40	36	X13
Tennant Rd., Pais. PA3	29	H13
Tennant St., Renf. PA4	17	M10
Tennyson Dr. G31	54	AA14
Tenters Way, Pais. PA2	45	H14
Tern Pl., John. PA5	43	C16
Terrace Pl. (Camb.) G72	67	DD17
Terregles Av. G41	50	T15
Terregles Cres. G41	50	T15
Terregles Dr. G41	50	T15
Teviot Av. (Bishop.) G64	11	Y6
Teviot Av., Pais. PA2	45	G16
Teviot Cres. (Bears.) G61	7	Q7
Teviot St. G3	34	T12
Teviot Ter. G20	21	U10
Sanda St.		
Teviot Ter., John. PA5	43	C16
Thane Rd. G13	19	Q9
Thanes Gate (Udd.) G71	69	GG17
Castle Gate		
Tharsis St. G21	36	X11
Third Av. (Millerston) G33	24	BB9
Third Av. G44	51	V16
Third Av. (Kirk.) G66	13	CC7
Third Av., Renf. PA4	31	M11
Third Gdns. G41	50	S14
Third St. (Udd.) G71	57	GG16
Thirdpart Cres. G13	18	N8
Thistle Bk. (Lenzie) G66	13	CC6
Thistle Cotts. G13	19	R9
Crow Rd.		
Thistle St., Pais. PA2	46	J15
Thistle Ter. G5	52	W14
Thomas Muir Av. (Bishop.) G64	23	Y8
Thomas St., Pais. PA1	45	H14
Thomson Av., John. PA5	43	D14
Thomson Dr. (Bears.) G61	7	R5
Thomson Gro. (Camb.) G72	54	BB16
Thomson Pl., Clyde. G81	5	M5
Thomson St. G31	37	Y13
Thomson St., John. PA5	43	D15
Thomson St., Renf. PA4	31	M11
Thorn Brae, John. PA5	44	E14
Thorn Dr. (Bears.) G61	7	Q5
Thorn Dr. (Ruther.) G73	65	Z18
Thorn Rd. (Bears.) G61	7	Q5
Thorn St. G11	34	S11
Dumbarton Rd.		
Thornbank St. G3	34	T11
Yorkhill Par.		
Thornbridge Av. G12	20	T9
Balcarres Av.		
Thornbridge Av. (Bail.) G69	40	EE13
Bannercross Dr.		
Thornbridge Gdns. (Bail.) G69	40	EE13
Thornbridge Rd. (Bail.) G69	40	EE13
Thorncliffe Gdns. G41	51	U15
Thorncliffe La. G41	51	U14
Thorncroft Dr. G44	64	W18
Thornden Cotts. G14	18	N9
Dumbarton Rd.		
Thornden La. G14	18	P10
Dumbarton Rd.		
Thorndene (Elder.), John. PA5	44	E14
Thornhill, John. PA5	44	E15
Thornhill Av. (Elder.), John. PA5	44	E15
Thornhill Dr. (Elder.), John. PA5	44	E15
Thornhill Gdns., John. PA5	44	E14
Armour St.		
Thorniewood Gdns. (Udd.) G71	57	HH16
Thorniewood Rd. (Udd.) G71	57	GG16
Thornlea Dr. (Giff.) G46	62	T18
Thornley Av. G13	18	P9
Thornliebank Rd. G43	62	S17
Thornliebank Rd. (Deaconsbank) G46	61	Q19
Thornliebank Rd. (Thorn.) G46	62	S18
Thornly Pk. Av., Pais. PA2	46	K16
Thornly Pk. Dr., Pais. PA2	46	K16
Thornly Pk. Gdns., Pais. PA2	46	K15
Thornly Pk. Rd., Pais. PA2	46	K16
Thornside Rd., John. PA5	44	E14
Thornton La. G20	21	U8
Thornton St. G20	21	U8
Thorntree Way (Both.) G71	69	HH18
Thornwood Av. G11	34	S11
Thornwood Av. (Kirk.) G66	12	BB5
Thornwood Cres. G11	19	R10
Thornwood Dr.		
Thornwood Dr. G11	33	R11
Thornwood Dr., Pais. PA2	45	H15
Thornwood Gdns. G11	34	S11
Thornwood Pl. G11	20	S10
Thornwood Quad. G11	19	R10
Thornwood Rd. G11	33	R11
Thornwood Ter. G11	33	R11
Thornyburn Dr. (Bail.) G69	56	FF14
Thornyburn Pl. (Bail.) G69	56	FF14
Three Ell Rd. G51	34	T12
Govan Rd.		
Threestonehill Av. G32	38	BB13
Thrums Av. (Bishop.) G64	11	Z7
Thrums Gdns. (Bishop.) G64	11	Z7
Thrush Pl., John. PA5	43	C16
Thrushcraig Cres., Pais. PA2	46	K15
Thurso St. G11	34	T11
Dumbarton Rd.		
Thurston Rd. G52	32	P13
Tibbermore Rd. G11	20	S10
Tillet Oval, Pais. PA3	30	J12
Tillie St. G20	21	U10
Tillycairn Av. G33	39	CC11
Tillycairn Dr. G33	39	CC11
Tillycairn Pl. G33	25	DD10
Tillycairn Rd. G33	39	DD11
Tillycairn St. G33	39	DD11
Tilt St. G33	38	AA11
Tintagel Gdns. (Chry.) G69	15	GG6
Tinto Dr. (Barr.) G78	59	L19
Tinto Rd. G43	62	T17
Tinto Rd. (Bears.) G61	6	P5
Tinto Rd. (Bishop.) G64	11	Z7
Fintry Cres.		
Tinto Sq., Renf. PA4	31	L11
Ochil Rd.		
Tinwald Av. G52	32	N13
Tinwald Path G52	32	P13
Tiree Av., Pais. PA2	46	J16
Tiree Av., Renf. PA4	31	M11
Tiree Ct. (Cumb.) G67	70	MM4
Tiree Dr. (Cumb.) G67	70	MM4
Tiree Gdns. (Old Kil.) G60	4	J5

138

139

Street	No.	Ref.
West Campbell St., Pais. PA1	45	H14
West Chapelton Av. (Bears.) G61	7	R6
West Chapelton Cres. (Bears.) G61	7	R6
West Chapelton Dr. (Bears.) G61	7	R6
West Chapelton La. (Bears.) G61	7	R6
West Chapelton Av.		
West Coats Rd. (Camb.) G72	66	AA18
West Cotts. (Gart.) G69	26	EE10
West Ct., Clyde. G81	4	K6
Littleholm		
West End Pk. St. G3	35	U11
West George La. G2	35	V12
West Campbell St.		
West George St. G2	35	V12
West Graham St. G4	35	V11
West Greenhill Pl. G3	35	U12
West La., Pais. PA1	45	H14
West Lo. Rd., Renf. PA4	17	L10
West Nile St. G1	35	V12
West Princes St. G4	35	U11
West Regent La. G2	35	V12
Renfield St.		
West Regent St. G2	35	V12
West Rd. (Kilb.), John. PA10	42	B14
West St. G5	51	V14
West St., Clyde. G81	18	N8
West St., Pais. PA1	46	J14
West Thomson St., Clyde. G81	5	L6
West Whitby St. G31	53	Z14
Westbank Ct. G12	35	U11
Gibson St.		
Westbank La. G12	35	U11
Gibson St.		
Westbank Quad. G12	35	U11
Gibson St.		
Westbank Ter. G12	35	U11
Gibson St.		
Westbourne Cres. (Bears.) G61	7	Q5
Westbourne Dr. (Bears.) G61	7	Q5
Westbourne Gdns. La. G12	20	T10
Lorraine Rd.		
Westbourne Gdns. N. G12	20	T10
Westbourne Gdns. S. G12	20	T10
Westbourne Gdns. W. G12	20	T10
Westbourne Rd. G12	20	S10
Westbourne Ter. La. G12	20	S10
Westbourne Rd.		
Westbrae Dr. G14	19	R10
Westburn Av. (Camb.) G72	67	CC17
Westburn Av., Pais. PA3	29	H13
Westburn Cres. (Ruther.) G73	52	X16
Westburn Dr. (Camb.) G72	66	BB17
Westburn Fm. Rd. (Camb.) G72	66	BB17
Westburn Rd. (Camb.) G72	66	BB17
Westburn Way, Pais. PA3	29	H13
Westburn Av.		
Westcastle Ct. G45	64	W18
Westcastle Cres. G45	64	W18
Westcastle Gdns. G45	64	W18
Westcastle Gro. G45	64	W18
Westclyffe St. G41	51	U15
Westend (Bears.) G61	8	S7
Maryhill Rd.		
Wester Cleddens Rd. (Bishop.) G64	11	Y7
Wester Common Dr. G22	21	V10
Wester Common Rd. G22	21	V10
Wester Common Ter. G22	21	V10
Wester Rd. G32	55	CC14
Westerburn St. G32	38	AA13
Westercraigs G31	36	X12
Westergreens Av. (Kirk.) G66	13	CC5
Parkburn Av.		
Westerhill Rd. (Bishop.) G64	11	Y6
Westerhill St. G22	22	W10
Westerhouse Rd. G34	40	EE11
Westerkirk Dr. G23	9	U7
Westerlands G12	20	S9
Ascot Av.		
Western Av. (Ruther.) G73	52	X16
Western Isles Rd. (Old Kil.) G60	4	J5
Western Rd. (Camb.) G72	66	AA18
Westerton Av. (Bears.) G61	19	R8
Westfield Av. (Ruther.) G73	52	X16
Westfield Cres. (Bears.) G61	7	R7
Westfield Dr. G52	32	P13
Westfield Dr. (Bears.) G61	7	R7
Westfield Dr. (Thorn.) G46	61	R19
Westfield Vills. (Ruther.) G73	52	X16
Westfields (Bishop.) G64	10	X6
Westhorn Dr. G32	54	BB15
Westhouse Av. (Ruther.) G73	52	X16
Westhouse Gdns. (Ruther.) G73	52	X16
Westknowe Gdns. (Ruther.) G73	65	Y17
Westland Dr. G14	19	Q10
Westland Dr. La. G14	19	Q10
Westland Dr.		
Westlands (Bishop.) G64	10	X6
Westlands Gdns., Pais. PA2	46	J15
Westminster Gdns. G12	20	T10
Kersland St.		
Westminster Ter. G3	35	U12
North Claremont St.		
Westmoreland St. G42	51	V15
Westmuir Pl. (Ruther.) G73	52	X16
Westmuir St. G31	37	Z13
Westpark Dr., Pais. PA3	29	H13
Westray Circ. G22	22	W9
Westray Ct. (Cumb.) G67	70	NN4
Westray Pl. G22	22	W8
Westray Pl. (Bishop.) G64	11	Z7
Ronaldsay Dr.		
Westray Rd. (Cumb.) G67	70	MM4
Westray Sq. G22	22	W8
Westray St. G22	22	W8
Westside Gdns. G11	34	S11
Partickhill Rd.		
Westwood Av. (Giff.) G46	62	S18
Westwood Gdns., Pais. PA3	29	H13
Westwood Quad., Clyde. G81	5	M7
Westwood Rd. G43	62	S17
Weymouth Dr. G12	20	S9
Whamflet Av. (Bail.) G69	40	FF12
Wheatfield Rd. (Bears.) G61	7	Q7
Wheatlands Dr. (Kilb.), John. PA10	42	B14
Wheatlands Fm. Rd. (Kilb.), John. PA10	42	B14
Wheatley Ct. G32	38	BB13
Wheatley Dr. G32	38	BB13
Wheatley Pl. G32	38	BB13
Wheatley Rd. G32	38	BB13
Whin Av. (Barr.) G78	59	L18
Whin St., Clyde. G81	5	L6
Whinfield Av. (Camb.) G72	54	AA16
Whinfield Path G53	60	P18
Whinfield Rd. G53	60	P18
Whinhill Rd. G53	48	P14
Whinhill Rd., Pais. PA2	47	L15
Whins Rd. G41	50	T15
Whirlow Gdns. (Bail.) G69	40	EE13
Whirlow Rd. (Bail.) G69	40	EE13
Whistlefield Ct. (Bears.) G61	7	R6
Whitacres Path G53	60	P18
Whitacres Pl. G53	60	P18
Whitacres Rd. G53	60	P18
Whitburn St. G32	38	AA12
White St. G11	34	S11
White St., Clyde. G81	17	M8
Whitecraigs Pl. G23	21	U8
Whitefield Av. (Camb.) G72	66	BB18
Whitefield Rd. G51	34	T13
Whiteford Rd., Pais. PA2	47	L15
Whitehall Ct. G3	35	U12
Whitehall St. G3	35	U12
Whitehaugh Av., Pais. PA1	31	L13
Whitehaugh Cres. G53	60	P18
Whitehaugh Dr., Pais. PA1	31	L13
Whitehaugh Path G53	60	P18
Whitehaugh Rd. G53	60	P18
Whitehill Av. (Stepps) G33	25	CC9
Whitehill Av. (Cumb.) G68	70	MM3
Whitehill Fm. Rd. (Stepps) G33	25	CC9
Whitehill Gdns. G31	37	Y12
Garthland Dr.		
Whitehill La. (Bears.) G61	7	Q6
Whitehill Rd.		
Whitehill Rd. (Stepps) G33	25	CC8
Whitehill Rd. (Bears.) G61	7	Q5
Whitehill Rd. (Kirk.) G66	25	CC8
Whitehill St. G31	37	Y12
Whitehurst (Bears.) G61	7	Q5
Whitehurst Pk. (Bears.) G61	7	Q5
Whitekirk Pl. G15	6	P7
Whitelaw St. G20	20	T8
Whiteloans (Both.) G71	69	HH18
Wordsworth Way		
Whitemoss Av. G44	63	U18
Whitesbridge Av., Pais. PA3	45	G14
Whitesbridge Clo., Pais. PA3	45	G14
Whitestone Av. (Cumb.) G68	70	MM2
Dungoil Av.		
Whitevale St. G31	37	Y13
Whithope Rd. G53	60	N18
Whithope Ter. G53	60	N18
Whithorn Cres. (Mood.) G69	15	GG6
Whitlawburn Av. (Camb.) G72	66	AA18
Whitlawburn Rd. (Camb.) G72	66	AA18
Whitlawburn Ter. (Camb.) G72	66	AA18
Whitriggs Rd. G53	60	N17
Whitslade St. G34	40	EE11
Whittingehame Dr. G12	19	R9
Whittingehame Dr. G13	19	R9
Whittingehame Gdns. G12	20	S9
Whittingehame La. G13	19	R9
Whittingehame Dr.		
Whittliemuir Av. G44	63	U18
Whitton Dr. (Giff.) G46	62	T18
Whitton St. G20	20	T8
Whitworth Dr., Clyde. G81	5	L7
Whitworth St. G20	21	V9
Whyte Av. (Camb.) G72	66	AA17
Wickets, The, Pais. PA1	47	L14
Wigton St. G4	21	V10
Wigtoun Pl. (Cumb.) G67	71	PP2
Wilderness Brae (Cumb.) G67	71	PP2
Wilfred Av. G13	19	Q8
Wilkie Rd. (Udd.) G71	69	HH18
William St. G2	35	V12
William St. G3	35	U12
William St., Clyde. G81	5	L5
William St., John. PA5	43	D14
William St., Pais. PA1	46	J14
William Ure Pl. (Bishop.) G64	11	Y5
Williamson Pl., John. PA5	44	E15
Williamson St. G31	53	Z14
Williamson St., Clyde. G81	5	L6
Williamwood Dr. G44	63	U19
Williamwood Pk. G44	63	U19
Williamwood Pk. W. G44	63	U19
Willock Pl. G20	21	U8
Willoughby Dr. G13	19	R9
Willoughby La. G13	19	R9
Willoughby Dr.		
Willow Av. (Bishop.) G64	23	Y8
Willow Av. (Lenzie) G66	13	CC5
Willow Av. (Elder.), John. PA5	44	F15
Hillview Rd.		
Willow Dr., John. PA5	43	D15
Willow La. G32	54	BB15
Willow Pl., John. PA5	44	E15
Willow St. G13	19	R8
Willowbank Cres. G3	35	U11
Willowbank St. G3	35	U11
Willowdale Cres. (Bail.) G69	56	EE14
Willowdale Gdns. (Bail.) G69	56	EE14
Willowford Rd. G53	60	N18
Wilmot Rd. G13	19	Q9
Wilson Av. (Linw.), Pais. PA3	28	E13
Wilson St. G1	36	W12
Wilson St., Pais. PA1	46	J14
William St.		
Wilson St., Renf. PA4	17	M10